GREAT MEN
DIE TWICE

ALSO BY MARK KRAM

Ghosts of Manila

ALSO BY MARK KRAM, JR.

Like Any Normal Day

GREAT MEN DIE TWICE

THE SELECTED WORKS OF MARK KRAM

EDITED BY MARK KRAM, JR.

ST. MARTIN'S GRIFFIN ≋ NEW YORK

www.stmartins.com

"At the Bell"; "The One-Minute Angels"; "There Ain't No
Others Like Me"; "Manila-for Blood and for Money"; "Lawdy,
Lawdy, He's Great; "But Only a Farce in Tokyo"; "On the
Throne Behind the Power"; "Not the Greatest Way to Go"; "A
Wink at a Homely Girl"; "To the Brink-and Beyond"; "All of
the Best"; "No Place in the Shade"; and "Why Ain't I in the
Hall?" are reprinted courtesy of *Sports Illustrated*.

Designed by Omar Chapa

The Library of Congress Cataloging-in-Publication Data is
available upon request.

ISBN 978-1-250-06499-8 (trade paperback)
ISBN 978-1-4668-7700-9 (e-book)

St. Martin's Griffin books may be purchased for educational,
business, or promotional use. For information on bulk
purchases, please contact the Macmillan Corporate and
Premium Sales Department at 1-800-221-7945, extension 5442,
or write to specialmarkets@macmillan.com.

First Edition: June 2015

10 9 8 7 6 5 4 3 2 1

For Andrew Blauner

Contents

Foreword

BY MARK KRAM, JR.

A vexing sense of unattained expectations prevented my father from collecting these pieces himself. Whenever I prodded him to do so, he would always shrug and say they would have to be rewritten, if not fully, then in part. There was no persuading him. When he read his own work, his eye always fell to a line that could have been worded better, a paragraph that wandered astray, a beginning or ending that was not as acutely observed as it should been. Even his stirring coverage of the Thrilla in Manila would leave him chewing on the stem of his pipe in consternation—this, the very piece that had for years been looked upon as the apotheosis of event reporting. Yet Dad would only toss it aside and scoff, "I could have done more with the ending." In this way and others, he could be maddening.

The New York Times obituary of Dad in June 2002 saluted his work in *Sports Illustrated* by calling him one of its "most lyrical writers of the 1960s and 1970s." But no one I can think of characterized him better than John Schulian, the star sports columnist of a generation later who described him as "a poet of the dark nights in sports." Given his evocative way with words and the shadows that enveloped his work, Dad would have found some appeal in that description. On an *SI* staff overflowing with talent—Dan Jenkins, Frank Deford, Jack Olsen, Bud Shrake, a young Roy Blount Jr., and an always overlooked personal favorite, Robert Cantwell—this eccentric young man from Baltimore with the literary appetite chronicled the exploits of Muhammad Ali, Joe Frazier, and scores of others who then populated what A. J. Liebling anointed "the Sweet Science." Although Dad would become internationally known for his observant eye on the boxing beat, he also pitched in an array of long-form pieces that helped create the voice of *SI*. Bill Veeck, the colorful baseball owner who was also an eclectic reader, was once quoted in his admiration of Dad, "I wish, just once in my life, I could write five hundred words as well as that man."

What I find astonishing as I look back on his life is that he sprang from an environment that encouraged none of this. In the two-story row house where he was reared in East Baltimore, the only reading matter was the folded-over racing page that his dad labored over in his quixotic search for two-horse parlays before he headed off to the assembly line at General Motors. While Dad had been a superior athlete at Calvert Hall College High School, academically he finished tenth from the bottom of his class—although he did pick up some Latin and discovered later that it helped him grasp the organizing principles of English. He played some baseball in the army, signed a minor league contract with Pittsburgh, but soon ended up back home with a young wife, a baby (me), and a variety of blue-collar jobs, living above a small fish store owned by my maternal great-grandparents. Only then did he begin reading with the intent to better himself: John Steinbeck, James T. Farrell, Nelson Algren, and an array of others whose work would point the way.

The Baltimore Sun hired him in the fall of 1959, but not without some subterfuge by Dad that would become family lore. The sports editor there asked him if he had any writing samples. Dad handed him a paragraph he had composed on a portable typewriter that his mother had purchased for him. The editor looked at it and asked my father, "Well, do you have any college?" Dad told him yes, he had attended the University of Georgia. However, he had only spent a few weeks there before he dropped out. But with the help of a friend, John (Jack) Sherwood, later a fine feature writer for *The Washington Star,* Dad wired himself a telegram that stated in part, "George M. Kram has completed three years of undergraduate study at the University of Georgia." He signed it *Dean of Men.* The sports editor glanced at it and gave him the job. Dad promptly dropped his given name, George, adopted mine, and began writing under the palindrome Mark Kram (which is why I am not technically a "junior").

Under an asphyxiating cloud of pipe smoke, Dad worked his way up at the *Sun* from a high school reporter to a sports columnist. His thrice-weekly space, Another Day, became a laboratory for him. An introvert who found himself awkward in social settings, he tended to be standoffish on the job until evening fell, when he would unwind over a few too many drinks at the bar. Instead of joining the pack at the big sporting events in a city that was absorbed with the Colts and the Orioles, he went off on his own, used his eyes and ears, and fashioned eight-hundred-word pieces that would later seem to him unbearably florid. But whatever his early prose lacked in discipline, he had a passion for the language that he showered on pool hustlers, down-and-out boxers, and ex–rodeo stars. An admiring copy editor at *The Evening Sun* sent some of the pieces to Ray Cave, a former colleague who had worked in Baltimore before becoming an editor at

SI. Dad was called up to New York for an interview in the fall of 1963.

Given his unconventional background, Dad could not help but feel out of his element when he walked into the Time-Life Building. Handed a job application, there was no running to Western Union when he came to the space that asked for his college experience. Like a man applying for a bank loan he knew he had no chance of getting, Dad sadly wrote, *None*. In his interview with a human resources manager, an Ivy Leaguer who sniffed at the overreaching applicant before him as if he had a week-old sandwich in his coat pocket, Dad sank in his chair as the executive looked over the form and said dismissively, "What? No college? No, no. This will not do at all." Dejected, Dad reported the encounter to *SI*'s managing editor, André Laguerre, who waved his hand and said with a gravelly chuckle, "Fuck him. This is *my* magazine." Dad started in January 1964.

Like every other writer *SI* rounded up back then, Dad fell under the spell of Laguerre, who had been an aide to Charles de Gaulle in World War II. When Dad delivered his first story—a profile of NHL star Gordie Howe—it was rewritten by an editor who told him, "You have to understand. You're the wood; I'm the carpenter." Dad tapped his head and replied, "It doesn't sound like wood to me." Laguerre told Dad that neither version worked but assured him, "My money is on you. Always remember that." But Laguerre was no pushover. When he discovered that his headstrong young writer had restored some wording that an editor had changed, Laguerre gave him an earful. "Oh, he chewed me out terribly," Dad once told me. "A half an hour later, I was sitting in my office and he called, as if nothing happened, and said, 'Mark, join us for a drink?' He never harbored a grudge." When Dad reminisced in a Letter from the Publisher how he had outfoxed the *Sun* with that phony telegram, Laguerre only laughed. He

protected Dad from the corporate politics that could have up-
ended him in the early stages of his development and quelled the
anxieties within him that years later did just that. Dad said, "I
loved the man."

   SI under Laguerre became prized literary turf. The celebrated *New Yorker* writer Joseph Mitchell reminded Dad of that
when they had lunch one day. Believing by the late 1960s that
sports had become too confining, Dad asked Mitchell if he had
any chance at joining the staff at *The New Yorker.* "That could be
arranged," Mitchell told him. "But why would you want to?"
Dad stayed at *SI* in part because of the latitude Laguerre gave
him, but also in part because of the working relationship with
Senior Editor Pat Ryan, whom Dad regarded as a lovely woman
and truly fine editor. Besides—and this would prove to be a
double-edged sword—*SI* was a freewheeling place and open-
handed with expenses, which Laguerre had calculated as added
income to offset the low salary even his better writers tended to
be paid. Upon taking an ocean liner to Europe on assignment
instead of flying, which he simply could not bring himself to do
in the early 1970s after experiencing an emergency landing in
London, Dad submitted an expense account with a charge that
became *SI* legend. Boat: $10,000.

   Imagine *Mad Men* set not in the advertising world but at a
weekly magazine, a place where the greatest sports staff of any
generation was attended by an open bar and hot-and-cold-
running stewardesses. But those jaunty days vanished with the
ouster of Laguerre in 1974. While Dad did some of his better
work for his replacement, Roy Terrell, an ex-marine fighter pilot who was uneasy with the boozy culture that had permeated
SI, Dad spiraled into a deep depression and remained so spooked
by flying that he could not board a plane to cover Ali-Foreman
in Africa. He became so undependable that Terrell had to be

persuaded by Cave to assign him to the Thrilla in Manila. Dad gulped down some tranquilizers and flew with Ali, who crept up behind him on the plane, began to rattle his seat, and said in a horror-movie voice, "Ali and Mark Kram, we're going to *die, die,* you hear!" But both survived to chisel out a place in history: Ali in the boxing ring, and Dad when he sat down at his typewriter. "Mark came through in spectacular fashion," Cave told me. "The story he did was more than splendid. He rose to the occasion. And it was the last occasion."

Terrell fired him in the spring of 1977. By then divorced from my mother (he met his second wife in Manila), Dad was swept up in a crooked boxing tournament promoted by Don King. Rumors spread that he took a payoff from King to solve his money problems, which had become increasingly steep in his effort to support two families. An *SI* investigation did not reveal any financial link to King, but did uncover ethical breaches that warranted a determination of "gross misconduct." Years later Dad admitted that he did receive a small payment from King for screenplay proposals that the promoter hoped would open the door to Hollywood. In the years that followed, Dad did two books that did not sell, a handful of screenplays that were not produced, and an occasional *Playboy* piece commissioned by Rob Fleder, a talented young editor there who remembered him when. In an interview with *Inside Sports,* Veeck said of his old friend, "Journalism prefers simon-pure mediocrity to a touch of tarnished genius."

How punishing those years were. With a second family to feed, he found himself under an avalanche of debt, which ultimately forced him into a bankruptcy. Somewhere along the line, it became accepted wisdom that he had been blackballed in the writing trade. By then a sports writer myself, I was aware of the wild stories that were circulating about him and could not help but feel profound shame; only years later did I come to understand that journalists are unreliable couriers when it comes to the troubles of one of their own. Although I would not agree that Dad was blackballed per se by the events that had ensnared him at *SI*, I think it would be accurate to say that he did not do himself any favors by the way he comported himself. He had a foul temper. In keeping with the unsavory heritage of the Kram men, not one of whom has lived to the age of seventy because of alcohol addiction, Dad became aggressive when he overindulged. At a Manhattan party in 1970, he brawled with Norman Mailer: Mailer came away from it with a black eye, but not before biting Dad in his side. What I would learn far later is that Dad drank to quell the panic attacks that had afflicted him since childhood and left him reeling with rubbery legs, a light head, and nausea. In a personal reflection he wrote on panic attacks later in life, Dad observed that drinking only caused his symptoms "to rebound more fiercely the next day."

Only when Dad began to see a doctor to allay his anxiety with antidepressants did he find any authentic footing. *Esquire* articles editor David Hirshey began throwing him assignments in the late 1980s and the early 1990s. When Hirshey became an executive editor at HarperCollins, he invited Dad to expand a biography he had been writing on Ali into the May 2001 book *Ghosts of Manila: The Fateful Blood Feud Between Muhammad Ali and Joe Frazier.* Sides were divided over the controversial book, which was perceived by some as an attack on Ali, yet the book received some glowing reviews and prompted the British actor Terence Stamp to send Dad a letter on hotel stationery: *Eminent. Ghosts of Manila is splendid. Your text is as sequined to your subject as a Cole Porter lyric.* By then, if you asked him, Dad would explain that he had lived an "unexamined life" during his years at *SI*—and do so with genuine regret. He scaled back his drinking and

became pleasurable company. Hirshey had signed him to do a
book on Mike Tyson, and I joined Dad in Memphis for the Len-
nox Lewis–Tyson bout in June 2002. We could not have enjoyed
ourselves more that week, which I remember now as full of barbecue joints, cold beer, and $20 cigars. I feel lucky to have had
that time with him. He died the following week of a heart attack
at sixty-nine.

It pleases me to think his work will live on in this collection. I have divided it into five parts. The first is a stand-alone
Esquire profile of Ali that appeared in 1989 called "Great Men
Die Twice"—which is to say, once as great and again as men.
Part II, "The Boxing Beat," begins in 1971 with the piece Dad
wrote for *SI* called "At the Bell" in advance of Ali–Frazier I, includes his coverage of the Thrilla in Manila, and follows Ali
through his less than stellar effort against Ken Norton at Yankee Stadium in 1976. Part III, "In the Telling," showcases five
bonus pieces he wrote for *SI,* which includes his cranky yet af-
fectionate portrait of his hometown, Baltimore, and a lovely
profile of the old Negro League baseball star Cool Papa Bell,
who Dad had always looked upon as a favorite. Part IV, "Gigs,"
covers the blend of sports and off-sports subjects he did for
Esquire, including a profile of the hurdler Edwin Moses and an
essay on Marlon Brando. Part V closes with a stand-alone piece
he did for *GQ* on the death of an anonymous boxer, which I think
echoes with the tragic circumstances that engulfed Ali and under-
scores the uneasiness with which Dad had ultimately come to
look upon boxing. As he once told me, "You find yourself at a
point where you want to turn your head."

Although Dad would never have got to this book himself—
as I said, the perfectionist in him would not have allowed it—I
long hoped to do something like this. As a boy, while he was off
trotting the globe on assignments, I would clip his articles from

SI and arrange them in order, just as one would oversee a prized baseball-card collection. I had placed him on a pedestal, and there he stood until 2005, when, with the eyes of an adult, I undertook a writing assignment that compelled me to probe his inner world. Only then did he become a figure of flesh and blood, which allowed me to appreciate his work even more. Not every piece was the gem I once imagined it to be. Some were far from it. But when he hooked into a story that called upon his literary skills, he labored hard and well, stretching his ability as far it would go and producing a body of work that shines in a way that journalism seldom ever has. These are some of his best.

PART ONE

GREAT MEN DIE TWICE

(MUHAMMAD ALI)

Esquire
June 1989

There is the feel of a cold offshore mist to the hospital room, a life-is-a-bitch feel, made sharp by the hostile ganglia of medical technology, plasma bags dripping, vile tubing snaking in and out of the body, blinking monitors leveling illusion, muffling existence down to a sort of digital bingo. The Champ, Muhammad Ali, lies there now, propped up slightly, a skim of sweat on his lips and forehead, eyes closed, an almost imperceptible tremor to his arms and head. For all his claims to the contrary, his surface romance with immortality, Ali had a spooky bead on his future; he never saw it sweeping grandly toward him but bellying quietly along the jungle floor. "We just flies in a room," he liked to say, moving quickly across the ruins of daily life, plane crashes, train wrecks, matricide, infanticide; then after swatting half of humanity, he'd lower his voice and whisper, as if imparting a secret, "We just flies, that's all. Got nowhere to fly, do we?"

Images and echoes fill the room, diffuse and speeding, shot

through with ineluctable light and the mythopoeic for so long,
the glass darkened to a degree no one thought possible; his immense talent, his ring wisdom, his antipathy for chemicals, argued against destructibility; all he would ever do is grow old.
For twenty years, while he turned the porno shop of sports into
international theater, attention was paid in a way it never was
before or has been since. The crowds were a wonder to behold.
Kids scaled the wings of jets to get a glimpse of him; thousands,
young and old, tailed him in masses during his roadwork. World
leaders marveled at the spell he cast over the crowds. "If you
were a Filipino," joked Ferdinand Marcos, "I'd have to shoot
you." The pope asked for his autograph; sure, he said, pointing
to a picture, but why ain't Jesus black? A young Libyan student
in London sat on his bed, kept him up half the night with dithy-
rambic visions of Muslim revolution. "Watch, one day you will
see," said Mu'ammar Qaddafi. Half-asleep, Ali said, "Sheeeet,
you crazy." Leonid Brezhnev once dispatched a note to an official at *Izvestia:* "I would like to see more on Muhammad Ali.
Who is this man?"

The Ali Watch: how absurd that it would one day drop
down here on a little hospital on Hilton Head Island, South
Carolina. The nurse dabs his face dry. What is he thinking?
Never has his favorite phrase sounded so dismally precise: *My,
my, ain't the world strange.* If he could root back through the maze
of moment and incident, would he find premonitory signs sticking out like dire figurations of chicken entrails? Does he remember King Levinsky, one of the many heavy bags for Joe
Louis, in the corridor after the Miami Beach weigh-in? Boldly
colored ties draped Levinsky's neck (he sold them on the street),
his synapses now like two eggs over light, in permanent sizzle,
as he tried to move into stride with a young Cassius Clay. Over
and over, like a one-man Greek chorus, Levinsky croaked, eyes

spinning, spittle bubbling from his lips, "He's gonna take you, kid. Liston's gonna take you, make you a guy sellin' ties....Partners with me kid, ya kin be partners with me." Does he remember a shadowed evening in his hotel room a day or so after the third Joe Frazier fight, moving to the window, his body still on fire from the assault? He stood there watching the bloodred sun drop into Manila Bay, then took a visitor's hand and guided it over his forehead, each bump sending a vague dread through the fingers. "Why I do this?" he said softly. Does he remember the Bahamian cowbell tinkling the end of his final, pathetic fight, a derisive good-bye sound stark with omen? What is he thinking?

Ali poses a question, his eyes closed, his lips parting as if he were sliding open manhole covers. "You die here...they take you home?" he asks. The nurses roll their eyes and smile, struck by his innocence; it has nothing to do, they know, with morbidity. He is not joking either. The practical aftermath of death seems to stimulate his curiosity these days; nothing urgent, mind you, just something that begins to get into your mind when you're watching blood move in and out of your body for half the day. Though he is very much a mystic, there is a part of Ali that has always found security and a skewed understanding of life in the quantifiable: amounts, calibrated outcomes, the creaking, reassuring machinery of living. The night before in the hotel lounge, with his wife, Lonnie, beside him, bemusedly aghast, he grilled a pleasant waitress until he knew how many tips she got each week, how many children she had, the frequency of men hitting on her, and the general contour of her reality. "She have a sad life," he said later. The nurse now cracks with a deadpan expression, "You die, we take you home, Muhammad."

Still, a certain chiaroscuro grimness attaches to their surreal exchange and cries out for some brainless, comic intervention. He himself had long been a specialist in such relief when he

would instantly brighten faces during his favorite tours of pris-
ons, orphanages, and nursing homes. When down himself (very
seldom), he could count on a pratfall from his hysterical shaman,
Drew "Bundini" Brown, on the latest bizarre news from his
scheming court, maybe a straight line from some reporter that he
would turn into a ricocheting soliloquy on, say, the disgusting
aesthetics of dining on pig. No laughs today, though.

"Don't make him laugh," a nurse insisted when leading a
writer and a photographer into the room. "Laughing shakes the
tubing loose." The photographer is Howard Bingham, Ali's closest friend; he's been with the Champ from the start, in the face of
much abuse from the Black Muslims. Ali calls him "the enemy"
or "the nonbeliever." His natural instinct is to make Ali laugh;
today he has to settle for biting his lower lip and gazing warily
back and forth between Ali and his nurses. He doesn't know what
to do with his hands. Ali had requested that he leave his cameras
outside; just one shot of this scene, of Ali on his back, the forbidding purge in progress, of fame and mystique splayed raw, would
bring Bingham a minor fortune. "He doesn't want the world to
see him like this," says Howard. "I wouldn't take the picture for a
million dollars."

The process is called plasmapheresis. It lasts five hours and
is being conducted by Dr. Rajko Medenica. The procedure,
popular in Europe, is a cleansing of the blood. Ali is hooked up
to an electrocardiograph and a blood-pressure monitor; there is
always some risk when blood is not making its customary passage. But the procedure is not dangerous and he is in no pain,
we are told. Two things, though, that he surely can't abide about
the treatment: the injection of those big needles and the ceaseless tedium. When he was a young fighter, a doctor had to chase
him around a desk to give him a shot, and chaotic mobility to
him is at least as important as breathing. Bingham can't take his

eyes off Ali; the still life of his friend, tethered so completely, seems as incomprehensible to him as it would to others who followed the radiated glow of Ali's invulnerability. The nurses cast an eye at his blood pressure and look at each other. His pressure once jumped twelve points while he watched a TV report on Mike Tyson's street fight with Mitch Green in Harlem. It's rising a bit now, and the nurses think he has to urinate. He can't bear relieving himself in the presence of women; he resists, and his anxiety climbs.

"Ali," one of them calls. His eyes remain closed, his breathing is hardly audible. The nurse calls to him again; no response. "Come on now, Ali," she complains, knowing that he likes to feign death. "Now, stop it, Ali." He doesn't move, then suddenly his head gives a small jerk forward and his eyes buck wide-open, the way they used to when he'd make some incoherent claim to lineage to the gods. The nurses flinch, or are they in on the joke, too? Eyes still wide, with a growing smile, he says to the writer weakly: "You thought I dead, tell the truth. You the only one ever here to see this and I die for ya. You git some scoop, big news round the whole world, won't it be?" He leans his head back on the pillow, saying, "Got no funny people round me anymore. Have to make myself laugh." The nurse wants to know if he has to urinate. "No," he says with a trace of irritation. "Yes, you do," the nurse says. "Your pressure…" Ali looks over at Lonnie with mischievous eyes. "I just thinkin' 'bout a pretty woman." The nurse asks him what he'd like for lunch. "Give him some pork," cracks Bingham. Ali censures the heretic with a playful stare. Ali requests chicken and some cherry pie with "two scoops of ice cream." He turns to the writer again: "Abraham Lincoln went on a three-day drunk, and you know what he say when he wake up?" He waits for a beat, then says, "I freed whoooooooo?" His body starts to shake with laughter. The nurse yells, "Stop it, Muhammad!

You'll drive the needles through your veins." His calms down, rasps, "I'll never grow up, will I? I'll be fifty in three years. Old age just make you ugly, that's all."

Not all, exactly; getting old is the last display for the bread-and-circuses culture. Legends must suffer for all the gifts and luck and privilege given to them. Great men, it's been noted, die twice—once as great, and once as men. With grace, preferably, which adds an uplifting, stirring, Homeric touch. If the fall is too messy, the national psyche will rush toward it, then recoil; there is no suspense, no example in the mundane. The captivating, aspiring sociopath Sonny Liston had a primitive hold on the equation of greatness. "Clay [he never called him Ali] beeeg now," Sonny once said while gnawing on some ribs. "He flyin' high now. Like an eagle. So high. Where he gonna land, how he gonna land? He gonna have any wings? I wanna see." Sonny, of course, never made it for the final show. Soon after, he checked out in Vegas, the suspicion of murder hovering over the coroner's report.

Who wanted to ask the question back then or even be allowed to examine in depth its many possibilities? It was too serious for the carnival, immediately at odds with the cartoon bombast that swirled around Ali, the unassailable appeal of the phenomenon, the breathtaking climb of the arc. Before him, the ring, if not moribund, had been a dark, somber corner of sports, best described by the passing sight of then-middleweight-king Dick Tiger, leaving his beat-up hotel wearing a roomy, black homburg and a long pawnshop overcoat, a black satchel in his hand, heading for the subway and a title fight at the Garden. But the heavyweight champions—as they always will—illuminated the image sent out to the public. There was the stoic, mute Joe Louis, with his cruising menace; street fighter Rocky Marciano, with his trade-unionist obedience; the arresting and dogged Floyd Patterson, who would bare his soul to a telephone pole at the sight of a pencil; all unfrivolous men who left no doubt as to the nature of their work.

With the emergence of Muhammad Ali, no one would ever see the ring the same way again, not even the fighters themselves; a TV go, a purse, and sheared lip would never be enough; and a title was just a belt unless you did something with it. A fighter had to *be;* a product, an event, transcendental. Ali and the new age met stern, early resistance. He was the demon loose at a holy rite. With his preening narcissism, braggart mouth, and stylistic quirks, he was viewed as a vandal of ring tenets and etiquette. Besides, they said, he couldn't punch, did not like to get hit, and seemed to lack a sufficient amount of killer adrenaline. True, on the latter two counts. "I git no pleasure from hurtin' another human bein'," he used to say. "I do what I gotta do, nothin' more, nothin' less." As far as eating punches, he said, "Only a fool wanna be hit. Boxin' just today, my face is forever." Others saw much more. The ballet master Balanchine, for one, showed up at a workout and gazed in wonder. "My God," he said, "he fights with his legs, he actually fights with his legs. What an astonishing creature." Ali's jab (more like a straight left of jolting electricity) came in triplets, each a thousandth of a second in execution. He'd double up cruelly with a left hook (rarely seen) and razor in a right—and then he'd be gone. Even so, it took many years for Ali to ascend to a preeminent light in the national consciousness. In the sixties, as a converted Black Muslim, he vilified white people as blond, blue-eyed devils. His position on Vietnam—"I ain't got no quarrel with those Vietcong, anyway. They never called me nigger"—was innocent at first, but then taken up as if he were the provocateur of a national crisis. The politicians, promoters, and sweeping sentiment converged to conspire against his constitutional right to work; states barred him from fighting. He resisted the draft and drifted into exile. Three years later he returned, heavier, slower, but with a new kind of fire in his belly. Though he had defeated heavyweight champion Sonny Liston and defended his title nine times, Ali had never had a dramatic constituency before. Now a huge one awaited him, liberals looking for expression, eager literati to put it into scripture, worn-out hippies, anyone who wanted to see right done for once. The rest is history: the two symphonic conflicts with Joe Frazier; the tingling walk with him into the darkness of George Foreman. Then, the Hegelian "bad infinite" of repeating diminishing cycles: retiring, unretiring, the torture of losing weight, the oiling of mushy reflexes. The margins of dominance compressed perilously, and the head shots (negligible before exile) mounted.

Greatness trickled from the corpus of his image, his career now like a gutshot that was going to take its time before killing. His signing to fight Larry Holmes, after retiring a second time, provoked worried comment. After watching some of Ali's films, a London neurologist said that he was convinced Ali had brain damage. Diagnosis by long distance, the promoters scoffed. Yet among those in his camp, the few who cared, there was an edginess. They approached Holmes, saying, "Don't hurt him, Larry." Moved, Holmes replied, "No way. I love Ali." With compassion, he then took Ali apart with the studied carefulness of a diamond cutter; still, not enough to mask the winces at ringside. Ali failed to go the route for the first time in his career. Incredibly, fourteen months later, in 1981, his ego goaded him to the Bahamas and another fight, the fat jellied on his middle, his hand-speed sighing and wheezing like a busted old fan; tropic rot on the trade winds. Trevor Berbick, an earnest pug, outpointed him easily. Afterward, Angelo Dundee, who had trained Ali from the start and had to be talked into showing up for this one, watched him slumped in the dressing room, then turned away and rubbed his eyes as certain people tried to convince Ali that he had been robbed and that a fourth title was still possible.

The public prefers, indeed seems to insist on, the precedent set by Rocky Marciano, who quit undefeated, kept self-delusion at bay. Ali knew the importance of a clean farewell, not only as a health measure but as good commercial sense. His ring classicism had always argued so persuasively against excessive physical harm, his pride was beyond anything but a regal exit. But his prolonged decline had been nasty, unseemly. Who or what pressured him to continue on? Some blamed his manager, Herbert Muhammad, who had made millions with Ali. Herbert said that his influence wasn't that strong.

Two years after that last fight, Ali seemed as mystified as everyone else as to why he hadn't ended his career earlier. He was living with his third wife, the ice goddess Veronica, in an LA mansion, surrounded by the gifts of a lifetime—a six-foot, hand-carved tiger given to him by Teng Hsiao-ping, a robe given to him by Elvis Presley. Fatigued, his hands tremoring badly, he sat in front of the fire and could only say, "Everybody git lost in life. I just git lost, that's all."

Now, five years later, the question *why* still lingers, along with the warning of the old aphorism that "we live beyond what we enact." The resuscitation of Ali's image has been a sporadic exercise for a long time now, some of it coming from friends who have experienced heartfelt pain over his illness. Others seem to be trying to assuage a guilt known only to themselves, and a few are out to keep Ali a player, a lure to those who might want to use his name in business; though the marketplace turns away from billboards in decline. Not long ago, a piece in *The New York Times Magazine* pronounced him the Ali of old, just about terminally perky. Then, Ali surfaced in a front-page telephone interview in *The Washington Post*. He appeared to have a hard grasp on politics, current states' rights issues, and federal judgeships being contested—a scenario that had seemed as likely as the fusillade of laser fire Ali said Muslim spaceships would one day loose on the white devils.

Noses began to twitch. What and who was behind the new Ali, the wily Washington lobbyist who had the ear of everyone from Strom Thurmond to Orrin Hatch? The wife of Senator Arlen Specter even baked Ali a double-chocolate-mousse pie. For a good while, most of these senators, and others, knew only the voice of Ali on the phone. Dave Kindred, a columnist for *The Atlanta Journal-Constitution* who has known Ali since his Louisville days, concluded that it was most likely Ali's attorney, Richard Hirschfeld, widely regarded as a brilliant impersonator of Ali, who had made the calls. (Hirschfeld has refused to comment on whether or not he did so.) Hirschfeld and Ali had cut up a lot of money over the years on numerous enterprises (funded by other people), from hotels to cars, most of them failing. Ali's lobbying seemed to center on a federal judgeship for a Hirschfeld friend, and a federal lawsuit in which Ali sought $50 million in damages from his "wrongful conviction in the 1967 draft evasion case." He lost the suit but succeeded in getting Senator Hatch and others to explore a loophole that might remedy the verdict. Ali eventually had to materialize (with Hirschfeld hard by his side), and many on Capitol Hill were unable to match the man with the voice. One of Sam Nunn's aides, noting Ali's listlessness and Hirschfeld's aggressive quizzing, wondered, "Is Ali being carted around like a puppet?" Certainly a serpentine tale; but had Ali been a collaborator all along?

At his farm in Berrien Springs, Michigan, Ali sits at the end of a table in the living room. The 247 pounds of weight have made him a bit short of breath. He's battled his appetite (two, three desserts, meals back-to-back) and sedentary lapses for years. Several months before, he had been almost sleek, thanks to fourteen-mile walks and his wife's efforts to police him at the table. But what is disturbing is the general profile of his condition.

For a long time now, he had appeared indifferent to the ravages of his problem. But he dispels that notion when asked how seriously he considered a dangerous brain operation in Mexico before his family talked him out of it. "Scale of ten," he says, "a six." The answer reflects the terrible frustration that must exist within him, the daily, fierce struggle with a body and mind that will not capitulate to his bidding. He sits there, his hands shaking, his movements robotic, the look on his face similar to what the marines call a thousand-yard stare.

Why is it, do you think, that after all these years, the dominant sound around Ali is silence? Look at the cataract of noise caught by TV soundmen, look at the verbosity that snared some novelists into thinking he was a primitive intelligence capable of Ciceronian insight. Part of the fever of the times; if the Black Panther Huey Newton, posing with a rifle and spear, could be written up as a theoretical genius, and his partner, Bobby Seale, interpreted as a tactical wizard, then how much a symbol was Ali, the first to tap and manifest glinting black pride, to dispute with vigor erosive self-laceration.

The fact was that he was not cerebral; he was a reflex of confusing emotions and instant passions. He did have street cunning, most of it aimed at keeping himself a mystery. "People like mystery," he used to say. "Who is he? What's he all about? Who's he gonna be tomorrow?" To that end, he tossed the media rabble dripping hunks of redundant, rote monologue; his loudness provided a great show and diverted probing questions. By

nature, he was a gentle, sensitive man, and even in the throes
of angry threats against whites it was hard to hide a smile, for
he loved what the blacks call "selling wolf tickets," tricking
people into fear. The Black Panthers used that gambit well, and
the TV crews followed their presence. Thinking of all of this,
how could someone so alien to ideas, and thought, who communicated privately, in scraps and remote silences, be capable of
fooling Washington politicians? Absurd, of course, but then the
question emerges: Did he allow himself to be used?

"How about all those phone calls," he is asked.

"What calls?" he responds vacantly.

"To politicians, this past summer."

"You can't believe that," he says. "Man wrote that, he's
cracker from way back in Louisville. Always hated blacks."

"But the piece had the goods."

"I'm signin' my autographs now," he says. "This is the only
important thing in my life. Keepin' in touch with the people."

"Were you used?"

"Spend a hundred dollars on stamps every week. Give 'em
all my autograph that write me."

"Were you used?"

"For what?"

"To influence your lawsuit."

"I ain't worried about money," he says.

"Maybe you just want to be big again. Remember what you
told Elvis. 'Elvis, you have to keep singin' or die to stay big. I'm
gonna be big forever.'"

He smiles thinly. "I say anything shock the world."

"You like politics now?"

"Politics put me to sleep."

"You were at the Republican National Convention."

"You borin' me, putting me to sleep."

"Reagan, Hatch, Quayle, they would've clapped you in jail in the old days."

His eyes widen slightly. "That right?" He adds, "I'm tired. You better than a sleepin' pill."

But don't let the exchange mislead. Ali is not up to repartee these days, never was, really, unless he was in the mood, and then he'd fade you with one of his standard lines ("You not as dumb as you look"). He speaks very, very slowly, and you have to lean in to hear him. It takes nearly as hour to negotiate the course of a conversation. Typically, he hadn't been enlightening on the Capitol Hill scam. Over the years, he has been easily led, told by any number of rogues what his best interests were. If the advisers were friends who appealed to his instinct to help them move up a rung, he was even more of a setup. Later, Bingham says, "Ali was pissed about that impersonation stuff. He had no idea." Why didn't he just say that he didn't make the calls? "You know him," he says. "He'll never betray who he thinks has tried to help him. The idea that people will think less of him now bothers him a lot."

If there was ever any doubt about the staying power of Ali, it is swept aside when you travel with him. His favorite place in the world—next to his worktable at his farm—is an airport. So he should be in high spirits now; he'll be in three airports before the day's over. But he's a bit petulant with Lonnie, who aims to see that he keeps his date at Hilton Head Island. He can't stand hospitals. They get in the way of life. He found it hard to ever visit his old sidekick Bundini when he was dying. Paralyzed from the neck down, Bundini could only move his eyes. Ali bent down close to his ear and whispered, "You in pain?" The eyes signaled "yes." Ali turned his head away, then came back to those eyes, saying, "We had some good times, didn't we?" Bundini's eyes went up and down. Ali talks about this in the Chicago airport. He's calmed down now, sits off by himself, ramrod-straight and waiting. He wears a pinstripe suit, red tie, and next to him is his black magician's bag; he never lets it out of his sight. The bag is filled with religious tracts already autographed; which is the first thing he does every day at 6:00 a.m., when he gets up. All he has to do is fill in the person's name.

His autograph ritual and travel are his consuming interests. He'll go anywhere at the ring of a phone, and he spends much time on the road. Perhaps the travel buoys him; he certainly gets an energy charge from people. Soon they begin to drop like birds to his side. "You see," he says, "all I gotta do is sit here. Somethin', ain't it? Why they like me?" He is not trying to be humble, he is genuinely perplexed by the chemistry that exists between himself and other people. "Maybe they just like celebrities," he says. Maybe, he's told, he's much more than a celebrity. He ponders that for a moment and says, "That right?" By now, a hundred people have lined up in front of him, and a security guard begins to keep them in line. Ali asks them their names, writes, then gives them his autographed tracts. Some ask him to pose for pictures, others kid him about unretiring. "Kong [Mike Tyson], I'm comin' after you." Near the end, he does a magic trick for a lady, using a fake thumb. "Where you going, Muhammad?" she asks. He thinks, and then leans over to the writer and asks, "Where we going?" The lady's eyes fill, she hugs him and says, "We love you so much." What is that so movingly draws so many people—his innocent, childlike way, the stony visual he projects, set off against his highly visible symptoms?

That night over dinner, Ali's eyes open and close between courses. He fades in and out of the conversation, has a hint of trouble lifting the fork to his mouth. His every day includes periods like this, he's in and out like a faraway signal. Sometimes he's full of play. He likes to swing his long arm near a person's ear, then create a friction with thumb and forefinger to produce a cricket effect in the ear. Then the play is gone, and so is he. "One day," Lonnie is saying, "I want someone to catch his soul, to show what a fine human being he is." Ali says, head down, "Nobody know me. I fool 'em all." Lonnie is Ali's fourth wife. She was a little girl who lived across from Ali's old Louisville home when he was at the top. She is a woman of wit and intelligence, with a master's degree in business administration. She plans his trips, is the tough cop with him and his medicine, and generally seems to brighten his life. Ice cream dribbles down Ali's chin. "Now, Muhammad," she says, wiping it away. "You're a big baby." He orders another dessert, then says, "Where are we?" A blade of silence cuts across the table.

Bingham says, "Hilton Head Island."

Ali says, "Ya ever wake up and don't know where you are?" Sure, he is told, steady travel can make a person feel like that for an instant; yet it is obvious that short-term memory for him is like a labyrinth.

Ali's day at the hospital is nearly over. He will soon be counting down the minutes. Right now, he's in high spirits. A nurse has secretly slipped him some strips of paper. He has a complete piece of paper in his hands. He crumples the paper, pretends to put it in his mouth, then billows his cheeks until he regurgitates tiny pieces all over his chest. "Ain't magic a happy thing," he says, trying to contain his giggling. When Dr. Medenica comes, Ali jokes with him. The doctor goes about examining the day's results. He looks at the bags of plasma: 15,000 cc have been moved through Ali. Floyd Patterson has expressed dismay over the current treatment. "No brain damage?" Floyd has said. "Next you'll be hearing he was bit by a cockroach. He's gonna kill Clay.... He'll drop dead in a year."

Medenica bridles at the comment. "He's rather ignorant. I'm going to have to call that man." Ali wants to know what Patterson said. Nobody wants to tell him. "Tell me," says Ali. Everyone looks at each other, and someone finally says, "Floyd says you'll drop dead in a year." Ali shrugs it off: "Floyd mean well."

It is Medenica's contention that Ali suffers from pesticide poisoning. Though his work has met with some skepticism in the medical community, Medenica is respected in South Carolina. His desk is rimmed with pictures of prominent people—a senator, a Saudi prince, an ambassador—patients for whom he has retarded death by cancer. He is supposed to have done wonders for Marshal Tito of Yugoslavia. Tito was so grateful, he arranged funding for Medenica's clinic in Switzerland. When he died, the funds were cut off and Medenica was left with bills and criminal indictment by the Yugoslavians and the Swiss. "Don't ask how Ali got the pesticides," Medenica says.

Plasmapheresis is a solid treatment for pesticide poisoning, which occurs more than ever these days. The blood cleaning removes the immune complex, which in turns removes toxins. But how can Medenica be so sure that Ali's problem is not brain damage? Dr. Dennis Cope, of UCLA, has said that Ali is a victim of "Parkinson's syndrome secondary to pugilistic brain syndrome." In short, he took too many head shots. Medenica, though, is a confident man.

He predicts Ali will be completely recovered. "I find absolutely no brain damage. The magnetic resonator tests show no damage. Before I took him as a patient, I watched many of his fight films. He did not take many head blows."

Is he kidding?

"No, I do not see any head blows. When he came this summer, he was in bad shape. Poor gait. Difficult speech. Vocal cord syndrome, extended and inflamed. He is much better. His problem is he misses taking his medicine, and he travels too much. He should be here once a month."

Finally, Ali is helped out of his medical harness. He dresses slowly. Then, ready to go out, he puts that famous upper-teeth clamp on his bottom lip to show determination and circles the doctor with a cocked right fist. His next stop is for an interferon shot. It is used to stimulate the white blood cells. Afterward, he is weak, and there is a certain sadness in his eyes. On the way to the car, he is asked if the treatment helps. He says, "Sheeeet, nothin' help."

The Lincoln Town Car moves through the night. Bingham, who is driving, fumbles with the tape player. Earlier in the day, he had searched anxiously for a tape of Whitney Houston doing "The Greatest Love of All," a song written especially for Ali years ago. He had sensed that Ali would be quite low when the day was over, and he wanted something to pick him up. The words, beautiful and haunting, fill the car.

"You hear that," Bingham says, his voice cracking. "Everything's gonna be just fine, Ali."

The dark trees spin by. There is no answer. What is he thinking?

PART TWO

THE BOXING BEAT

1 —At the Bell . . .

(ALI-FRAZIER I)

Sports Illustrated
March 8, 1971

He will be the first in the ring, so look at him with honest eyes because you probably will never see such an impeccable talent again. Assessed by the familiar standards—size, speed, intelligence, command, and imagination—he is without peer and there is nothing he cannot or will not do in a ring. In the esthetics of boxing, Muhammad Ali transcends the fighter. He is a Balanchine, a Dalí, the ultimate action poet who has lifted so primordial an act to eloquent, sometimes weird, beauty. But for all his gifts, it is his fear of failure, of the moment, that is his real strength. All fighters have it, but few shape it into such a positive force. It seems to be the catalyst, the thing that detonates his intense public displays, his psychological war dance that opens the floodgates for his talent.

Move across now to the other corner and there you will see the finest gladiator—in the purest sense of the word—in heavyweight history. To picture Joe Frazier once must recall what happened to Jerry Quarry when he elected to work within Frazier's perimeter. It was like the *Wehrmacht* crossing into Russia—and the end was the same. Even the most cynical of boxing people look at Frazier and rhapsodize about his drilling aggression, his volume of threshing-blade punches that make you forget his short arms. He does not have the single, crumpling punch of Marciano, or the sudden ferocity of Dempsey, but he is more mobile than either, and much better to watch. It is that animal joy he exudes; one has the feeling that he has watched a man bring honesty, a nobility of spirit to his work.

Like deadly weaponry projected from opposite ends of the earth, Muhammad Ali and Joe Frazier collide Monday night at Madison Square Garden for the final sorting out of the heavyweight championship of the world. In itself, that is enough, but there is much more here than a title. This is *the* international sporting event of our age, one of the great dramas of our time created by a unique permutation of factors: Ali's unjust exile, his sudden pyrotechnic presence and the political climate that demanded that return; the $2.5 million for each fighter, a bold, brilliant promotional gamble; the beautiful evolution of Joe Frazier; and the reality that both Ali and Frazier might retire no matter what happens.

The thrust of this fight on the public consciousness is incalculable. It has been a ceaseless whir that seems to have grown in decibel with each new soliloquy by Ali, with each dead calm promise by Frazier. It has magnetized the imagination of ring theorists and flushed out polemicists of every persuasion. It has cut deep into the thicket of our national attitudes, and it is a conversational imperative everywhere—from the gabble of big-city saloons and factory lunch breaks rife with unreasoning labels, to ghetto saloons with their own false labels.

No two peoples consider or respond to the ring with the same emotion. It is a rite of blood and manhood to the Latins, and what they bring to it is hysteria. Because of their innate, quiet pugnacity, the English see it intimately, the same way the French see themselves pridefully in the works of Racine and Molière at the Comédie-Française. As for the Swedes, who banned it, they never could make up their minds about the ring, and with their heavy sadness they always seem suspended between shame and a zealous need to be in communion with a victim. How the Russians approach the ring cannot be gauged accurately, but there seems small doubt about what they would do with a champion in the propaganda market.

Americans are the most curious in their reaction to a heavyweight title bout, especially one of this scope. To some, the styles and personalities of the fighters seem to provide the paraphernalia of a forum; the issue becomes a sieve through which they feel compelled to pour all of their fears and prejudices. Still others find it a convenient opportunity to dispense instant good and evil, right and wrong. The process is as old as boxing: the repelling bluff and bluster of John L. against the suavity and decorum of Gentleman Jim; the insidious malevolence of Johnson vs. the stolidity of Jeffries; the evil incarnate Liston against the vulnerable Patterson. It is a fluid script, crossing over religion, war, politics, race, and much of what is so terribly human in all of us.

The fight—mainly an athletic spectacular for many, though it provokes almost unbearable anticipation—also appears to have released manic emotion. The disputation of the New Left comes at Frazier with its spongy thinking and push-button passion and seeks to color him white, to denounce him as a capitalist dupe and a fifth columnist to the black cause. Those on the other fringe, just as blindly rancorous, see in Ali all that is unhealthy in this country, which in essence means all they will not accept from a black man. For still others, numbed by the shock of a sharply evolving society, he means confusion; he was one of the first to start pouring their lemonade world down the drain.

Among the blacks there is only a whisper of feeling for Frazier, who is deeply cut by their reaction. He is pinned under the most powerful influence on black thought in the country. The militants view Ali as the Mahdi, the one man who has circumvented what they believe to be an international white conspiracy. To the young he is identity, an incomparable hero of almost mythological dimension. They all need him badly, and they will not part with him easily. They know that if ever a fighter lived who could smash their symbol into fragments it is Joe Frazier. Out of anxiety, a sense of dread, they respond with the most synthetic of accusations: Frazier is the white man's champion, contrived and manipulated to destroy what is once again so close to the black man's heart and soul.

"When he gets to ringside," says Ali, "Frazier will feel like a traitor, though he's not. When he sees those women and those men aren't for him, he'll feel a little weakening. He'll have a funny feeling, an angry feeling. Fear is going to come over him. He will realize that Muhammad Ali is the real champ. And he'll feel he's the underdog with the people. And he'll lose a little pride. The pressure will be so great that he'll feel it. Just gettin' in the ring alone with thousands and millions of eyes lookin' at you in those big arenas, and those hot lights comin' down that long aisle. It's going to be real frightful when he goes to his corner. He don't have nothing. But me...I have a cause."

It is one thing, however silly it may be, for a black man to impugn Frazier, but it is the worst sort of presumption for whites to denigrate him. Contrasted to Ali's past, Frazier's much more expresses the hard reality—other than politics—of what the black man's life has been and is. Quality of life to Frazier meant a plow, hours and days in the subtropical heat, calluses as big as hen eggs on his hands, and just enough to eat from a table crowded by a huge family. He was raised in South Carolina's Beaufort County—where the government first gave black people "forty acres and a mule," where a recent survey found abysmal poverty and a high percentage of parasites in the blood of black children, more than 50 percent of whom are infected. "Was I a Tom there . . . then?" asks Frazier.

Ali's early days in Louisville were those of a gifted prodigy rather than those of a ghetto kid. He was from a small family, and he lived and ate well. Work was foreign to him; he spent the summer on the baronial manor of William J. Reynolds, where he concentrated on boxing, playing and occasionally removing the leaves from the Reynolds swimming pool. He was paid $7 a day, and according to a policeman named Joe Martin, who shaped his early training, "He drank a gallon of milk a day. They had this milk machine out there where you just pulled the spigot." Ali seems to have been cut off from the harshness of black life. He talked big, dreamed great scenarios, and then found a way to translate them into reality—thanks to the sizable lift given to him by the same kind of white syndicate that has helped Frazier.

What the two reflect seems lamentably lost amid ideologies, emotions, and a cross section of idiocy. Out of the ring, the true character of the fight is that Frazier and Ali encompass much of the best that sometimes is, and more often should be, in all of us—white and black. First, there is the courage of Ali, his obstinacy in the face of rank injustice and rejection. One may question his early motivation (which he himself did not fully understand) and, even now, ponder the argument that is so often posed about Thomas à Becket: Is a man less a saint because he tries to be a saint? After a while it was obvious that Ali was seeking political martyrdom. He got it, and he grew steadily and genuinely with his deed. His vision came high. He lost a fortune in his exile, all for a cause that has been neutralized by the slide of events and the vise of opinion.

If Ali, as some admirers think, is a man of the future, a man whose wiring is so special that he reacts unlike any other yet seen, then Joe Frazier is a rare copy of the old, revered, indomitable man. He came north out of Beaufort, pointed himself in a direction, survived the corruptive influence of North Philadelphia, and, with radar accuracy, reached his target. The country, the blacks, need an Ali, and so also is there much room for a Frazier. He feels just as deeply about his people, but he does not know the levers of political action, does not have the imagination for social combat. He understands only the right of the individual to be an individual, to survive and grow and be free of unfair pressures.

They have broken camp now, Ali in Miami, where critics blinked at his usual desultory gym work; Frazier in Philadelphia, where he was just as industrious as ever. But camps seldom reveal what will happen in a fight, and this one defies speculation. Certain points, however, may be made. Frazier must be extremely careful in the early rounds, especially in the first two, when he usually has not quite achieved the pulsating rhythm that is so vital to his style. One can expect Frazier to crowd Ali, to cut his punching radius, and to deal with Ali's height by trying to beat him to the body and arms in the hope of bringing the head down to a more workable level. It is unlikely that Frazier will gamble with many right hands to the head, for this would expose him to Ali's wicked flash of a left hook. He will have to absorb some pain from Ali's jab, but he must slip it quickly or he will never be able to put his fight together.

The possibility of a Frazier decision is not absurd as it may seem—aggressiveness means points and Joe will definitely take the fight to Ali. In the end, though, the question, which Ali

alone can answer, is, How much does he have left? He gave us
no real evidence in the Quarry fight. He did what he had to do,
but he did not labor long enough for any studied appraisal. He
did get a lot of work against Oscar Bonavena, and what was seen
was hardly vintage Ali. "The Bonavena fight saved him," says
his trainer, Angelo Dundee. "He needed a tough, long fight and
he got it. He's never been better. He will be something to watch."
Even if he is, Ali will still be in for a hard night against the stark
fact of Frazier—cut off from the insulation of his fantasy world
in which there is seldom any fact.

It behooves him to listen to the wise counsel of his mother,
who stopped off to kiss him good-bye before leaving for the Bahamas.

"Baby," she said, "don't underestimate this Frazier. Work
hard. I'm too nervous."

"Don't worry, Mom," Ali said, "I'll be in top shape. He's a
bum."

"Sonny . . . he's no bum," she said, and then kissed him again.

Whatever the result, there is ample precedent to support
the possible occurrence of the unexpected, the ludicrous, the
bizarre, especially in an Ali fight. Going all the way back to
Johnson-Willard, which many still believe Johnson threw,
heavyweight title bouts have often been shrouded in contro-
versy. It remained for Ali, with some help, to make the improb-
able familiar: the two Liston spectacles; the Chuvalo bout, in
which he allowed himself to be beaten to the body; the welter of
claims of foul tactics when he was in with Terrell; and the night
Patterson gimped about the ring because of a back injury and
Ali cruelly taunted him. Critics and spectators are usually confused by these moments, and the reaction is often the growl of
fix, for the most part an obsolete word in boxing today and certainly unrealistic in this fight.

Still, the prospect of odd incident, even a close decision for Frazier, offers the potential for trouble, and one can already sense sinister vibrations. So the fight cannot afford the slightest murkiness: no breaches of rules and no confused interpretation of the rules. The referee, who should be black and not allowed to score, must be in absolute control; for him, scoring is diverting. Any bungling, any laxity in supervision, is beyond consideration.

So now, with only the hallucinatory ranting of Ali to amuse us and whip the passions of his legions, we can only wait for the climax of the ring's strangest era. Wait and wonder if Ali will fulfill what he calls his divine destiny and deliver as romantic a moment as sport has ever known. Wait and feel the loneliness of Joe Frazier's position, sense his quiet desperation to remove the last obstacle in his life. Wait... as the drama tightens like a knotted rope in water.

2 The One-Minute Angels

(CORNERMEN)

Sports Illustrated
February 17, 1975

It was not necessary to look like Charley Goldman to work a corner in boxing, but whenever he was not there something seemed to be missing, as if you were looking at a wall from which a favorite picture had just been removed. From the sideshow feet to the derby, which crowned a head reminiscent of van Gogh's potato eaters, Charley was right out of central casting. He was the perfect embodiment of the public image of the cornerman, a wandering sect that scratched out survival with swab sticks, stopwatches, pails full of humbug, muttlike loyalty, and a compulsive attention to detail.

His looks aside, old Charley was notable mainly because—all things equal—he brought an edge to a fighter. As for the others, most remained just pasty faces moving through yellow light, a parade of dead men with towels over their shoulders and worn satchels in their hands. By day, you looked for them at Stillman's, a temple of higher learning renowned for its foulness of air and the breed's inclination to despoil; by night, in the grayness of an Automat, hunched behind very white coffee and a piece of arid cheesecake. Acclaim would only have confused their rigid, solitary lives.

In the old days only a few were more than parenthetical drops in news reports. Some of those who counted: Whitey Bimstein, the Hippocrates of trainers; Bill Gore, the architect of Willie Pep; avuncular Jimmy August, who worked with the late Dick Tiger; Ray Arcel, the quiet tactician who spent too much of his career picking up victims of Joe Louis. They were invaluable to their clients (Charley Goldman gave life to the stone legs of Rocky Marciano), but their rewards were modest compared with the earning power and celebrity of the best of those who followed them.

Three trainers now stand at the top of their trade: Angelo Dundee, who has worked with Muhammad Ali from the start; Gil Clancy, who has Emile Griffith and Jerry Quarry, among others; and Eddie Futch, who handles Joe Frazier and once salvaged the ruin that was Ken Norton. Neat, trim, little men, none of them resembles or even vaguely reminds one of the old elite, most of whom would have stiffened in a restaurant that smelled of anything more than beefsteak and onions. But the new guard is generally comfortable with what currently passes as civilization, as well as the versatility required by the contemporary ring.

Today boxing demands an ample brainpan of those who handle the best. There is none of that cursory stuff of jotting figures on the backs of envelopes or sticky bar napkins. You keep an eye on the lawyers (don't even blink) and you keep an eye on the math. The trainer is often now the manager, too. The job requires caution, even with the fighters. They are not the same fellows who used to walk around with lumpy ears and thick tongues and answered to any old name ("bum," for one) and later wondered, childlike, where the money went. The new fighters have names, sensitivities, a sense of the meanness that the ring can be; they also have the money.

Clancy was once a phys-ed teacher in Brooklyn; he boxed in the service and later became a trainer for the Police Athletic League. Dundee was a street kid in South Philly; he did his internship at Stillman's, where trainers swapped stories about cuts as if they were at a convention of plastic surgeons. Futch is one of the few professional boxers ever to make it as a big-time trainer. After a heart condition ended his fighting career, he studied under the great Chappie Blackburn, who tutored Joe Louis. The common ground of Clancy, Dundee, and Futch is success. They have the quality fighters, yes, but they also know how to control, to motivate, to run a corner with acumen.

Begin with Eddie Futch, the quiet, gentle ex-lightweight who is probably the least known of the three. His style is pianissimo, yet his ability to transmit knowledge that sticks is incomparable. "If I had a good one now, a young one now," said the late Jack Hurley long ago in an LA gym while watching Futch explain a move, "there's only one man I'd have to have, and that's Eddie Futch. The man's a master." Eddie says he doesn't think of himself as "any kind of master," only a man who has patience. If necessary, he will spend six months teaching a kid a left hook. He will break down every move in the ring as if it were a problem in long division, and if he sees it all come together only once, it is enough for him. Of all the punches, he says, the left jab is the most vital to a fighter. "There are four, five different jabs," he says, "and they all look easy. But they don't learn 'em easy."

The late Yank Durham got most of the credit for Joe Frazier, and a lot of it was deserved. Durham's strength was in the back room of negotiations. Still, Futch played a key role in making Frazier a fighter and carefully mapped the tactics. For years he would think of ways to dismantle Muhammad Ali, who was to him a rare and fascinating bird that he wanted to cage for one long moment. It took a while, but Eddie would be the only trainer to beat Ali—first with Frazier in the most dramatic, maybe the best, title fight of this century; then again with Norton, who had been merely a worker in the fields until Eddie picked him up. The key to victory was the same: relentless and steady pursuit.

Futch ran a cool corner the night Frazier beat Ali, whose own corner seemed to be in chaos. Ali is used to it, may even prefer it that way. Yet such an atmosphere does not usually help a fighter. "If a corner gets rattled," says Eddie, "it's a cinch the fighter will, too." He says the best corners are the ones that are noticed least. "*Control,* that's the word," he says. "Control of the fighter. Control of yourself."

Angelo Dundee works out of the Fifth Street Gym in Miami. He is the trainer the public knows best, mainly because he has had more fighters on television than anyone else, is often hired for instant analysis between rounds, and is united visually with Ali in the public mind. When left alone, that is, when he is not working with Ali, Dundee runs a sharp corner, complemented by two seconds who are the best in the business: Luis Sarrea, the wordless Cuban, and Dr. Ferdie Pacheco, for whom boxing is one of many avocations.

The charge that Dundee tampered with the ropes in Zaire (making them sag, to allow Ali to play them beautifully) is not true, but the trick is not beyond him. He is expert at prefight detail—not only ropes and canvas but publicity and propaganda.

Working in Ali's corner has been exasperating for Angelo, whose only balm is the money and a closeness to an authentic legend. Ali trains Ali, and he sometimes is a ruthless, heartless conditioner. The situation reduces Dundee almost to being a figurehead, a gregarious, eminently quotable press guide, a mediator of camp wrangles, a watcher of the camp's body politic. And a few remember that it was Angelo who saved at least two major fights for Ali. But his role with Ali does not diminish him. He is quick of mind. He can follow a fighter's most convoluted thoughts. He knows how to get a response. And he has no peer as a cutman—or as a survivor in a tattered way of life.

Gil Clancy has not done badly, either. He operates from a gym on the Lower West Side of Manhattan, a place barren of the slightest comfort. Clancy's face is not warming. It suggests sadism (because his one eye is impaired), and seldom can you measure his mood. He is more private than Futch or Dundee, more within himself, forever wary. Yet he is an emotional man in a gym or in a corner, and the joke is that you can always tell a Clancy fighter: he is black-and-blue from his own trainer. "Working with Emile Griffith for twenty years can do that to a man," says a friend. Griffith is the essence of professionalism: disciplined, willing, and durable. In the ring he can also be a study in limp concentration. Because of it, his fights often flirt with dullness and defeat.

"Once Griffith tames a guy," says Clancy, "he seems to lose interest. That's what happened against Benny Paret. I had burned it into Emile's mind that once he got inside, he should punch, punch, punch, and never stop! He never looked better. Then he goes blank again. He gets hit in the sixth and gets up at the bell. He comes back into the corner, and I look for a long time into his eyes. And then I slapped him across the face so hard my hand stung. Sadly, everybody knows what happened after that." Caught on the ropes, under one of the most uncompromising attacks ever seen in a ring, Paret was knocked out and later died.

Clancy has worked in the corners of more than two hundred fighters, including one so nervous he left his trunks in the dressing room. "That's all right," Clancy says. "I like emotional fighters. If they're way up, I don't have to be." Incompetence and sloppiness in a corner tick Clancy off. "All that pummeling of a fighter to refresh him is not often necessary," he says. "Nor is all that water. Sometimes you'd think they were loading up a camel. I remember Oscar Bonavena, with two relatives in his corner. He's tough enough to handle by himself. He kept saying, *'No agua, no agua,'* but they kept pushing the bottle up to his mouth and throwing buckets of water on him like he was on fire. They nearly drowned him. I had to yank the stuff away from them."

Such confusion, which unsettles most fighters, emphasizes the need for tighter controls over cornermen. As it is, anybody can get a license to work in a corner; the anybodys range from boxers' personal gurus to local druggists and the uncle from Waycross. Before a bout it is difficult to tell who will be working the corner of some fighters because of the swarm of people flapping about them; the latest trend is to personal bodyguards. When the bell rings, only three people should appear in the corner, hopefully men who can go about their duties with swift precision. As the sixty-second rest interval speeds by, there is no time to guess what has to be done. The corner should know when the fighter prefers water, know what it takes to revive him.

"You can feel quite foolish at times," says Dr. Pacheco. "Long ago, when I was learning under Angelo, I was working with Branca Otero. He came back to the corner at the end of the eighth round looking like he had just come off the Bataan death march. I unscrew the top of the ice bag and empty it, ice cubes and all, into his jock. He stands up for the ninth and just looks at me. Then, with a dagger in his voice, he says, 'Was that absolutely necessary?'"

A corner usually consists of a principal and two seconds. The principal, the manager/trainer, is the only one who talks. The other two carry equipment, Adrenalin, Q-tips, towels, a bucket, water bottles, all the accoutrements of the trade. Ten seconds before the bell rings signaling the end of the round, the principal is up on the top step with the stool, waiting for the fighter. With a swipe of the towel he wipes off the fighter's face, removing grease and sweat, and almost simultaneously he takes the mouthpiece and hands it to a second to be washed. He reapplies Vaseline to brows and cheekbones, talking calmly about the next round. His seconds have stretched out the fighter's trunks and have him gulping deep breaths of air.

Certain rules should never be broken. The word *tired* is banned from conversation in any form, even when referring to an opponent. Fighters sag visibly when the word is mentioned. Also, when the fighter sits down in his corner, he should not be allowed to stretch out his arms on the ropes. His arms should be folded in front of him, giving the impression of stoicism. Sponge baths and ice bags are not to be used until late in a fight. Such ministrations made early may convey to the fighter that he is wilting, that he needs maximum help. All of this makes sense, but there is also much charming nonsense concerning the handling of a fighter, so many slaphappy, old-time dicta and so much brittle advice. For example:

Sex is a killer: "It's rooned more good fighters than booze." Or, "It takes de legs right outta a fighter."

A boxer should get up at dawn and run: No sane reason has ever been given. Luis Rodriguez ran at night before supper, and he was remarkably durable.

Conditioning, getting a fighter ready, is a trainer's most delicate test, and for the boxer it is a masochistic ritual if ever there was one. The fighter brings his body, sometimes misshapen by excess, and the trainer brings his whips. Some trainers have been too malleable, some have used hobnails on their boots, and others have been indifferent. Toward the end of his career,

George Chuvalo, that most splendid masochist, walked out of his camp when he could no longer stand the taunts of his handler. Few fighters like to train. Gene Tunney, for whom training was nearly a religion, was an exception, and so was the early Rocky Marciano, who would start work nine months before a bout. It is a lonely time. The body hurts, and it is easy to wallow in self-pity.

All the work used to be done in spare, wooded isolation, but now the big fighters are more public, close to the scent of perfume and unending distraction, often in the garish ballrooms of hotels. But there is only so much you can do to condition a fighter: the rest is up to him and his state of mind, specifically in the area of *will*. Tunney had it, Marciano had it, and so do Ali and Frazier. Because of their single-mindedness, if he were around today, Whitey Bimstein would call them "nanimals." A lot of fighters think they qualify for that description, but few ever do. Inside, they are often frail men who lean toward hypochondria, and like most men who must live in constant communion with their bodies, they are forever looking for the *secret*: maybe a swallow of goat's milk and calf's blood; something, anything, to make them superhuman.

Cuts also are the object of much hocus-pocus. Every gym has its witch doctor; every fighter has a trainer with a formula that will stop a river of blood. The fact is that too many cutmen are clumsy butchers.

The location of a cut dictates the treatment: a cut eyelid is more serious than a cut ear; a cut on the bridge of the nose rolls up skin and is a nonstop bleeder; lips that are cut through are ugly and difficult to handle; nose splits are rare but terrifying (e.g., Marciano's in his September 1954 title fight with Ezzard Charles). But in general, says Dundee, the procedure for handling a cut is this:

"You wipe off the grime and ring dirt and apply Adrenalin on it with a Q-tip, then apply pressure with both fingertips. This is the most important part of the treatment, pressure for at least twenty seconds. The Adrenalin causes the end arteries to clamp, and the pressure causes small slots, or stoppers, to form on the ends of the constricted vessels. Some cutmen use bismuth powder to further clot the blood. Then a thick coagulant paste is applied. It has a cementlike quality that forms a tamponade. The first minute of the next round might see this punched out, but enough remains to stop the bleeding. The fighter returns to the corner, and the process is repeated over and over."

Dundee says the worst cut he has ever had to handle was a slash over the left eye suffered by Florentino Fernandez in a fight with Jose Gonzales; it later required sixty-four stitches. Gil Clancy remembers Rocky Rivero in the Fernandez bout in 1963: "He had a six-inch cut under the chin. It looked like a second mouth." And of those who were there, who could ever forget Leotis Martin, whose lip was nearly sheared off, left hanging, by Jimmy Ellis in their 1967 Houston encounter. It makes one wonder about Ernest Hemingway, who would handle a fighter occasionally back in Idaho and once said, "I enjoy working the corners, handling the cuts, the fat eyes, the fat ears...."

If you have a fighter who cuts easily (Henry Cooper had no equal), there is not much that can be done before a fight. Old-time fighters used to soak their faces in brine, a practice that has long since been abandoned.

A few fights have been won by a quick-witted cornerman when all was seemingly lost. Three such incidents stand out in memory, all involving Angelo Dundee. In his first bout with Cooper in 1963, Ali ran into one of Henry's famed left hooks. The bell saved him. Dundee then discovered that Ali's glove was ripped. Ali didn't even know he had gloves. Dundee was

given time to get another glove. It took ten minutes, more than
enough time for Ali to put his head back together. "The last time
a glove ripped in England," said one critic, "was when Henry
the Eighth's falcon got fresh with his hand."

Then there was Ali's first fight with Liston, when Ali, blinded
by wintergreen from Sonny's shoulder, wanted to quit, and
Dundee shoved him back into the ring. And again Dundee, this
time handling Willie Pastrano as Pastrano defended his world
light-heavyweight title in England against Terry Downes. Willie
was being soundly whipped. Downes was quite tired; so was
Willie, and for some reason he was mad at Angelo. In the corner,
Dundee berated Pastrano viciously. Willie glowered and started
to lunge at Dundee.

"You mad at me?" Dundee bellowed at his man. "Don't be
mad at me! I ain't takin' your title! There's the chump over there
you should be mad at! He's takin' your title, sucker!" The aroused
Pastrano knocked out Downes in the eleventh round.

It is doubtful that the ancient Captain Barclay, a pioneer of
precise training methods early in the nineteenth century,
would have been as abrasive as Dundee. He liked to refer to
the business as pugilistic art. His formula for training was conceived with great care; to him there was no higher calling than
to prepare a man for combat. After the Captain's time the trade
evolved first toward shoddiness, when, among other things,
trainers would tape hands with lethal bicycle tape and would
use razor blades to relieve swelling, and then to what is now
(for the most part) humaneness and competence. The Captain
would be pleased.

And so would Charley Goldman, who treated all of his
fighters as if they were made of porcelain. His advice was endless:
never buy diamonds off anyone on the street; only a sucker git
hit with a right hand. At the end of his life at eighty-five, Char-

ley lived alone in one room on the Upper West Side of Manhattan. The fixtures of his work were all over that room: Q-tips, beat-up satchels, old, chewed-up mouthpieces with a thin coat of dust. He used to sit there, his gnarled little hands clasped, and speak of Rocky Marciano. "I was the trainer of Rocky Marciano," he liked to say. He was not being boastful. He just wanted to make sure it was part of the record, for that was all he had left. And then one day they found him in his room, dead and wearing an old robe of Rocky's. Greater love hath no trainer.

3

"There Ain't No Others Like Me"

(DON KING)

Sports Illustrated
September 15, 1975

"Space is not space between the earth and the sun to one who looks down from the windows of the Milky Way." He pulls on a Montecruz Supreme, releasing a smoke ring that flutters above his head like a broken halo. "It was but yesterday that I thought myself a fragment quivering without rhythm in the sphere of life. Now I know that I am the sphere, and all life in rhythmic fragments moves within me." Having rid himself of these thoughts, the big man, the main man, the "impresario of the Third World" (name him, and you can have him, say his critics), turns and booms, his voice ripping across the skyline of Manhattan, "Yes, I do have an ego! I am!" Then, humbly, he adds, "But no man is an island, ya deeg?"

One could swear he heard the world sigh with relief, so glad it is that the orator admits to being human. "I am quintessential!" he begins again. He does not say of what he is quintessential, and it does not matter, his eyes seem to say; the word fits his mood. Words are always hovering above anyone who happens to be within ocean's distance of Don King, words fluttering in the air like crazed bats. But nobody waits for the next word, his next sentence of impeccable incoherence. They wait for his next move, that next gale of a gamble that knocks reason senseless and has powered him in a few short years from a busted-out life to the summit of his business—which you can also have if you can name it.

Call him a boxing promoter, but that does not explain what he does; it only gives him a label. Nobody knows exactly what he does or how he does it, and his adversaries, who underestimated him so badly, now flinch at the sound of his impact. The clattering telex in his office tells much more: Baby Doc Duvalier, the president for life, hopes that King can visit Haiti to discuss a situation of mutual interest; a spokesman for President Mobutu Sese Seko of Zaire has shown much interest in King's idea for a future project. King does not deal much with private capital, he works with governments, Third World countries whose rulers find King to be a useful catalyst. He says, "Henry Kissinger can't get in the places I can."

The power of the world, says King, "is slowly shifting, and you don't have to be no prophet like . . . who was that old dude? Yeah, Nostradeemusss. It's right in front of your nose, if you wanna look. But I don't care about politics. Just call me a promoter. Not the first black one. Not the first green one. But *theeee* promoter, Jack. There ain't no others, 'cause they've only had three in the history of the world: P. T. Barnum, Mike Todd, and you are lookin' at the third. Nobody kin deny it. They mock me at their peril."

Some do, though—with passion. They look upon him as a blowhard, a mountebank—and look at the way he dresses, like an MC in a cheap nightclub. "Just an uppity nigger, right?" says King. But the facts bite back in his defense: he has raised

$35 million in less than a year for his boxing spectaculars; he has made more money for Muhammad Ali "than Ali done in all his previous fights in his whole career." With the Ali-Foreman fight—and for only $14 million ("most of which they got back")—he brought "dignity and recognition and solidarity" to Zaire, a place "where people thought it was ridden with savages." And in a few weeks King will bring to the universe Ali vs. Joe Frazier for the heavyweight title in Manila. How's that for quintessential, his long pause seems to ask.

What he did not do and what he might do in the future are equally dramatic, according to King. With oil money from Saudi Arabia, he was on the brink of buying Madison Square Garden before deciding it was a bad investment. "It's become a turkey of a building," he says. He is now thinking of purchasing a major movie company. But more immediate is his sudden thrust into big team sports and music as a packager and manager of careers. He says that he has already signed eighty-five black pro football players, with more to follow in basketball and baseball. Overnight, it appears, he could become one of the most powerful men in all of sports.

"I won't be creatin' any wars," he says. "We just wants in on the middle of all that high cotton."

But for now, right this minute in Tokyo, or Zaire, or Cairo, or London, or in the back streets of Cleveland, whether among the right and polished sportsmen, or those who leg the numbers up dark alleys, Don King *is* boxing, the man with the show, the man with the fistful of dollars and the imagination to match. Quickly, with a lot of street genius, enough brass for a firehouse, and the messianic support of Herbert Muhammad (Ali's manager, who has an inscrutable genius of his own), King has managed to reduce the ring's power structure to rubble, and he is left all alone in his cavernous office atop Rockefeller Center to commune with the gods and play with his own ideas as if they were toys.

Boxing promoters have seldom been so singular; most of the big ones have been nearly invisible as personalities. The color, it seems, was left to the scufflers who kept their offices under their hats, would step on a nickel if a kid dropped it, and would smoke a cigar down to its last gritty and defiant end. In one sense, the big ones weren't promoters, not in the way of a Tex Rickard, his mind as sharp as his familiar diamond stickpin, or a Mike Jacobs, with his clacking false teeth and pawnbroker's shrewdness—they were names who worked up front. In the last decade or so, all those who have come along have been money-men who happened to be in control of the heavyweight champion. The list is long: Roy Cohn, the Bolan brothers, the Nilon brothers, Bill Fugazy, and that most resilient of night creatures, Bob Arum.

Limousines, hot dogs, the law, these were their businesses, and they drifted like clouds across a big moon. The ring was an amusing subsidiary, a playground in which to exercise their already fully developed roguishness; they left nothing behind, and if they were not completely anonymous, they were as dull as their gray suits. Now there is Don King, who used to stick out like a single hatchling turtle trying to make the sea in full view of sly crabs and deadly frigate birds. That image has been smashed, replaced by something close to King Kong skipping across the jagged teeth of Manhattan's skyline. He will be heard. He will be seen. He thinks a low profile is something you get in a barbershop.

"Nobody wanted to be up front before me," says King. "They all wanted to sit back, collect their money, and play their dirty tricks on each other and even the ones who worked for them. But I'm out there, Jack. You can see me, and if you don't, then

you're color-blind. My name's on everything. This ain't no
No-Name Productions. It's Don King Productions. I *perform*. And
when I don't perform, then I gotta go, too."

All right, let's look at the record over the one and a half
years King has been a front-rank promoter. First, there was
Foreman vs. Ken Norton in Venezuela; give it a rating of two
garbage cans. Norton was timid, King's partners behaved like
sharks, and Foreman was his usual self; that is to say, his presence did not radiate. It was pure chaos. Next, Ali vs. Foreman in
Zaire. Give it three stars. It was a brilliant victory for Ali, cere-
brum over inept strength; it was genuinely exciting, and if the
figures did not excite accountants, they did not disappoint
them, either. On the negative side was government censorship,
and again the attitude of some of King's associates, who tried
(and in some cases managed) to cheat the press out of a charter-
plane refund. King went on his own with Chuck Wepner vs. Ali,
Foreman vs. the Infirm Five up in Toronto, Ron Lyle and Ali in
Las Vegas, and Ali against the catatonic Joe Bugner in Malaysia.

The artistic merit of these four productions is dubious.
"How did I know Foreman would go berserk in Toronto?" says
King. "But I'll take the blame. It was a good idea, but I didn't
think George would make a farce of it." The business aspect is
brighter. Wepner took a loss, but television picked up the tab for
the Toronto show and Lyle; Toronto held its own against Con-
nors vs. Newcombe in the TV ratings, and the Lyle fight had an
enormous pull in numbers. Bugner in Malaysia lost a few dollars, too. "What can you do?" says King. "Here's a big strong
dude with the chance of a lifetime, and he stands in the ring like
a thousand-year-old mummy."

Essentially, King works for Muhammad Ali, the hottest
property in the world, and for Herbert Muhammad, a hard real-
ist who could not care if King's skin was Technicolor; when Her-

bert looks at a promoter, he sees only green. Herbert gave King his chance, but he would not stay with him if King didn't produce. Herbert never really believed King would deliver, yet he could not deny a black brother a chance to fail. But King did not fold, and as Herbert watched, King produced the figures, the action, the credibility, the continuity that Herbert demanded. "He's a hard taskmaster," says King, "but he's taught me much." King has survived.

The trio gets along well. Ali introduces King as "a businessman—and former gangster." Often bemused, Herbert looks on quietly from the background. He is sensitive to any nuance suggesting that King is the brains behind Ali. Recently, when Ali conned the press into thinking he was retiring, King said he was going to Malaysia to intercede, to use his influence on him. "What's this?" asked Herbert. "You got everybody thinkin' you're the manager of Ali. I'm paranoid 'bout that, Donald." Herbert tries to tone down the excessive side of King, and that is like trying to rein a runaway team of Clydesdales. The excesses, the props, have become King's style.

Harold Lloyd had his lensless glasses, W. C. Fields his voice, and Clark Gable those ears. Several distinctions—familiar things that have become a part of his character—mark Don King. His hair looks like a bale of cotton candy just retrieved from a coal bin. He must hold the record for time spent in a tuxedo; he easily beats out Tony Martin, the recognized champion. Then, there is his jewelry. To look at King is to look into the sun or to gaze at a mobile Cartier's. On one finger is a meat block of a diamond ring that cost $30,000, on his pinkie is a $3,000 number, and on his wrist is a $9,000 watch. Add to all of this his voice and language, a thunderous roll that blends black slang with newspeak words like *infrastructure, interface,* and *input,* a grandiloquent soliloquy that he will suddenly interrupt to summon up the ghosts of the Apostle Paul, François Villon, the moonstruck Khalil Gibran, and King's favorite, Shakespeare.

Now King, at age forty-four, has found a headquarters, an address to match the man. The suite of offices, including two boardrooms, is located on the sixty-seventh floor of the prestigious RCA Building, just two floors up from the famous Rainbow Room and close enough to the sky to grab a star. The rent is $60,000 a year, and the furniture cost him $40,000. The move by King shook those who follow such things, not to mention the fight mob, which was used to dealing in the back rooms of bars, or in five-story walk-ups. "I'm not walkin' up to the top of *that* place," said one manager. Clearly, the offices have done what King hoped they would do.

"They're all out there wonderin'," he says. "They're wonderin', 'What's that crazy nigger doin' up there? He must be doin' somethin'.' The place has become a magnet."

King has made people pay attention, so much so that his reception room looks like the last lifeboat leaving the *Titanic,* and his messages run to two hundred a day. He tries to see everyone, from inventors who have machines with strange powers or a solution to the aging process of the body, to the lowliest fight managers, who look up and around the place as if they were in a spaceship—all of the schemers and dreamers looking for that peg to hang the world on. King spends an average of fifteen hours a day in his office, some of it in the effort of staying atop office intrigue. And well he should, for he had made himself vulnerable.

King's high command is a good example of how things work in boxing promotion. For instance, one never lets a grudge get in the way of making money. Working with him are Henry Schwartz, Mike Malitz, and, of all people, Bob Arum, once King's avowed enemy. Schwartz was King's former boss at Video

Techniques. He first brought King on the scene, made him a vice president, and thought of him as "my black interface." Which, as King says now, was another way of saying "chump." But King could not be held on a leash, and soon he went on his own, leaving behind such disgraceful practices as extra charges for equipment; closed-circuit exhibitors were badly mauled by Video on the Zaire fight. "Schwartz has got nothin' to do with the business end now," says King, "but he's valuable when it comes to technical stuff like satellites."

Malitz is a familiar face; he was long the right arm of Bob Arum. Malitz is a pro. He has no equal as an orchestrator of closed-circuit television. He knows where the money is, and he knows how to collect. King needs Malitz, but why Arum? "He has a brilliant legal mind," King says unconvincingly. The fact is that King has no choice but to cut Arum in on the promotion. The Manila connection, a personage named Thomas Oh, had dealt with Arum first, having been led to believe that Arum could deliver Ali. King had been trying to put the fight on in New York. Failing, he went to his sources in Manila, who did not have the clout of Thomas Oh. Finally, learning that Arum did not have Ali, Oh had to deal with King. Now Arum's only chance was to bring Thomas Oh and King together. They sat down, but King held out as long as possible, looking for money elsewhere, mainly because of Arum's presence in the deal. Herbert Muhammad was impatient. He wanted a contract from King, or else he was going with still another rival promoter, Jerry Perenchio.

King saved promotional face by hooking up with Thomas Oh at the last minute, so Arum, the man who used to "control" Ali in a promotional sense, is once more in the thick of things. King fought long and hard to break Arum's grip, and here Arum is, back in the middle of the money, right in the middle of King's own operation, sitting on his shoulder like a wise and patient owl observing a field mouse who has gotten too big.

But a hired hand in King's office says, "There's no way King's going to get hurt. So far he's done the impossible for Herbert and Ali. If Herbert ever does sink him for a white man, he's going to look pretty bad after the way King's performed. And as far as this promotion is concerned, King won't be caught napping. The secret of closed circuit is who gets to the money first, and that's King now. King and Arum have absolutely nothing in common. King has his faults. He's too loud. His tired black line can wear you out. But he's a decent human being, generous and sensitive. One day he must have had his driver twenty hours. So he's going into his hotel, and then turns back and presses a hundred-dollar bill in the driver's hand. Another promoter would have borrowed twenty dollars from the driver!"

The main person King must keep an eye on is himself. It is an old truth that the bigger the man, the easier the con. King's feathers must be preened, his ego stroked; grafters with larger plans usually jump at the chance, and then they become much more. Loyalty is almost nonexistent in boxing, but King has what little there is. He did not have to ask for it or pay for it. It was given to him because he was strong and fair, and his followers saw him as a deliverer from the tyranny of Madison Square Garden. "He's made a mole out of Teddy Brenner, and he's put Mike Burke in his pocket," says Paddy Flood, a manager. "The Garden doesn't count anymore." But there are some who believe King's ego and his ambition have leaped out of hand. "He don't listen too good anymore," says another manager.

"It's all subjective," says King. "They don't understand that up here is like bein' in a war every day. I'm so tired most of the time, I goes home and falls into bed."

It is a Sunday afternoon. He sits beneath a large portrait of

Ali. He has been talking about his early life, about the roaches in the tenements that he would spray furiously with bottles of white poison, and still they kept coming; about all the days he spent running to deliver squalling chickens from Hymie's Chicken Shack to the slaughterhouse knife; about his reign as a regent of the numbers in Cleveland; about Benny, one of his predecessors, who used to equip his numbers runners like an army preparing for winter invasion. "He used to buy a whole supply of galoshes and hats and overcoats and hand them out to his men," says King.

King is not wearing a shirt, and his massive chest is moist with sweat. It is a hot day in New York, and he does not like air-conditioning. An angry scar crawls up his chest, a gift from his prison days when an incompetent doctor turned a simple cyst surgery into an awful mess. It is obvious, as he stretches and prowls throughout the room, that he likes the space of his office. King knows all about space, for it was only six years ago that he was put into the hole at the Ohio Penitentiary with only bread and water and a Bible and darkness; he read the Bible by light that slithered through cracks, and then he would use it as a pillow. "I had no trouble in prison, except for that one time a guy hit me in the mouth," says King. "They don't need much excuse to do anything they want to you."

King was in prison because he killed one of his runners in a fistfight, just an ordinary scrap. The memory of it haunts him, and so do the four years he got, a severe sentence for the kind of charge that a lot of people have beaten over the years.

"I went up on manslaughter," says King, "and I expected to be paroled early. But they made me do four years in the joint. These parole flops cut the heart right out of me. My numbers reputation was held against me."

The details, the moments of prison life, are engraved in his mind: being led by foot chains off the bus; the sixty-man floor at the Marion Reformatory where nightmares came to life in sound, and King would stay awake as long as he could so he would not have to enter subconscious hell; the six-by-twelve cell, where they made you wash out of the toilet bowl, and the smell of sulfur in the water made you sick; the look on the face of his wife, who drove four hundred miles every weekend to see him—and the riot.

"It was over," says King, "and we're standin' there naked, and a guy named Bradshaw was standin' there, too...just standin' there. I'll never forget how the kid from the National Guard got nervous. Bradshaw, he was doin' what he was told. But the kid got scared and he pulled the trigger, and there was Bradshaw's stomach running down to his crotch. Solitary? Perversions? You don't know the kind of depravity that stalks a prison!"

King looks over at a picture of his wife and kids taken on his big farm in Ohio. "That's the only place where the war stops," he says. His wife, Henrietta, runs the farm. "She don't go for no nonsense," he says, recalling how once his son's marks in school tailed off, and she personally shaved off all his hair.

King gets up and walks out onto the balcony. Down below, sixty-seven floors, evening falls on the town like a dirty handkerchief. High up there, he is a long way from a six-by-twelve cell, he is a man with the power to raise $35 million in a year, the man who can deliver Muhammad Ali—for now. And then he shouts up to the sky, "If I do not perform, Mr. Rockefeller, I will not jump off your building!" Raising his hand as if he were Emperor Jones, his voice booms again: "But if the Milky Way were not within me, how should I have seen it or known it?"

A star winks back at him.

He says. Winking.

4 —Manila—for Blood and for Money

(ALI-FRAZIER III)

Sports Illustrated
September 29, 1975

His metaphysical baggage by now lashed down to a handy place in his mind after a numbing twenty-one-hour trip above a world that seems to have assigned him a regency never before known by a fighter, Muhammad Ali sits in the presidential suite looking out at the great ships of the world anchored in Manila Bay. The sun punches up slowly over the water, and the beauty of the scene is not lost on this man whose mind wanders forever and confusingly between the poles of simpleton and primitive genius. "Just look at those ships," he says, "think of all the monsoons they must have fought through to get here, all the mighty oceans that could have snapped them in half." "My, my," he says softly. "Ain't the world somethin'. Too beautiful for an ignorant and ugly man to be king of."

A day later, with the wind and rain whipping against the windows of another hotel suite across town, Joe Frazier, the man who would be king, lies on his bed, trying to articulate the hurt that has burned through his heart and mind for so long that the words come in spasms. And if words could consign a man to everlasting hell, Muhammad Ali would be damned right that very moment. Frazier tries to find control, tries futilely to reach back for equilibrium, leaning on country Baptist teachings and his own clear and gracious nature, which sticks out, oddly moving, like a common dark stone on a white mantelpiece. "I don't want to knock him out here in Manila," he finally says. "I want to hurt him. If I knock him down, I'll stand back, give him a chance to breathe, to get up. It's his heart I wants."

So after a long five years that have seen two fights between them (the first a brilliant drama), that have seen Ali become an instrument of international politics and economics, have seen the proud foot soldier Frazier manhandled in the second fight, perhaps the rawest of sports feuds will come to a public end when Ali and Frazier meet for the third time next week in Manila. Listen to Ali about the fight, and the firmament is ablaze. Listen to Frazier, and you feel the sun on an open field that has to be worked, touch the blisters on his hands.

It is a proposition of the heart and blood for Frazier, an offering to Allah and another chance to light up the lives of the world's disenfranchised for Ali, but beyond all of this is that most unromantic of motives—money. If the bout goes fifteen rounds, Ali will receive $4 million for forty-five minutes' work, and Frazier will get $2 million. The revenue from closed-circuit television will surely break all existing records. As promoter Don King says, "This ain't just a sportin' event. This here is a dramatic contribution to the world's economy. Waiters will be waitin'. Bartenders will be tendin'. The brothers and sisters gonna be buyin' new clothes. Why, I got enough people on my payroll alone for this here happenin' to buy a jet plane and go back and forth to New Orleans up until the year 2000. Jack, this is the ennnnnnd."

When the sun comes up in Manila on October 1 (in New York it will be 6:00 p.m., September 30), thousands will have been camping overnight outside the Coliseum. The top ticket costs $300; the lowest price, for a bleacher seat, is $2. A crowd of twenty-eight thousand, the largest for any athletic event in Philippine history, is expected, and what it will see at 10:30 a.m. will be a rare thing: two of the most luminous heavyweights in ring history in the kind of showdown that seldom comes once in a lifetime, not to mention thrice. There is nothing contrived here. This is not an electronic toy conceived in network boardrooms and then sent out and made to look like a dramatic sporting conflict.

Even so, it is doubtful that Ali and Frazier will match their first fight, a masterpiece of courage and talent and high tension that left one damp with sweat and tingling many hours later. Never before had two big men given so much so artfully and completely. And no one will ever forget the sight of Ali, finally crumbling under one of Frazier's cruel left hooks, his feet kicking high toward the ring lights. The knockdown hurt Ali's chances for a decision, and in the end Frazier, his face looking like a gargoyle's, was the champion. Frazier spent days in the hospital, and it was rumored that he would never be the same again. He did not do much to refute those rumors in his second meeting with Ali.

No title was at stake in January of 1974, but still the private limousines were parked two deep around Madison Square Garden, and the crowd came with the first fight exploding in its memory. No one cared that Ali had lost to Ken Norton once and barely beaten him another time, or that George Foreman had knocked down Frazier six times in two rounds. In this fight, Ali walked a thin line between ring generalship and slovenly style. Clinching whatever he could (he started 114 of them), Ali found a way to disrupt Frazier's attack. But there was not much of the old Joe visible. His thrilling aggression was gone, the ceaseless bob and weave almost nonexistent, and had the referee not blundered, thinking the bell had sounded, and prematurely separated them, Joe might have been knocked out in the second round. His lance had clearly dropped near to the ground. Was he through? Maybe not, but he was near the end.

Since then, Frazier has fought a total of fourteen rounds in two fights, Ali forty-nine rounds in four fights. "He ain't in no shape for a man like me," says Ali. Yet, Frazier looks very sharp in his daily workouts in the Folk Arts Theater, a beautiful structure that juts into Manila Bay. Every day about two thousand people pay the equivalent of $1.25 to watch him snort and hammer his way through an assortment of sparring partners. The crowd always seems stunned by his animalism, by the toughness of his 217 pounds. Then Frazier goes to the ring apron and fields questions from the Filipinos before singing into the mike: *You tried to shake it off / Ooh, but you just couldn't do it / 'cause there was a soul power in my punch / and like a good left hook I threw it / one minute you were standing so tall / the next second you began to fall.*

Ali hears that Frazier sings at his workouts and he says, "Are you kiddin'? That man can't sing. He's the only nigger in the world ain't got rhythm." That kind of talk has finally and irrevocably eroded Frazier, but nothing has disturbed him more over the years than Ali's recent taunts. Over and over Ali shouts, "Joe Frazier is a gorilla, and he's gonna fall in Manila." The gorilla label, with all its inherent racism, stings. Frazier glances at a picture on his dresser. "Look at my beautiful kids," he says plaintively. "Now, how can I be a gorilla? That's a dirty man. He's just like a kid when you play with him. He don't wanna stop, and then ya gots to whup him to make him behave. That's what this jerk Clay is like. Well, I guess he gonna talk. Ain't no way to stop him, but there will come that moment when he gonna be all alone, when he gonna hear that knock on the door, gonna hear it's time to go to the ring, and then he gonna remember what it's like to be in with me, how hard and long this night's gonna be."

The condemned man, Ali, is not hurrying through any last meal. Indeed, he seems to be preoccupied by his appeal to the masses. "My personality has attracted the world," he says. "My personality has gone so far till America can't afford me anymore. The American promoters can't have me no more 'cause they can't bid against so many countries. My personality and the power that Allah has given me has gone so far out that America is cryin' and the Garden is dyin'. When I was a little boy, I used to say, 'Daddy, one day I'm gonna make four thousand dollars on the *Gillette Cavalcade of Sports*.' Can ya imagine—four thousand dollars! That's what I pay my cooks for a bonus. No nation can contain me anymore."

Or, if bored by his universal radiance, Ali will begin speechifying. The monologues are dead certain to clear a room. Especially when the subject is Allah. Through the years he has put together about ten speeches, most of them written by the kitchen light of his fight camp. He listens to tapes that carry his messages: "He is beyond the reach of range and time.... He sees though He has no eyes. He created everything without a model, pattern, or sample." Ali turns down the volume. "I get this in my mind," he interjects, "and I have real power over Joe Frazier. I can whup him. Allah knows if I win, I'll keep doin' His preachin' for Him. That's why I win all the time. I'm using my fame to talk about this man. The world's mystified by me. It likes to be mystified. You know, stuff like Batman and Robin, Dracula, the Wolfman, Mary had a child without a man.

"I train myself spiritually. Frazier's fightin' for money. I'm fightin' for free people. How many suits I got? One, two maybe. No watch, no ring, one pair of shoes. I've got Eldorados and Rolls-Royces, but I don't drive 'em anymore. Where's a man's wealth? His wealth is in his knowledge. If you don't think I'm wealthy, go talk to Joe Frazier and try to carry on a conversation. He's illiterate. I spoke at Harvard. They wanted me to be a professor of poetry at Oxford. I'm shockin' the world. But even I, Muhammad Ali, don't amount to nothin' more than a leaf in the wind. Ain't nothin' yours, either. You own nothin'. Not even your kids. You die, and they will be callin' somebody else Daddy when your wife remarries."

It is endless, this religious backwater through which all his listeners must wade. It is as if he believes that being the heavyweight champion is not enough and that the Filipinos want much more from him. The simple truth is that they want nothing more than to gaze upon him. Each day more than eight thousand of them shove their way into the theater to watch him work. Thousands more line the streets when he goes to an official function, and at five in the morning—an hour after the end of the curfew but still pitch-dark—bands of them accompany him on his roadwork, creating a charming scene of tenacious, small men trying to match the giant stride for stride along the boulevard by the bay. Once he stepped into a hole and turned and shouted, "Watch out for the hole." He ends his running on the steps of the Hilton, and there he sits in the dark in a gray sweat suit and black boots, tilting a large bottle of orange juice to his mouth. The sweat drops off him as he leans back on his elbows. He looks at the faces around him, listens to the heavy silence. "Look at their expressions," he whispers. "Ain't no man worthy of that kind of love."

At this time, he is likely to talk about boxing. He can feel his body, listen to its music as he tries once more to make it reach for the high note of condition. "You been watchin' my gym work?" he asks. "Don't pay any attention to it. I'm nothin' in a gym. I just use it to experiment, you know that. This fight is goin' to be won out here in the mawnin', and on that heavy bag. I hadn't worked on the heavy bag for a long time, until George Foreman in Africa. I kept hurtin' my hands all the time. They've never been in the best of shape, and the bag I had was brutal on 'em. Ya hit that old bag with a baseball bat and the bat breaks in two. This one is especially made in Mexico, and it's easy on the hands. It got me sharp for Foreman, seemed to give me strength. I never let it out of my sight now. I sleep with it in my room. My men carry it personally on and off planes. I am strong, and I kin feel it all hummin' inside me. That heavy bag has done a miracle. I got my punch back."

He sits there for a long time and then retires to his room. He is alone now, meaning that the rooms are not filled with the moochers and odd characters he has picked up during his career. He does not like to be alone. He needs his audience to abuse or charm. But now he is alone, except for his man, his mute body servant from Malaysia. Ali looks over at him and says, as if he were an old sergeant major out of Kipling, "Look at him, he's so obedient. Always says, 'Yessir, yessir.' He'll go fetch anything for you. He'll even take your shoes off for you. He's civilized."

Ali arises and picks up a large book that has been written about him. "I haven't read ten pages in all the books written about me. I can't read too good; a bad speller, too. I read one page and turn it and get tired. I just look at the pictures. I know that sounds dumb." He reads for a long minute, following each word with his little finger. "Oh, I wish I could read better." The frustration of a child is in his voice, and then it turns to anger as he is asked about the *gorilla* tag that he has pinned on Frazier. "The way I've been talkin' black power," he says, "nobody can get on me for bein' ignorant or racist. Why does he call me Clay? That's my nigger slave name. He's insultin' my name and my religion. He ain't nobody. I made him. Now he's just an old has-been. He envies me. When he was a kid, I was the champ. He's an old man now, long before his time, and I'm still the champ."

Frazier has avoided any personal collision with Ali. His trainer, Eddie Futch, does not want his man ruffled. Frazier and Futch refuse to be suckered into public exchanges with Ali. They think of nothing but the fight. Futch is particularly concerned about the choice of referee. It is sure to be a bitter issue. "It's the most vital aspect of the bout," says Eddie. "I want a referee who's goin' to break Ali every time he starts leanin' in and holdin'. Give us this, and Joe Frazier will once more be heavyweight champion of the world."

Neither man will offer a prediction. Frazier never has and does not intend to start now: "I don't believe in predictin' I'm gonna knock a man out, because if you tell me you're gonna push me out that window at midnight, I'm gonna sit there and watch you along about eleven fifty-nine." Ali says, "I'm too old for that stuff now. This is a serious fight. I'm goin' to be classical. None of this Russian-tank stuff, none of the rope-a-dope. I got too much at stake here. I got sixteen million dollars in fights waitin' for me."

Too many questions preclude a private choice. Can Ali once more orchestrate his body to his will against a man who has always tested both severely? Is he really in shape? Has he maintained the form he showed against Joe Bugner in Malaysia last July? Some close to him say no, say that women and the problems that come with them have seriously disrupted his concentration.

What about Frazier? Is this gallant man finally at the end of the line? Can he summon up one last measure of his old self, the kind of Frazier who made the heart pump wildly and the hands clammy?

For both Frazier and Ali, a sense of finality creeps into their words as the bout nears. "This is a big gatherin'," says Frazier. "And I don't like big gatherin's. It's like when we were all back home in South Carolina, and all of us, all the relatives, would be havin' a fish fry in the backyard, and everybody would be laughin', but my mama would be sittin' there lookin' sadly out. She didn't like big gatherin's. Big gatherin's mean death."

Lost in a long silence, Ali comes out of it and suddenly says in a barely audible voice, "I'm goin' to have another test soon. It's time. Things have been goin' too good lately. Allah must make me pay for my fame and power. Somebody may shoot me, who knows? I might be kidnapped and told to renounce the Muslims publicly—or else. 'Okay, shoot me,' I'll have to say. I feel somethin' out there. My little boy might die. He might get run over by a car the day before the fight. Allah's always testin' you. He don't let you get great for nothin'. It ain't no accident I'm the greatest man in the world." Then he looks at those ships in the bay, and who knows what wondrous and strange things are gliding through so unpredictable a mind. Only this is certain now: ahead lies the hatred of Joe Frazier, and Ali must journey through it. And it is a trip that few men should wish to make.

5   "Lawdy, Lawdy, He's Great"

(ALI-FRAZIER III)

Sports Illustrated
October 13, 1975

It was only a moment, sliding past the eyes like the sudden shifting of light and shadow, but long years from now, it will remain a pure and moving glimpse of hard reality, and if Muhammad Ali could have turned his eyes upon himself, what first and final truth would he have seen? He had been led up the winding, red-carpeted staircase by Imelda Marcos, the First Lady of the Philippines, as guest of honor at the Malacañang Palace. Soft music drifted from the terrace as the beautiful Imelda guided the massive and still heavyweight champion of the world to the long buffet ornamented by a huge candelabra. The two whispered, then she stopped and filled his plate, and as he waited, the candles threw an eerie light across the face of a man who only a few hours before had survived the ultimate inquisition of himself and his art.

The maddest of existentialists, one of the great surrealists of our time, the king of all he sees, Ali had never before appeared so vulnerable and fragile, so pitiably unmajestic, so far from the universe he claims as his alone. He could barely hold his fork, and he lifted the food slowly up to his bottom lip, which had been scraped pink. The skin on his face was dull and blotched, drained of that familiar childlike wonder. His right eye was a deep purple, beginning to close, a dark blind being drawn against a harsh light. He chewed his food painfully, and then he suddenly moved away from the candles as if he had become aware of the mask he was wearing, as if an inner voice were laughing at him. He shrugged, and the moment was gone.

A couple of miles away, in the bedroom of a villa, the man who has always demanded answers of Ali, has trailed the champion like a timber wolf, lay in semidarkness. Only his heavy breathing disturbed the quiet as an old friend walked to within two feet of him. "Who is it?" asked Joe Frazier, lifting himself to walk around. "Who is it? I can't see! I can't see! Turn the lights on!" Another light was turned on, but Frazier still could not see. The scene cannot be forgotten: this good and gallant man lying there, embodying the remains of a will never before seen in a ring, a will that had carried him so far—and now surely too far. His eyes were only slits, his face looked as if it had been painted by Goya. "Man, I hit him with punches that'd bring down the walls of a city," said Frazier. "Lawdy, lawdy, he's a great champion." Then he put his head back down on the pillow, and soon there was only the heavy breathing of a deep sleep slapping like big waves against the silence.

Time may well erode that long morning of drama in Manila, but for anyone who was there, those faces will return again and again to evoke what it was like when two of the greatest heavyweights of any era met for a third time and left millions limp around the world. Muhammad Ali caught the way it was: "It was like death. Closet thing to dyin' that I know of."

Ali's version of death began about 10:45 a.m. on October 1

in Manila. Up to then his attitude had been almost frivolous. He would simply not accept Joe Frazier as a man or as a fighter, despite the bitter lesson Frazier had given him in their first savage meeting. Aesthetics govern all of Ali's actions and conclusions; the way a man looks, the way he moves, is what interests Ali. By Ali's standards, Frazier was not pretty as a man and without semblance of style as a fighter. Frazier was an affront to beauty, to Ali's own beauty as well as to his precious concept of how a good fighter should move. Ali did not hate Frazier, but he viewed him with the contempt of a man who cannot bear anything short of physical and professional perfection.

Right up until the bell rang for round one, Ali was dead certain that Frazier was through, was convinced that he was no more than a shell, that too many punches to the head had left Frazier only one more solid shot removed from a tin cup and some pencils. "What kind of man take all those punches to the head?" he asked himself over and over. He could never come up with an answer. Eventually he dismissed Frazier as the embodiment of animal stupidity. Before the bell Ali was subdued in his corner, often looking down to his manager, Herbert Muhammad, and conversing aimlessly. Once, seeing a bottle of mineral water in front of Herbert, he said, "Whatcha got there, Herbert? Gin! You don't need any of that. Just another day's work. I'm gonna put a whuppin' on this nigger's head."

Across the ring Joe Frazier was wearing trunks that seemed to have been cut from a farmer's overalls. He was darkly tense, bobbing up and down as if trying to start a cold motor inside himself. Hatred had never been a part of him, but words like "gorilla," "ugly," "ignorant"—all the cruelty of Ali's endless vilifications—had finally bitten deeply into his soul. He was there not seeking victory alone; he wanted to take Ali's heart out and then crush it slowly in his hands. One thought of the moment days before, when Ali and Frazier with their handlers between them were walking out of the Malacañang Palace, and Frazier said to Ali, leaning over and measuring each word, "I'm gonna whup your half-breed ass."

By packed and malodorous jeepneys, by small and tiny taxis, by limousine and by worn-out bikes, twenty-eight thousand had made their way into the Philippine Coliseum. The morning sun beat down, and the South China Sea brought not a whisper of wind. The streets of the city emptied as the bout came on public television. At ringside, even though the arena was air-conditioned, the heat wrapped around the body like a heavy, wet rope. By now, President Ferdinand Marcos, a small, brown derringer of a man, and Imelda, beautiful and cool as if she were relaxed on a palace balcony taking tea, had been seated.

True to his plan, arrogant and contemptuous of an opponent's worth as never before, Ali opened the fight flat-footed in the center of the ring, his hands whipping out and back like the pistons of an enormous and magnificent engine. Much broader than he has ever been, the look of swift destruction defined by his every move, Ali seemed indestructible. Once, so long ago, he had been a splendidly plumed bird who wrote on the wind a singular kind of poetry of the body, but now he was down-to-earth, brought down by the changing shape of his body, by a sense of his own vulnerability, and by the years of excess. Dancing was for the ballroom; the ugly hunt was on. Head up and unprotected, Frazier stayed in the mouth of the cannon, and the big gun roared again and again.

Frazier's legs buckled two or three times in that first round, and in the second he took more lashing as Ali loaded on him all the meanness that he could find in himself. "He won't call you Clay no more," Bundini Brown, the spirit man, cried hoarsely from the corner. To Bundini, the fight would be a question of where fear first registered, but there was no fear in Frazier. In the third round Frazier was shaken twice and looked as if he might go at any second as his head jerked up toward the hot lights and the sweat flew off his face. Ali hit Frazier at will, and when he chose to do otherwise, he stuck his long left arm in Frazier's face. Ali would not be holding in this bout as he had in the second. The referee, a brisk workman, was not going to tolerate clinching. If he needed to buy time, Ali would have to use his long left to disturb Frazier's balance.

A hint of shift came in the fourth. Frazier seemed to pick up the beat, his threshing-blade punches started to come into range as he snorted and rolled closer. "Stay mean with him, champ!" Ali's corner screamed. Ali still had his man in his sights and whipped at his head furiously. But at the end of the round, sensing a change and annoyed, he glared at Frazier and said, "You dumb chump, you!" Ali fought the whole fifth round in his own corner. Frazier worked his body, the whack of his gloves on Ali's kidneys sounding like heavy thunder. "Get out of the goddamn corner," shouted Angelo Dundee, Ali's trainer. "Stop playing," squawked Herbert Muhammad, wringing his hands and wiping the mineral water nervously from his mouth. Did they know what was ahead?

Came the sixth, and here it was, that one special moment that you always look for when Joe Frazier is in a fight. Most of his fights have shown this: you can go so far into that desolate and dark place where the heart of Frazier pounds, you can waste his perimeters, you can see his head hanging in the public square, maybe even believe that you have him, but then suddenly you learn that you have not. Once more the pattern emerged as Frazier loosed all the fury, all that has made him a brilliant heavyweight. He was in close now, fighting off Ali's chest, the place where he has to be. His old calling card—that sudden evil, his left hook—was working the head of Ali. Two hooks ripped with slaughterhouse finality at Ali's jaw, causing Imelda Marcos to look down at her feet, and the president to wince as if a knife had been stuck in his back. Ali's legs seemed to search for the floor. He was in serious trouble, and he knew that he was in no-man's-land.

Whatever else might one day be said about Muhammad Ali, it should never be said that he is without courage, that he cannot take a punch. He took those shots by Frazier and then came out for the seventh, saying to him, "Old Joe Frazier, why I thought you were washed-up." Joe replied, "Somebody told you all wrong, pretty boy."

Frazier's assault continued. By the end of the tenth round it was an even fight. Ali sat on his stool like a man ready to be staked out in the sun. His head was bowed, and when he raised it, his eyes rolled from the agony of exhaustion. "Force yourself, champ!" his corner cried. "Go down to the well once more!" begged Bundini, tears streaming down his face. "The world needs ya, champ!" In the eleventh, Ali got trapped in Frazier's corner, and blow after blow bit at his melting face, and flecks of spittle flew from his mouth. "Lawd have mercy!" Bundini shrieked.

The world held its breath. But then Ali dug deep into whatever it is that he is about, and even his severest critics would have to admit that the man-boy had become finally a man. He began to catch Frazier with long right hands, and blood trickled from Frazier's mouth. Now Frazier's face began to lose definition; like lost islands reemerging from the sea, massive bumps rose suddenly around each eye, especially the left. His punches seemed to be losing their strength. "My God," wailed Angelo Dundee. "Look at 'im. He ain't got no power, champ!" Ali threw the last ounces of resolve left in his body in the thirteenth and fourteenth. He sent Frazier's mouthpiece flying into the press row in the thirteenth and nearly floored him with a right in the center of the ring. Frazier was now no longer coiled. He was up high, his hands down, and as the bell for the fourteenth sounded, Dundee pushed Ali out saying. "He's all yours!" And he was, as Ali raked him with nine straight right hands. Frazier was not picking up the punches, and as he returned to his corner at the round's end, the Filipino referee guided his great hulk part of the way.

"Joe," said his manager, Eddie Futch, "I'm going to stop it."

"No, no, Eddie, ya can't do that to me," Frazier pleaded, his thick tongue barely getting the words out. He started to rise.

"You couldn't see in the last two rounds," said Futch. "What makes ya think ya gonna see in the fifteenth?"

"I want him, boss," said Frazier.

"Sit down, son," said Futch, pressing his hand on Frazier's shoulder. "It's all over. No one will ever forget what you did here today."

And so it will be, for once more had Frazier taken the child of the gods to hell and back. After the fight Futch said, "Ali fought a smart fight. He conserved his energy, turning it off when he had to. He can afford to do it because of his style. It was mainly a question of anatomy, that is all that separates these two men. Ali is now too big, and when you add those long arms, well…Joe has to use constant pressure, and that takes its toll on a man's body and soul." Dundee said, "My guy sucked it up and called on everything he had. We'll never see another one like him." Ali took a long time before coming down to be interviewed by the press, and then he could only say, "I'm tired of bein' the whole game. Let other guys do the fightin'. You might never see Ali in the ring again."

In his suite the next morning he talked quietly. "I heard somethin' once," he said. "When somebody asked a marathon runner what goes through his mind in the last mile or two, he said that you ask yourself, 'Why am I doin' this?' You get so tired. It takes so much out of you mentally. It changes you. It makes you go a little insane. I was thinkin' that at the end. Why am I doin' this? What am I doin' in here against this beast of a man? It's so painful. I must be crazy. I always bring out the best in the men I fight, but Joe Frazier, I'll tell the world right now, brings out the best in me. I'm gonna tell ya, that's one helluva man, and God bless him."

6 . . . But Only a Farce in Tokyo

(ALI-INOKI)

Sports Illustrated
July 5, 1976
The *tsuyu*—the rainy season that wraps around your head like a wet towel—hugged Tokyo last week, and when it did not rain, the narrow, crowded streets were choked by a heavy mist, adding mystery to a week neck-deep in the stuff. The Lockheed affair broadened its shadow and a pair of earthquakes rattled buildings, but all talk centered on what came to be known as the War of the Worlds, the latest in the kind of popcorn nonsense that was, on the surface, blood kin to Evel Knievel and his death cycle—the ego going amuck.

Why Muhammad Ali needs more attention from a world he says he owns is beyond a normal mind, but here he was last Saturday morning in Budokan Hall, up against a wrestler by the name of Kanji Antonio Inoki. Nobody knew what to make of it. Would it be a hoax? Could Ali get hurt? What would the final rules be? Was Inoki truly a man of the samurai tradition, a man who could stick his hand down the throat of a pig and pull out its heart?

Concerned much more with the form of things than with content, the Japanese, who have produced the half-million-ton tanker and the world's smallest television set and tape recorder, have now given us a sporting event that will go down as the dullest in history. Among other things, it was declared a draw. No, it was not a hoax; it was not prearranged in any way (indeed a bit of neat choreography might have helped). But it was more like a tea ceremony, or watching a man getting a haircut, than a fight.

Inoki turned out to be a fraud of the first rank—not even a good illusionist, as some are in his trade. He was just an ordinary wrestler with a good pair of legs and a lot of money with which to accommodate his strange whims, one of which was to challenge Ali. For fifteen rounds he moved around the ring on his back—like a crab with his belly up. For his part, Ali clowned, sticking his tongue out and gesturing to Inoki to stand up and punch with him, meanwhile staying close to the safety of the ropes. The rules said Ali could stop the action—action?—by grabbing the ropes. The scene left one to meditate on his own sanity and the Japanese word *wakarimasen*, which means "I can't understand."

Nobody among the ten thousand people at Budokan, some of whom paid $1,000 for a ringside ticket, could understand. What they saw was an Ali who, in a few brief intervals when Inoki stood up, threw only six punches in the entire fight. That's a million dollars a punch. Only a couple of them landed, and both were harmless jabs. Meanwhile, Inoki spent the time slithering about trying to get a leg in back of Ali's left leg. The result was that Ali was kicked about sixty times on his leg. His shin was bloodied and the back of his leg was covered with hematomas. His corner began to work on the leg early, applying ice bags and Vaseline; it could have been the first fight ever stopped because of a cut leg.

The Ali-Inoki affair was supposed to settle once and for all that old and idiotic saloon argument: Who would win a match between a wrestler and a boxer? Granted, it is not one of the burning questions of our times, but whip it up to an adjectival soufflé, add the name of Ali, throw in some inscrutable oriental claptrap, and you have James Cagney going against a bullet-headed black belt on a Tokyo wharf for God and country. The curiosity level grew high, and popcorn sold by the ton.

A crowd of 32,897 turned up at New York's Shea Stadium to view the match on closed-circuit television, and millions of others watched throughout the world, all of them corroborating what H. L. Mencken once said: "People know what they want, and they deserve to get it... good and proper." They also confirmed what Ali said before the match: "All the inventions in the world, all the new things comin' out every day, but I find a loophole. A new thing." It is Ali's contention that the world is bored, and that he alone provides it with relief.

Maybe so, but Ali is currently walking a thin line between being a supreme talent, a magical figure with a pull and draw never before experienced, and being an impossible bore. He has been badly overexposed. His theatrics are stale; each line he speaks seems to come from a man with a key in his back.

So why did he need a Japanese wrestler? Six million dollars is part of the reason, but there is more. By some weird reasoning—perhaps only a rationalization for taking the money—he talked himself into believing that the prestige of his sport was somehow at stake here. Ali also believes that he must constantly astound the planet, that his beauteous ring gifts are not enough. He talks often of the mythological Hercules, little knowing that intelligence was conspicuously absent in much that Hercules did. Too hot, Hercules points an arrow at the sun and threatens to shoot it. Tossed by the waves, he tells the waters to be calm or else he will punish them.

After he arrived in Tokyo, Ali began to hear stories of how Inoki could maim him for life. He became annoyed and said, "I intend to wear the kind of gloves I use on the heavy bag. With these gloves, over taped fists, a man could easily get killed. I fear for Inoki. I also fear for his family."

The Ali camp was apprehensive. "I don't know what to think of all this," said trainer Angelo Dundee. "This could get nasty."

Bitter meetings over the rules followed, and it was finally decided that Inoki could not use his hands or feet in karate fashion.

The rules clearly did not favor Inoki, and he did what any sensible man would do: stay on his back, far away from the Ali jab that rams out in one twenty-fifth of a second. Being on his back did not help Inoki win the crowd's favor—or increase his chances of becoming a genuine national hero, one of the reasons he guaranteed Ali $3 million just to show up in Tokyo.

He seemed a pathetic figure in his dressing room as large tears dropped from his eyes; he could not speak. The money—an estimated $2 million—he had made apparently was not enough to console him. Besides the desire to become a hero, what else had he hoped to gain? To restore prestige to the floundering sport of professional wrestling in Japan? To set up a big tour of the US? He sat there, his huge jaw drooping like a sinking aircraft carrier, and one could only hope that he would be reunited with an elder sister, who he said had lost contact with the family twenty years ago.

"I hope all this publicity brings us together again," he said before the fight.

It would have been better for him to take out a classified ad.

As it is, he and Ali have left at least one spectator to ponder over and over the words of the mystic Lafcadio Hearn, writing of Japan:

"Remember that here all is enchantment, that you have fallen under the spell of the dead."

He can say that again.

7 On the Throne Behind the Power

(HERBERT MUHAMMAD)

Sports Illustrated
September 27, 1976

Glance at a man, and you find his nationality written on his face, his means of livelihood on his hands, and the rest of his story in his gait, his mannerisms, shoelaces, and in the lint adhering to his clothes. So insisted Dr. Joseph Bell, the Edinburgh surgeon who taught Sir Arthur Conan Doyle and was the real-life model for Sherlock Holmes. "The trouble with most people is that they see, but do not observe," the doctor used to say, while lecturing doggedly on the vast importance of little distinctions, the endless significance of trifles. He himself could detect from a man's hat that his wife did not love him, from a man's cane that he feared being murdered. Nothing much got by Dr. Bell, but it would be long odds that he could unravel Herbert Muhammad.

If you had not seen him before, not known what he does, what would observation tell of Herbert as he sits in his apartment overlooking New York's Central Park? His handshake is limp, his hand is soft. He is black—a smooth, sort-of-bloodless

black. There is no hair, except for his mustache and neatly bar-
bered sideburns. There is no joy in his eyes—or sorrow—nor is
there anything sinister in them, either. When he gets up, his
gait is slow and weary, that of a man who is not physical, or at
least of a man who does not like to walk. His tie is quiet, his suit
plain and slightly baggy. You can tell he must be a prodigious
eater, for he is a very round man—the kind of roundness that
bears witness to long and determined dining. No shoelaces. No
lint. What to make of him, Dr. Bell? Who is Herbert Muhammad, and why are people saying such awful things about him?

A good question, one that a lot of people have been asking
for more than a decade now. "Herbert is the invisible man," says
an old friend. "Has been for years. Sometimes you think you
see something, but look back and all you have is a three-piece
suit and a hat, brim up, pushed down over a pair of eyes." Others think of him as a grown-up member of Our Gang, or maybe a
King Farouk. The more erudite liken him to certain subatomic
particles that cannot be seen even through the most powerful
of microscopes; their existence is known only by their effects.
With Herbert, two effects are always apparent: fear and silence.

Herbert Muhammad is the force behind the most easily
recognizable figure of our time—Muhammad Ali, a man who
will have earned $50 million before his career ends, $15.5 million this year alone. As a boxing manager, Herbert is antithetic to
the breed. He doesn't smoke a big cigar, he uses no unpleasant
names for his fighter, and he displays an almost complete lack of
knowledge of the ring; he may know that there are three minutes in each round, but that's it, say some Herbert watchers.
The one thing Herbert does know is money; he knows the little
trapdoors hidden in a deal and can shoot the eyes out of a bad one
while half-asleep. Ali needs a Herbert Muhammad.

No better description of Herbert's style can be given than

that which evolved out of a phone conversation between him and Don King, once the exclusive promoter of Ali. As usual, King was doing most of the talking. Frustrated, he finally began to spin a parable with the passion of a stumping preacher.

"Ever hear of the lion," he roared on the phone, "who was so powerful that he couldn't hunt no more because all those other animals were wise to him? He can't get a meal anywhere. So he comes across this zebra, and he says, 'Zebra, huntin' is pretty slim out there. But if the two of us combine our talent, we could make all these other animals a real bonanza for us. With your speed and my power—you round 'em up and I knock 'em out—we gonna have all we want, all the booty we want.' So the two became partners, and business was great. And after a couple of weeks, the lion and the zebra are sittin' around the fireplace at night, and the lion says, 'Brother Zebra, you sure did a good job for us. How we gonna split up this booty?' The zebra says, 'We both worked, my speed and agility, your power and cunning—I think fifty-fifty could be fair.' Now, ya know what happened? The lion jumped on the zebra and ate him up."

King went on, and now the lion has struck a deal with a wolf, who "howls in the dark of night." The lion and the wolf go to work. The two acquire twice as much as the lion and zebra did, and once more the lion is surveying the spoils, sitting there, picking his teeth. "Brother Wolf," he says, "you did a tremendous job. You worked twenty-four hours a day, you're a real hustler. Now how we gonna split up all this booty?" The wolf, recognizing the lion's superiority, said he thought sixty-forty would be all right with him. The lion jumps on the wolf and eats him up. Then the lion, who is soon hungry again, goes to Brother Fox. The fox is reluctant to deal with the lion, but he is pressed hard. The lion and the fox are immense successes in their hunt, garnering ten times more than the lion ever did before. The lion is elated and says, "Brother Fox, you truly a hustler, you really know what you're doing. Now how we gonna split up this pile of booty, old brother?" The fox rummages through the pile and takes out a leg of lamb. "I'll take this," he says, "and you can have the rest."

"Brother Fox," says the lion, "where did you learn to be so fair?"

Looking in the direction of the fire, the fox says, "From those shiny bones over there of Brother Zebra and Brother Wolf!"

King's bluster and comic charm might have eased the sting of that little tale, but the implication was clear: Herbert was the boss, and a greedy one at that. It was obvious that King had thought that Herbert needed him, that he did all the work with Ali, that he was obtaining the incredible purses for him, yet he was willing to settle for scraps from Herbert; he merely wanted to be appreciated by Herbert. The two would later part company, but looking back now at that conversation, one remembers the sudden jolt from hearing Herbert Muhammad being spoken to in such a manner. For Herbert had always been a remote figure, forever changing his phone numbers, always off to one of his many houses or apartments around the world, refusing to be interviewed; Herbert was creepy, man, so the word went. Leave him be.

"Why write about Herbert?" a Muslim asked last May during a taxi ride to the stadium in Munich where Ali was to fight Richard Dunn in the early-morning hours.

"Because Herbert is the man who makes the deals," the Muslim was told, "the biggest deals in the history of sport for one athlete."

"Forget about him," the Muslim said. "It's not worth it. All you get is trouble."

"What kind of trouble?"

"The worst kind," he said, almost whispering.

"Hey, nobody's here in the taxi except the two of us. You can talk."

"No, I can't," he said. "Herbert is everywhere."

When he is not "everywhere," Herbert, forty-eight, lives with his wife in a big house in Chicago's Woodlawn section near the University of Chicago. Ali has recently bought a house down the street from him. Designed by an Arabian architect, there is a heavy Middle Eastern ambience to Herbert's home; it is filled with exotic rugs and pictures and things like flowers on the backs of camel statuary and strange candelabra. Across the street from Herbert's is the house of his late father, Elijah, where his older brother and the leader of the Muslims, Wallace D. Muhammad, now lives (Herbert's other two brothers occupy the houses next to him). "All of his spare time," a friend says of Herbert, "is spent supervising alterations on his house. He never stops making it over. He seems to get a kick out of it."

Herbert, who is known universally by his first name, lives quietly, seldom entertaining at home. He does not have many visitors, except for his five sons, all of whom are married. He spends a lot of time reading from his extensive library—mostly works on philosophy, economics, and religion—which includes some extremely rare volumes. Often, when he has lectured Ali, the champion would say, "Hey, that's great stuff. Where did you learn that?" Herbert would tell him that it came from one of his books, and Ali would ask to borrow it. "Can't do it; it's too rare, Judge," Herbert would say.

Herbert is out of the house by 7:00 a.m., usually in a dark suit, off to work—most of which is done over two phones in his Cadillac. Nobody seems to know much about his private life, other than that "he chooses his friends very carefully" and seems to be forever on a diet. "He loves to eat," says a friend named

Hassan, "but when he had to give up somethin' he loves, I've never seen anybody with more willpower." Herbert is just as stubborn about his privacy.

"I don't want people comin' up to me while I'm at dinner," says Herbert, who doesn't like to be startled by the sudden appearance of a strange face (he is well protected at fights). "Most of the world thinks Angelo Dundee is the manager of Ali. When I go to a town, I have to call up Angelo to get me into places. But that's fine with me. I only care if Ali and the bank know me."

Mystery implies romance—but not so with Herbert. "You can sum up Herbert in three words on the head of a pin—dull, dull, and dull," says a man who has had dealings with him. That must be a comforting description for someone who has spent most of his life caught in the weft of intrigue and accusation, who has been hounded by the dogs of white justice. "We've never had a day's rest," he says. "I've had more bugs put in my rooms and on my phones. Privacy was just a word to me." Herbert was not just a boxing manager back then. He was a prince of the Nation of Islam, the Black Muslims, the son of Elijah Muhammad, the leader of the sect that made a lot of whites, as well as blacks, cringe at what might be hiding behind a phrase like "white devil."

Images of the Mau Mau, of crazed storm troopers, of bloodbaths. were widespread in the racially bitter sixties. Overreaction, maybe, but there was no question that Elijah, the Messenger of Allah, never leaving his compound in Chicago, enforced iron discipline among his people, preached and imposed separatism and militancy. The Black Muslims had two faces. One suggested a placid, committed people determined to exist by means of their will and acumen; they had their own successful businesses—fish stores, bakeries, farms, etc. The other face spread fear in the form of the Fruit of Islam, a coarse, rude, and humorless elite corps who wore black leather gloves and overcoats; all of them knew judo.

"Exaggeration," says Herbert now. "My father was not a violent man. He was gentle. He fought hard to make the black man proud of himself. I saw my father fight off all kinds of people. I saw them come and go." In many ways Herbert is much like his father, who was serious and formal, a man who kept a close watch on his time. Herbert does not abide fools or crackpots for long, either. "Herbert did what his father liked," says Hassan. "He communicated well with his father. There's a lot of Elijah in Herbert. He never bucked his father on anything." Once Elijah walked into the family garage and saw Herbert, then a young boy, punching a speed bag. Elijah delivered a stern lecture. "I don't want you around the ring, boxing for any little fat white man with a big cigar," he said. "Don't be around any sports world. Sport is the ruin of our people. Turns them into children who're used and then left broken. Stay out of it."

Herbert's youth was uneventful, except when he was eighteen. He was working at his first job, painting numbers on office doors, when he was arrested for failing to register for the draft; beginning with Elijah, who did four years in the pen for draft resistance, contempt for the draft runs in the family. Later, Herbert ran a Muslim bakery, the Muslim newspaper *Elijah Speaks*, and a photography studio where he did portraits of Nasser, Martin Luther King Jr., Roy Wilkins, and others. "Photography—I'm crazy about it," says Herbert. "I wish I could do it again. I like to play with light and shadows. To develop pictures. See the wrinkles in an old man's face coming out." It was in his studio that Herbert first met Cassius Clay in the early sixties, and no two men working together would ever be more dissimilar.

Clay was not Ali yet but had been recruited for the Muslims by Malcolm X. At the time, the white Louisville syndicate owned Clay's contract. Impressed by Herbert, Clay the convert also knew the advantage of being allied with a member of the "royal family" and kept after Herbert to manage him. Herbert was wary of his father and of his views on sports—boxing, in particular. After Clay beat Sonny Liston for the title and became Muhammad Ali, the Louisville syndicate was out. Herbert became the closet manager, seldom seen or heard, except in the hushed hallways of hotels, whispering to other Muslims. Soon Ali made Malcolm X an ex-friend and ex-confidant. Told to be "responsible" by Malcolm (who had broken with the Muslims over ideological differences) before going on a trip to Africa with Herbert, Ali said, "Malcolm didn't seem too responsible to me. Man, did you get a look at him? Dressed in that funny white robe and wearing a beard, and walking with that cane that looked like a prophet's stick. Man, he's gone. He's gone so far he's out completely."

Turning to Herbert, he then said, "Doesn't that go to show, Herbert, that Elijah is the most powerful? Nobody listens to that Malcolm anymore."

Herbert became Ali's manager officially in 1966. By this time, Malcolm X had been murdered, and the lover of photography came to despise being photographed. Herbert had a firm grip on Ali and tried to work on Ali's image, to bring it just a bit closer to Herbert's own conservative nature. The Ali Shuffle, which was introduced against Cleveland Williams in Houston, was forbidden. "It didn't add anything," said Herbert. Ali called Ernie Terrell an Uncle Tom, and Herbert zippered his mouth. And it was Herbert who urged Ali, who was alarmed at the heavy taxes he had to pay and fearful (even now) of becoming another Joe Louis, to fight more often. "Standard Oil doesn't try to sell a small amount of oil each year," Herbert told him.

At the time, two questions persisted in the white press:

Were the Muslims bleeding Ali white financially, and had Ali been coerced into refusing to be inducted into the army? "We never took a dime from Ali," Herbert says now. "He made and still makes donations to the religion, but no more than, say, Catholics or others give to their churches." As for the draft, Herbert says, "Nobody put any pressure on Ali. He made his decision independently. He was a Muslim. He loved my father." Ask those two questions of those who have been around Herbert and Ali, and the responses are all the same: silence. The awful things being said about Herbert Muhammad are the things that are not being said.

"Why don't your friends set the record straight?" Herbert is asked. "You say one thing; why don't they say the same thing, if that's the way it was? Why don't they say *any*thing?"

"People are funny," says Herbert. "Maybe they don't want to get involved. Maybe they're afraid what they say will be misinterpreted."

Take the exile, for example, when Ali's passport had been picked up, and the patriots barred him from fighting because of his stance on the draft. Ali's legal fees had wiped him out. There was still the money that the Louisville group had put in trust for him—15 percent of all his earnings. Ali tried desperately to get to this money, but he was not legally entitled to it until he was thirty-five. He borrowed heavily—even down to $10 and $20 bills—from his friends. Where were the Muslims and Herbert, who had taken a handsome 40 percent of all Ali's earnings? "We gave him money, did a lot of things for him," says Herbert, who used to have to meet Ali in secret on street corners when Ali was suspended from the Muslims by Elijah because he persisted in boxing. What sort of things? "That's between Ali and me."

The Ali-Herbert union is curious, unique and exemplary

in the ring, or for that matter in the entertainment business: the two really have nothing in common, except their religion. Ali is a public person, grows restless without the stage; Herbert is private. Ali has no regard for money; Herbert seems to care for little else. Ali is genuinely kind and giving; Herbert is often seen as cold and ruthless. Ali is a physical creature, will be all his life; Herbert is exquisitely sedentary. In the past, there were no notable rows between the two, hardly any harsh words. But Herbert was angry after the fight with Jimmy Young, berating Ali—rightly so—for his poor physical condition, describing him as a disgrace, and yelling at him behind closed doors, "From now on, you're going to listen to me."

Girls and sweets are Ali's implacable temptations. "I can't watch him forever," says Herbert. "Like he says: 'Herbert, you got to sleep sometime, and at night I can git out.'" Most of the time Herbert is an absentee manager. He comes into a town before a fight and stays in a hotel far from Ali's, while those he has hired to watch the champ cater to his desires. Early on, Herbert was a fixture in Ali's corner, but now the only time you see him is when he takes a seat below it. There he sits with a water bottle in front of him, shifting nervously while the wild dollar arithmetic of Ali's future spins through his head; sometimes he walks out in disgust or fright, as he did in the Young fight before the decision was announced. "I was scared, real scared," says Herbert. "Ali says he's never been more scared in his life."

On the surface, nothing seems to have snarled their relationship. "It's clear between the two of us," says Herbert. "Ali told me, 'Look Judge, I'll handle the boxing, you handle the lawyers and the promoters.' That's the way it is." Herbert is sensitive to Ali, he is aware of his antiboss attitudes, so they call each other Judge. Look beneath the surface, though, and you sense unrest, strain in their union. Among the causes are the tarnishing of Ali's name after his bout with the wrestler in Tokyo and the ultimate size of the purse; the frequency of Ali's fights, which he feels indicates panic and greed on Herbert's part as the two of them approach the end of Ali's career.

"Champ," one of Ali's people said to him while Ali was in a California hospital recovering from blood clots in his legs caused by the wrestler's kicks, "champ, don't you think that a man who is getting one-third of all you make, don't ya think he should be here with you? Does he care?" The man, of course, was Herbert, who gets a third as his end of the money now. Ali did not answer, but later complained angrily over the phone that he wound up with only $1.4 million of the $3 million guaranteed in the Tokyo contract. "Ali is unhappy," says Don King. "He says at least he got all his money when I was doin' the promotin'." If Ali is disturbed—he has not said anything publicly—it would add credence to the widely held belief by insiders that the death of Elijah set him free, that he is his own man now, that no longer can the name of Elijah be invoked to make him step smartly into line.

Herbert hates conflict, yet such talk does not bother him. "I was heartbroken over Tokyo," he says. "But I would do it again. All that money for an exhibition. How can you turn it down? But the event got out of hand and became dangerous. And I still don't believe Ali was publicly damaged. His fame is beyond that. As for the money, I'll take the blame. It was the first time that I did not get all the money up front and in the bank. It was a mistake." Herbert is aware of those who are trying to undermine him. "Go ask Ali one thing," he says. "Ask what he'd do if he had a problem and I wasn't around. He'd find me if he had to spend ten thousand dollars in phone bills."

Herbert says there have been a number of fights he never

wanted to take. Ali makes these decisions, Herbert says, pointing out that he told Ali after the Ron Lyle bout, "Maybe you
ought to pack it in, get out of the game ahead." Says Mickey
Duff, a London promoter, "Herbert's being smart. He has to fight
Ali a lot. Ali away from the ring would be his own worst enemy.
At this stage of his career, with his tastes and money habits, long
absences from the ring would be terrible. Ali stays in shape by
fighting. It's that simple." Herbert speaks bluntly of Ali's financial condition, noting that he will net about $7.5 million after
taxes this year, about $3 or $4 million after other expenses. He
says Ali is in fine shape with Internal Revenue, that there is no
reason why he should end up like Joe Louis.

"Look, I can't lock up his money," says Herbert. "I wish I
could have done what the Louisville group did—take that 15
percent. They did a good job for Ali. But I can't do that. I'd look
to Ali like I'm interfering, that I'm the boss getting in the way of
his money."

"Is his future secure?" Herbert is asked.

"Yeah," he says. "Ali's got about four million dollars in
property, and he could live off that alone."

"Why is he afraid of becoming another Joe Louis?"

"I don't know," Herbert says, "but I'll tell you this. I got one
million dollars in municipal bonds. I'd give it all to him before I
see him go broke. He go broke—I go broke."

For some, Herbert's sincerity is undeniable, while others
pass over what he says and look at Herbert as a businessman. "A
man who has made thirty-eight million dollars," says one,
"should now be worth close to one hundred million dollars, with
sound investments and good business direction. Ali's real estate isn't worth much, probably less than half of what he paid for
it. The Deer Lake camp, for instance, is totally unattractive as
real estate. He always comes up way short in deals he makes.

His friends get something for one dollar and sell it to him for two dollars. Some friends. Another thing—no good tax shelters have been set up for him." Is Herbert at fault here? Hardly, it seems, for he is not a money manager; he is the man who brings in the deals, sees to it that Ali gets every cent coming to him. Nobody tells Ali what to do anymore, especially with his money.

Before Herbert came along, the promoter was the man who wielded the mackerel, usually slapping fighters and managers in the face with it. For all his great power at the gate and his magnetism, Joe Louis took orders from Mike Jacobs. Al Weill, who was a matchmaker as well as a manager, dictated to Rocky Marciano and his camp; he never referred to Rocky by name or even by *champ*. He always could be heard saying, "Git the fighter in here; tell the bum I wanna see 'im." Herbert tells promoters what to do. "I don't owe them anything," he says. "I don't work for promoters. I work for one man—Muhammad Ali. I answer to him. It's my job to get the money for him, and if I don't, he has a right to know why."

Even so, Herbert seems to have blundered in the Tokyo bout, and there were a lot of rough edges around the Dunn fight. Both events took place after Herbert left Don King for his old promoter, Bob Arum. Arum says he was not the promoter in either fight, just the television conduit. "The German promoters," says Herbert, "reflect what's wrong with a lot of promoters. They were so eager, they were dreamers. They overpaid for a fight, and then they suffered. Look, it's simple; if you can't handle your business, you don't belong on the other side of the table with me." A stubborn and proud negotiator, Herbert does not bend easily to ultimatums, as promoter Jerry Perenchio discovered. "He made a good offer for the Zaire fight," says Herbert, "and then he said, 'That's it, you're not going to get one cent more, and nobody else will give it to you either.' Well, that made me determined to teach him a lesson." Offstage was Don King—with a few million more.

How Herbert handled King sharply defines the views, the thinking, of Ali's manager. Before the entrance of King, it was clear that Herbert had become restless. He was looking for a way to unload Arum, his longtime confederate, who had annoyed Herbert by suddenly moving "out front too much." King had also sold Herbert on his blackness, saying that Arum did not care about blacks or Ali, that the Muslims, of all people, should give a black man his chance to promote Ali. Herbert was amused by King—also quite skeptical—but he decided to gamble that King could deliver. Under pressure all the way, King got the money for the Zaire fight, and from then on the two collaborated on seven title bouts; eager to please Herbert and Ali, King inflated the market to a preposterous level.

"The pace became deadly," King says now. "More and more fights, no time to promote in between. I wasn't through with one fight when I had to find money for the next one. Herbert never leaned on a white promoter like he leaned on me, threatening always to go elsewhere if I didn't get what he wanted. I performed for Herbert and Ali, and they tossed me aside like a bum. Not the slightest loyalty."

As the fights went on, those around Herbert knew that King's promotional head would end up in a basket. As far as Herbert was concerned, King had taken his ego and twisted it into his own future as if it were a knife. King had become too big, upstaging Ali in the press and on television, until Herbert was certain the public believed King was the man behind Ali. In Malaysia, when Ali said he was going to retire, King innocently told the press, "No, he won't. I'm going over there now and unretire him." The comment enraged Herbert; he confided, "He's going to have to go." After that, Herbert used King brilliantly for five more fights, then went to Arum and Madison Square Garden for the lucrative Ken Norton–Ali fight in Yankee Stadium next week. King had worked toward this event, had sacrificed money (the huge purses left him little) for promotional continuity with Ali and Herbert, but the two of them had summarily turned him out. Did Ali, a highly sensitive athlete, loyal beyond belief, come to King's defense? "Herbert makes my business decisions," says Ali.

Herbert says, "Don King was never the exclusive promoter of Ali. I never worked for him. I don't owe him anything. I owe only Ali; I must be loyal only to him, to do the best I can do for him. King says he made millions for us. Well, where did he get the money? He never gave us anything. He could have had the Norton fight. I gave him more time than I would give any promoter to come up with the money. But he came up with it too late. We wanted a deal. We wouldn't wait for him forever. As for him being black, I don't believe in any fight game around Ali being black or white. Ali is universal."

Two words are always used to describe Herbert: ruthless and fair. "I've never seen a fairer man," says Dr. Ferdie Pacheco, the physician in Ali's corner. "Before the Tokyo fight, there were the old gripes, the blacks in the corner complaining about the whites in the corner. I went to Herbert and said, 'Herbert, we're not going to go through this old routine again.' And Herbert said, 'Tell me who's starting this stuff, and I'll straighten him out.'" Mickey Duff remembers, "I once got Ali an advertising spot in Germany years ago. I wasn't making much money then, and I asked the key man in Ali's camp for my commission, about two hundred and fifty dollars. He didn't want to pay me, but Herbert was standing right there and said, 'Look, give him the money, he earned it.'" The consensus is that "if Herbert owes you money, you get it"—without begging; he is aware of the dignity of those who work for him.

The dispute with King underlines a major concern of Herbert's. He wants his role with Ali clarified, to be put into perspective. He did not like Ali's autobiographical book and bucked the writer, Richard Durham, all the way. "For one thing," Herbert says, "I don't think it's a good book. Secondly, it doesn't really explain my role. A book lasts a long time. It's on a shelf forever. I want my children to know what I did for one-third of Ali's money." He opposes the script of the forthcoming movie of Ali's life—*The Greatest*—on the same grounds. "The role for Herbert can be made bigger," says a man from Columbia Pictures. "But what do you do with a guy who has been so antipublicity? No television interviews, no press interviews, no pictures, nothing. What do you have to go on? He can't be both anonymous and public." Yet, like the Muslims themselves, Herbert is trying to become more visible, trying hard to alter his image as the secret man of the secret people.

The Muslims, too, do not appear to be as guarded, as sinister, as they once were. Since Wallace D. Muhammad has become the leader of the Muslims, they seem nearly ecumenical as they search for the American mainstream. They no longer like being called Black Muslims—just Muslims. They have opened their religion to whites. They have declared sports and boxing permissible, defining them as a luxury. The once terrifying Fruit of Islam has been dismantled, so they say, and the trend is toward the spiritual rather than the material. "My father believed in materialism as bait for our people," says Herbert. "He wanted to show them that they, too, could acquire things through hard work and enterprise." He might also add that the once-profitable bakeries and fish stores are no longer prosperous, leaving the Muslims in financial trouble.

It is unlikely that Herbert himself will ever be in need of money. With much nerve and the hottest property in the world—created by the slide of political events and the growing voice of the Third World that so idolizes Ali—Herbert has become rich. In the end, what can be said of him and his work? The silence around him is a roar. He is ruthless, not an uncommon trait among men of success. He is fair, and he does not appear greedy. He only does what any manager should and must do: protect his fighter.

A man like Herbert—off his record, the smartest manager who ever lived—creates enemies, and it is doubtful that he could ever do anything to dispel the animus swirling about him, or those old speculations that never will die: (1) Ali has been raped financially by the Muslims; (2) Ali is held by the Muslims through terror. Both seem grossly incorrect, but only Ali knows the truth.

Who is Herbert Muhammad? The question nags, making one feel like the eminently deductive Dr. Bell when he was called upon by his students to relate a story of his genius.

Visiting a bedridden patient, Dr. Bell said, he had asked the man, "Aren't you a bandsman?"

"Aye," the man had said.

"You see, gentlemen, I am right," Dr. Bell had said, recounting how he had turned to his class with confidence. "It is quite simple. This man had a paralysis of the cheek muscles, the result of too much blowing at wind instruments. We need only to confirm. What instrument do you play, my man?"

The man had got up on his elbows and said, "The big drum, Doctor!"

8 Not the Greatest Way to Go

(ALI-NORTON III)

Sports Illustrated
October 11, 1976

Just a few hours before his title defense against Ken Norton last week, Muhammad Ali sat shoeless, his feet up on a kitchen table in an apartment on the Upper West Side of Manhattan, isolated from all the chiselers and half-wits who snap at his peace and concentration before a big fight, away from some of those parasites around him who call themselves aides and had hastened his recent decline. After thinking about suitable endings for his strange and incomparable career, Ali suddenly turned to his host and said, "Maybe I should reach up and pull down the mike in the middle of the ring and announce . . . 'Laaaaadies and gentlemen, you have seen the last of the eighth wonderrrr of the world. Muhammad retires.'"

"Nah, Nah," rasped Harold Conrad, an adviser to champions for decades, who had put Ali up for three days. "You did that in Manila, you did it in Malaysia. One more you said, always one more. Who would believe you?"

Three days later in exotic Istanbul, Muhammad Ali rattled

the world stage for the second time in a week—the first when he was given a controversial decision over Ken Norton in Yankee Stadium, this second time as he announced with the appropriate dramatic inflection, Wallace Muhammad (head of the Muslims in America) by his side to give it an official imprint, "Mark my words, and play what I say right now fully. At the urging of my leader Wallace, I declare I am quitting fighting as of now, and from now on I will join the struggle for the Islamic cause."

The announcement was a last, fitting tremor in a bizarre week in which occurred one of the worst heavyweight title fights in history; in which a champion who had finally become too old was brutally exposed and found to be a fragile mortal like the rest of us; in which a challenger with meager gifts was robbed of his moment by his own head as well as bad advice from his corner. It was a week that saw the arrogant Madison Square Garden put on a truly shabby fight promotion; a week that saw the dark and mean streets around Junkie Stadium erupt into anarchy and savagery, leading one to contemplate the line of e e cummings "What comma indeed comma is civilization?"

Quite properly, Ali's retirement was received with wide cynicism. Most observers see a grand design behind Ali's words, which seldom indicate what he really feels. They see it this way: Foreman fights Norton for the vacant title, Norton gets beaten (thus removing the stigma of Norton for Ali), and Ali "unretires" to challenge for the championship a third time, setting up the richest title bout ever. The logic seems sound.

"It's too premature," says Bob Arum, copromoter with Madison Square Garden, of Ali's announcement. "If the money's right, Ali will fight Foreman." Down in Texas, George Foreman remarks, "I'll only be satisfied when I knock Muhammad Ali out." Then, as an afterthought, he says, "Turkey goes right along with him. He's a turkey."

Others are certain that Ali means what he says. "I had no idea he was going to do this," says Angelo Dundee, who has trained Ali since his fight with Herb Siler back in 1960 in Miami Beach. "Nobody knows what he'll do. He's got me where I'll take anything that comes. If he makes a statement, I believe him." Says Ali's old promoter Don King, "He's through. I'm sure of it. He may play with the rest of us, but not with the chief minister, Wallace." Stunned, Joe Frazier, who may well have taken the last bit of greatness out of Ali back on that torrid morning in Manila a year ago, could only say of Ali's quitting, "He did?"

What happened? How did Ali's decision evolve in the space of a couple of hours? Following the Norton fight, there seemed to be a sharp division in Ali's thoughts. For the first time in his life he seemed almost speechless; the words came out softly, timidly, from a man who was looking into the bared teeth of true doubt about himself, about his work, about his future. "I got six million tax-free saved up," he said in his dressing room. "Drawin' seven percent interest. What I gotta keep on fightin' for? Wise for me to get out now. There's nothin' else to prove. This thing is dangerous." The next day at a press conference, sitting next to Norton, he quietly explained why Norton should fight Foreman first before a rematch, then privately said, "None of them niggers want Foreman. Only this nigger, me, can take him."

A Foreman-Ali match sometime in late spring appeared certain, even after he arrived at the airport in Istanbul. He told reporters that he "will leave boxing after my upcoming bout with George Foreman." He then went to noon prayers with Wallace Muhammad in the Blue Mosque. Next, at a press conference, Wallace turned to Ali and said, "Since he has indicated that he is seriously considering retiring from boxing and taking up the battle for truth, I want to ask him right now to pledge to retire from the ring and use his power—the fist of his tongue instead of the ring—for truth. He has the inspirational power to wake up the slumbering people of this world, and I am asking him now to retire."

Said Ali, "It has been my lifetime dream to become a champion and retire from the ring and then use my influence and fame for Allah. I have many people advising me to retire, and many people advising me to fight a few more times. I do not want to lose a fight, and if I keep boxing, I may lose. I may gain much money, but the love of the Muslims and the hearts of my people are more valuable than personal gain. So I am going to stop while everyone is happy and I am still winning. This [Wallace] is my leader, this is my spiritual teacher in Islam, and I want to retire anyway. Now he has advised me it will be wise. I have no confusion in my mind."

Perhaps there was only happiness and lucidity in Istanbul, but elsewhere around the world confusion and bad tempers simmered for days, especially among many of the 30,298 who had been at Yankee Stadium. The crowd had not only seen a bad fight, it had heard a decision that—for some fans and much of the press—was equal to the squalidness and general breakdown of law and order inside and outside the stadium. The decision for Ali—8–7, 8–7, 8–6–1—brought down the sky on him, and outrage, scalding hot, ran from the pages of the press, leaving Ali far from being the "people's champion," leaving him a decidedly unheroic figure. His manager, Herbert Muhammad, may well have been reexamining his often-repeated words: "I don't think anything can hurt Ali. He is beyond criticism. He is a legend."

Legends should be allowed to die slowly; at least that is what Ali seemed to want in his dressing room after the fight. But here it was, all the reality of this awful moment smothering him, each question like a knife thrust into his pride as an artist. My God, he seemed to be saying, they're going to strip me down bare right in this room and send me naked into the streets. He mumbled. He swore. He seethed inside. His head was down. Then a question came that released all the pounding hurt inside his head.

"How much longer can you fight with your mouth?" a huge black reporter asked.

"You're an Uncle Tom nigger to ask something like that," Ali snapped.

"I'm askin' you how long you can fight with your mouth," the guy pressed.

"Long enough to whup your black ass," Ali shot back.

Going into this fight, there were two questions—Ali's age and Norton's head—and the worst aspects of both would be confirmed, making it an unmemorable piece of physical art, yet an incendiary evening because of the ambiguity of so many rounds. There is no question now that Ali is through as a fighter. The hard work, the life and death of Manila, the endless parade of women provided by the fools close to him, have cut him down. Unlike the Jimmy Young defense, when he obviously was out of shape, there is no excuse for Ali's showing against Norton. He threw only one good combination all night. His jab, which once drained and depressed aggression, was only a nervous flick. But he was in excellent physical condition, and that along with a sure hand on his craft saved him.

Once more, as in his second fight with Ali, Norton's head got in the way. Here he is with a six-round lead going into the ninth, and he seems to unravel ever so slightly; he drops the ninth, and then four of the next six rounds to Ali, who has begun to dance and dictate the course of the fight with vast ring wisdom. Norton pursues ineffectively while Ali hand-fights,

keeping Norton off-balance, forever lodged in his turtle defense. It is the eleventh round, though, when Norton makes his
most serious mistake. He elects to parody Ali, to hang on the
ropes, to put his hands down, to exchange repartee. How foolish,
how insufferably wrongheaded. It is at this point when he should
have been his most physical, when abandon and fury were called
for, when he should have pushed Ali over the edge with the
considerable strength left in his superb body. "Nobody is going
to give us a gift against Ali," said Bob Biron, Norton's manager,
before the fight.

So they all knew this, Norton and his corner, led by Bill
Slayton. Now comes the fifteenth round, the pivotal round, the
one that can shove Norton over the top without argument.
"We've got to close the show," shouts Angelo Dundee, sending
Ali out. "Turn tiger, champ!" Thinking the fight was wrapped
up for Norton, Slayton moves him out with instructions not to
get careless. The result is that Ali fights for two minutes and forty
seconds, and Norton wakes up the rest of the way. As the round
ends, Norton stalks Ali back to his corner, shouting, "I beat you!
I beat you!" Led back to his own corner, he leaps for the sky along
with Slayton, both of them certain that the title has been won.
Shortly, the verdict comes, and Norton, his head wrapped in a
towel, is crying uncontrollably; sympathy pours down on him.

Norton got hold of himself later. "I wasn't even tired," he
said. "If I thought it was close, I'd have fought back harder and
more. When you fight Ali, you're behind at the start. It's obvious you have to knock him out to win. When it's that obvious,
you have to think the judges stole it. They made asses out of
themselves. The fight speaks for itself."

Ali did not think so: "You got to beat the champ, you gotta
whup him! Did he beat me convincingly? I had to beat Joe Frazier twice, Sonny Liston twice, George Foreman.... You can't

fight like Jimmy Young. You got to whup the champ! Drop me! Make me fall! Hurt me! Do you think I paid the judges? They never give me anything. I'm not a good American boy. I'm an arrogant nigger. They're white men. They wouldn't give it to me if I didn't win it!"

A well-worn bit of sophistry, this use of race, this donning of martyr's robes when backed against the wall, but Ali must know better, or he is as dumb as some think he truly is. In the past, Ali has always been given the best of it. He was allowed to hold Frazier by the back of the head (fifty-five times) in their second fight. He was given, rightly so, the benefit of doubt in the Young bout. "The only thing the people watch and the judges see," says Slayton, "is what Ali does in the ring. They don't see the other guy." That comment carries much truth, but it is also more than sufficient reason for a challenger to try to rip a title from a champion, to shock judges away from the hypnotic presence of Ali.

What is one to make of the decision? Do you take a title away from an Ali on a one-round difference in fifteen muddled rounds? Can a solid case be made for Norton? Those who saw him as the winner believe that no evidence has to be gathered for Norton, pointing out that scoring in the end is the ultimate delineator, scoring based on number and content of blows, aggression, ring generalship, and defense. The trouble is this: How can you score such a bad fight, how can one be so clear in such murky going? Scoring is always imprecise, and in this case it was almost impossible. In a close contest any judgment must be highly subjective. It hinges on tradition (the heavyweight title has changed hands only three times by decision since 1932). It involves sentiment and preference for style and the man—and with Ali, the mystique of the man.

Technically, on hard scoring, I gave the fight to Norton by

one round, but it was a troubled 8–7—without real conviction.
He was ahead 7–6 at the end of thirteen rounds, won the fourteenth big and ignored the fifteenth. The fourteenth and fifteenth meant the fight for Norton. Two of the judges, Barney
Smith and Harold Lederman, gave the fourteenth to Ali. "They
were playing catch-up," says Biron. "They had given too many
rounds early on to Norton, and now they were leaning hard
into the wind for Ali. In heaven's name, how can you give him
the fourteenth?" Even so, Norton was still alive on both cards
going into the fifteenth; it seemed the officials wanted a dramatic statement from him. "If Norton had started in the first
minute of that round," says Lederman, "and started with that
right hand, he would have been champion." Arthur Mercante,
the referee, says, "Aggression is one thing, but effective aggression is another. A lot of the time Norton was not effective."

If Norton was lethargic, the New York police were useless
outside the Stadium, this $100 million worth of concrete and steel
in the West Bronx; it might as well be in the most remote part
of New Guinea. On this night the cops chose the Stadium as the
scene of a job action over work schedules and deferred raises;
hundreds of them, off duty and on duty, turned the night into a
holiday for muggers, pickpockets, and general marauders. The
on-duty cops did nothing except laugh at—and sometimes join—
their off-duty colleagues who were blowing whistles and stopping traffic. Their eyes were turned away as one saw a man hit
over the head and then frisked rapidly while he was on the ground;
as one watched an arm reach into a limousine and pull out a necklace; as one looked on while three photographers were robbed of
all their equipment; as tickets were stolen right out of hands and
women were pawed. It was not a pretty sight.

Nor was it easy on eyes to see Ali on this night. He seemed
a pathetic figure, merely a master of illusion, groping with his

loss of reflexes; his feet knew precisely where to be, but his hands and mind seemed to be hooked up in some diabolical plot against him. He reminded one of Paul Léataud, who writes of man's relationship to his body, his image, in his *Journal*. "Damn it all!" he writes, after a woman remarks upon his age. "How impossible it is to see oneself as one really is!" That is much to ask of anyone, and it is no certainty that Ali can do it, either. If he has done it sincerely, looked into that shimmering glass at all that he was and is, if he has retired, then it would be a remarkable triumph of sense over ego. If not, then one wishes he somehow could get a picture of the image left by him in the ring at Yankee Stadium: that of a cat hung by its tail outside a window, trying to stick to the panes of glass with its claws, the sound grating and chilling and the spectacle altogether too cruel.

PART THREE

IN THE TELLING

1 A Wink at a Homely Girl

(BALTIMORE)

Sports Illustrated
October 10, 1966

A giant once, now a January sort of city even in summer, spring, and autumn. An anonymous city even to those who live there, a city that draws a laugh even from Philadelphia, a sneer from Washington, with a hundred taglines that draw neither smile nor sneer from the city. Baltimore: Nickel Town, Washington's Brooklyn, A Loser's Town, The Last Frontier, Yesterday Town.

"I'll take a sleeping pill, just in case," said a Briton, preparing to visit the city. "I want to make sure I can keep up with the pace."

So, it is October, and the town, which CORE made a target city in the summer gone (and failed to whip up one good, solid riot), is a World Series town, attracting attention it really does not enjoy, feeling a piston-like beat of the heart it has so seldom felt, and provoking—by just being what it is—more cackling from all those who came and found January in October.

All right, Jack, but don't knock it as a sports town, say the blue collars who are always in the side-street bars when shadows start climbing up factory walls. They say it next to a draft beer and a sports section opened to the racing page. From which the eyes never veer. Looking for a number or looking for an edge, looking for a chance to make tomorrow different from today, or just looking. By bar light or kitchen light, by neon or track light, with racing page or scratch sheet, with money or no money.

"Make sure," a publisher of one newspaper told his secretary, "I see the handle from the tracks every day. It gives me a good picture of the economy of the city."

"I've dreamed and I've schemed and I ain't never found any cream," the uncle used to tell his nephew. "Sonny, pray you grow up to be a bookmaker in this here town."

A racing town, then, but you can forget about charm and tradition, Old Hilltop and the Preakness, rolling acreage with dancing Thoroughbreds. That's for the Establishment, the Valley and Elkridge and all those who think they are a part of it, for the ones in good tweed with the F. Scott Fitzgerald rich-boy faces lined with exquisite dissipation who, forty-eight years old, are known within the circle as Skippy or Junior. Take the charm, the tradition, if you want it, because it's there; but deal around the other ones, the mobs that bust out of the steel mills, shipyards, and can factories, and try to reach the frozen face behind the window for the last two at Pimlico.

"In this here town, Sonny," said Uncle, who could talk about the loveliness of Saratoga even after getting wiped out, "only suckers and short arms and those with no arms [check evaders and nonspenders] go for the charm, and they ain't fillin' the closet of any track owner's wife with mink."

Racing, as even the bankrupt, dreamless ghosts of Pratt Street can see, is the silent giant of sports in this dudeless town, but the street-corner big mouth is pro football. College guys who wish they were back, high-school types who wish they had been, Valley dandy and Highlandtown scuffler—everybody has a piece of the Colts. Never try talking to a bartender after the Colts get busted up on television. Never scoff at the sophomoric cheering, from old ones who have never been young and young ones who don't want to grow old, that floods barrooms and lounges during a television game. Never knock the club, or you'll be knocked.

"Remember the big one with the Giants?" says one knocker. "Well, I had been putting the club down all year in this place where I hang, just to get a rise in the joint. So the Colts take the Giants, and that night I get nasty telegrams and a dozen phone calls telling me what a creep I am."

"John Unitas," says a newspaper copyreader, "never has a cold, he has pneumonia. He never has a sore leg, he has a broken leg. The smallest detail about the club is embroidered and turned into what they consider exciting conversation. Colts fans, the real ones, are the biggest bores in town."

A waterfront orphan in the eastern megalopolis, the city, it seems, relates to the Colts, and each autumn it waves them like a banner in front of all the lifted noses in the nation, in front of all those who used to motor through town on wine-soaked, fetid US 40 and then went home and pronounced the city just a tunnel between Philadelphia and Washington, in front of all those who came and left calling it a tapped-out bumpkin of a town smothered with sullied monuments to forgotten heroes of forgotten wars.

But it is not just that the team has won, it is the *way* it has won. Scratched up and head down from the hook, they took the Giants on one faraway December day. Then last season, chipless and light in the center of the table, they called the Packers and raised them with a halfback at quarterback and nearly made the bluff stick. Baltimore, with its massive inferiority complex, needs the Colts.

Class D sports town or big-league town, who can make a case? Unfriendly toward Navy, indifferent toward Maryland, the city gets no play from college football. Lacrosse is first-rate, but college basketball is an atrocity to be earnestly avoided. The hockey is minor league, and so are the fans. Say the same for attendance at NBA basketball. Nobody knows, or cares, that the Bullets are here, in this town full of nine-hole women golfers and dart throwers and pinochle players gone wrong.

"All the throwers and players are gone, Sonny," Uncle used to say. "Gone to fresh air and clothes that hurt an old man's eyes. They're all golfers now. In the old days they would have chased fire engines, too. That was big in this here town."

Once, too, it was a fighter's town, and a town full of pool hustlers and crapshooters who worked during jazzless hours. Five champions came out of the town: Joe Gans, who owned the old Goldfield Hotel; and Kid Williams, who owned only misery; Joe and Vince Dundee; and Harry Jeffra. Fight Night made it through the forties, but it died in the fifties, along with the pool-hall salesmen and the crapshooters and the last of the marks who fled when work in the war-production plants ebbed. The city, the diehards say, then went back to sleep.

Now, in this October, a World Series comes to a town that has a grand and rich past in baseball. John McGraw, Willie Keeler, and Wilbert Robinson worked here, when the city belonged to the old National League. Jack Dunn was the first to have Babe Ruth, a Camden Street urchin and a reform-school dropout. Dunn once brought the city seven straight International League pennants, and—so say the old men who sit in the public parks and play checkers and lament the passing of the five-cent draft beer—he had to sell all his players because the fans, bored, stopped coming to the park.

The city had Lefty Grove and Joe Boley and Max Bishop and Jack Bentley then, and later, in the forties, it would win a Little World Series with names that now are only recalled in trivia exercises: Kenny Braun, Blas Monaco, Stan Benjamin, Stan West, Bo Bo Barillari, and Bob Latshaw. Fifty-five thousand attended one of those Little World Series games in the old and vast stadium of weather-frayed wooden benches, and even now, when the moon is full, those who were there and those who were not dredge up a day of minor glory that Baltimore baseball has not felt since—and then call the newspaper.

"How many people were there that night?" the voice will ask.

"Fifty-five thousand," he is informed.

"You're crazy," the voice will say. "Had to be at least seventy thousand there."

Uncle could understand. "Sonny," he used to say, "every time you turn around, you bust into a monument which nobody ever looks at, but don't try to tear any of 'em down, and don't ever say 'The Star-Spangled Banner' sounds like it was written by a gent up to his ears with busthead."

"Was it?" he was asked.

"No, but you can bet only a Baltimorean could have written the 'Banner,' and if he was drinkin', it was beer, because this here town is a beer drinker of a town and a show-bet-on-a-favorite kind of town. Whack it one real good and it comes back at you with Lord Baltimore and the War of 1812. No power, but lots of foundation. They try to take you out with the past and with tradition."

Town with too much past and too little present, town with a big-league club in a boarded-up pub—all of this has been claimed since the St. Louis Browns metamorphosed into the

Orioles in 1954. Say it isn't so, but nobody knows. Baseball attendance in the sixth-largest city in the nation, where the Colts
often draw 35,000 for a scrimmage in August? From 1954 through
1965 the Orioles averaged 13,685 a game. Last year, third place:
781,649. This year, a pennant: 1.2 million—maybe.

True, the club and the city can build a two-pronged rebut-
tal: baseball competes with the dubious summer wonders of
Chesapeake Bay and the population's lust for "shore" living, and
the Orioles, unlike other big-league teams, do not have a large
hinterland from which to draw. The Eastern Shore, an antedi-
luvian settlement of oyster shuckers, does not help much; it has
long wanted to secede from the state and, in particular, Baltimore. Western Maryland thinks that it is in Pennsylvania and
hence throws its support behind the Pirates. Rap the gate
figures, if you want, but don't expect to be rapped back by an
Oriole fan.

If there is such a thing, the solid Oriole fan is a subterranean creature, the antithesis of the Colt fan. He has no identity.
Noiseless and spiritless, he reminds one of a guy who might
apologize for not buying a vacuum cleaner from a salesman
at the door. No insult can inflame him, and no losing streak
can distract him. He just goes to the games, and he is hardly
ashamed that restaurant, bar, and department-store windows
are not covered with imbecilic slogans and other displays of
pennant fever. The only noise he makes is directed at the absentee Oriole fans, who talk a lot but never go to the ballpark.

"Hell, why don't they bunt more?" says one absentee at an
East Side bar.

"Yeah, they never bunt," says a second absentee.

"Nobody bunts anymore," says No. 1.

"No runnin' or buntin' anymore," says No. 2.

"They ought to do something with Frank Robinson," says

No. 1. "He can't field. He's just been lucky. If he's so good, why isn't he back in Cincinnati?"

"They knew somethin' we ain't found out yet," says No. 2.

"Pardon me," interrupts a guy three glasses down, "when was the last time you two were at the stadium?"

"A couple of months ago when the Yankees—" starts No. 1.

"How come?" presses the interrogator.

"Why, there's no runnin' or buntin' anymore," says No. 2.

Uncle could understand that. "Sonny, the bunt solves all problems in baseball in this here town," he used to say. "It's a single-hitter's town and a bunter's town and a town with no heroes. 'If you're good, what're you doin' here?' is the way they feel in this town."

Uncle, who always thought that Babe Ruth had never been honored properly by the town, was wrong. It is a town with heroes, but it is suspicious of them. It does not embrace the hero quickly, but when it does, it elevates him to a point beyond simple hero. Then if the hero drops to one knee, becomes temporarily imperfect, he is shorn of his toga and garland until he proves that he can stand tall again, until he justifies the town's commitment of pride in him. The bond between Baltimore and the hero is sort of matrimonial in nature, fraught with all the emotions and pettiness of marriage; nowhere else does adulation dip and rise as it does in Baltimore. Only Art Donovan, the tackle, and Gino Marchetti, the defensive end, were, inexplicably, spared the sting of the town. Reticent and with a mechanic's attitude toward his work, John Unitas, if off form on Sunday, becomes a dartboard on Monday.

Paul Richards was no hero, but the people expected much from him. They did not understand that he was a teacher and a builder and that the Orioles desperately needed him. In the end they resented his genius. Hank Bauer came from the Yankees, and this is his big edge: they seem to stop before they knock anyone—or anything—that has been a winner in New York. Philadelphia, Washington, Boston—none of these places count in Baltimore. Frank Robinson has tapped their emotions, but not completely. He is the man whom they have been looking for since 1954, but they do not truly believe that they have him. It is as if they are all waiting for him to support their suspicions, waiting for their question to be answered: Why did Cincinnati get rid of him?

The town seems finally to have realized that Brooks Robinson is not counterfeit, and when his bat sags and his glove goes stiff, it forgives him. But that's because he came to them when he was quite young, and he belongs to them. He is, they feel, a Baltimore product, a "First," so to speak, and the city likes to remind others of its firsts: the First umbrella, the First city to receive the First message by Samuel Morse, the First to light its streets with illuminating gas, the First Mergenthaler Linotype, and the First ice-cream factory. It also might claim another first. It might be the first town ever to be embarrassed by the presence of a World Series.

"No chance," says Horse Thief Burke. "The people here got no beef with the city the way it is." The Thief, a former tout ("adviser," he says), who has been exiled from the tracks, acquired his name for picking up a rope—with a horse on the end of it. "I never stole a horse in my life," he told the desk sergeant. "Where would I hide it?" The Thief now runs a "bookstore" and spends his time watching *Search for Tomorrow* and telling people that, no, he does not have that *Dreams of an Egyptian Witch* number. "Why should people here have any beefs?" he says. "We got more tracks here than anywhere."

"Sure, but what about accommodations?" he is asked.

"What you mean, accommodations?"

"You know, hotels. The ones you sleep in." (The explanation is necessary, because the Thief remembers hotels as bivouacs for crapshooters.)

"So, we got one."

"No, there are three."

"One, three, twenty, who needs hotels to sleep? You can fall asleep right on a corner here."

"You mean it's dead?"

"Is Lord Baltimore? That's the way they like it here. No Series is gonna change it."

Once, in 1683, there was a Baltimore on the Bush River, but that settlement died when silt filled up the river; some Series visitors might leave thinking the original location was appropriate. Later, tobacco planters petitioned for a Baltimore on the Patapsco River (many citizens think the city is on Chesapeake Bay) and were given one, though first they had to quell a strenuous objection from one John Moale, whose land embraced the site of the settlement. Baltimoreans have dueled with change ever since. Finally the city did become a port of entry for tobacco, but even that failed. Wheat export saved it and pumped life into it.

A town of rolling land and dipping hills, a town of merchants, a town of rippling clipper-ship sails and rum-scented sailors, the settlement evolved into a city, the third largest in the country by 1858. All who came enjoyed it. "To my taste the women of Baltimore have more charm than the rest of the fair sex in America," said a French visitor. Barnum's Hotel, said Charles Dickens, "is the most comfortable of all hotels in the United States." Oliver Wendell Holmes called it "the gastronomical capital of the world"; visitors, looking for restaurants today, will wonder why.

Gracious living for Dickens and others, but for many Baltimore was a back-slum loudmouth, Mobtown, they called it, a

town of riots and brutes who were mainly volunteer firemen
and political yahoos. The volunteer firemen, who feuded often,
used to start fires deliberately and see which company could
get to the scene first. Often, when they did arrive, they forgot
about the fire and started brawling and flinging cobblestones at
each other. The elections were not as comic. In 1856, 8 persons
were killed and 250 wounded. The years brought many other
riots before Baltimore completed its ungraceful slide into the
twentieth century. After that, only the acidity of H. L. Menck-
en's column, The Free Lance, could incite the rabble.

Born in Baltimore in 1880, Mencken, a libertine, in a sense,
with a Katzenjammer mischievousness, became—and still is,
along with Babe Ruth—the city's most famous figure and, in his
time, its most abominated. Over a typewriter, with an Uncle
Willie cigar hanging from his lips and with glasses resting on
the tip of his nose, he went after "American piety, stupidity, tin-
pot morality and cheap chauvinism in all their forms." Outra-
geously irreverent, he flayed officialdom, labeled civic leaders
as Honorary Pallbearers and Baltimore's prominent citizens as
being first among the city's seven deadly curses. He only supported female suffrage because, he said, it would quickly "reduce democracy to an absurdity." He campaigned for bachelors
to be taxed a dollar a day simply because it was worth that to be
free, and when the Maryland General Assembly adjourned one
year, he wrote, "Let this be said for the legislature just hauled to
the dump: It might have been worse. And that, perhaps, is the
highest praise that can ever be given a dead cat."

Baltimore had only antipathy for Mencken, but he thought
warmly of the city. When he edited the *American Mercury* and
had to go to New York—which he despised—he was always impatient to return. He could relax in Baltimore, where he played
Beethoven with a group of amateur musicians called the Satur-

day Night Club and "ate divinely" out of Chesapeake Bay. Years later he joined the Maryland Club, a repository for many of the types that he used to flog in his column. Women were not permitted in the club, and Mencken reasoned to his astonished friends, "Why not! It does not even employ charwomen. If an older member falls ill and a trained nurse is necessary he is thrown into the street." Mencken died in Baltimore in 1956 in his house on Hollins Street, which even then was surrounded by blight. He had spent his entire life there, and now only a minority of citizens and the Enoch Pratt Free Library—one of the finest in the country—recall that a frolicsome giant of letters once towered over its somber skyline of spires and church steeples.

Town where Edgar Allan Poe is buried, where Thomas Wolfe died, and where F. Scott Fitzgerald brooded on Park Avenue, town where Francis X. Bushman was born, town that Father Divine had to leave to work his con, town where you can still buy a vote with a draft beer, town where a Bromo-Seltzer advertisement defaces the medieval tower of a building—Baltimore has not changed much since Mencken's time. Physically, it has been altered slightly, and more surgery has been done downtown. But Pratt Street, which faces the waterfront and is an encampment for drifters and grifters, remains unpromoted; even the Salvation Army has given up on Pratt Street.

Generally, the people resist rather than assist. Henry Barnes, now traffic commissioner for New York City, ran into their attitude when he was trying to solve traffic problems in Baltimore. A four-lane, two-way street, US 40 was a national highway that was being choked by double-parking and triple-parking in front of a popular fish house. Baltimoreans, who deify the crab cake, were furious that Barnes would even think of ending the congestion around the restaurant; it was sinful. "Man, we're here to buy some crab cakes," Barnes's men were told. "We just got to have some crab cakes. You're crazy if you think we're going any-place else. This is the best in town. Why don't you go and chase crooks and leave us crab-cake lovers alone." Barnes never did solve the problem, but the owner gave him carte blanche for free crab cakes for the entire Barnes family.

Beyond the crab cake, the monuments, and the people's re-luctance really to participate in the twentieth century, the lan-guage is the most unique aspect of the Baltimorean and his city. It is an aggravation composed of Southern Cracker, Brook-lynese, and Pennsylvania Dutch Singsong that makes a New Yorker, by comparison, sound like Laurence Olivier. For instance, Baltimore is Balamer or Balmer, the Irish are Ahrsh, one does not dial a number—one dolls. A place of business is a bidness, and an accelerator is an exhillerator, and you don't go to a drug-store, you go to a drukstore. Dusk is dust, Druid Hill Park is Druidl Park, a man's paramour waits for him on the lawn every evening. Our is air, barbed wire is bobwar, home is hame, a bureau is a beero, the government is the gummint, a car is a koor, a cruller is a crawler, asphalt is asfelt, orange juice is arnjoos, and any citizen who thinks this article is garbage will call it gobbidge. Some people claim that this language is only heard in East Baltimore, but you can hear it in the velvet sec-tions of town, too—that is, if you don't live there.

"Sonny, the only ones who don't mind hearin' that they talk that way," Uncle used to say, "are the ones in the tenth ward and in East Baltimore and South Baltimore, because they think all the other ones, the ones that live in the big houses outside of town, have to put on airs because they live in big houses. But we know they're Balamerans as soon as they open their mouths."

The tenth ward, which controlled politics in the city for years, is gone now, gone to inept second-story men and Negroes—they compose 40 percent of the population—who don't care to riot and aren't sure what CORE means. Besides, like most Baltimoreans, the Negroes have a group to look down on—the mountaineers, or hillbillies, or poor whites. Thousands of them, looking for work or just looking, move into the city and settle in pockets. They all have pallid faces with the same lost, lonesome look, and on a hot summer afternoon you can see them sitting on the steps in front of squalid row houses as if they were sitting under a tree in some faraway backland. They pick at their guitars and just watch the passing cars, and, sometimes, when you see a window shade lifted by a sudden wind and a kid's empty face behind it, you can understand their lonesomeness and lostness. A song tells about them, but it is only partially accurate. It tells of a man from Tennessee who lost his wife when she fell in love with the lights and streets of Baltimore. Never!

Baltimore, you see, is a lightless, no-night town, a kind of club basement, come-on-over-and-have-a-beer, one-night-out-a-week town. The Block, which the Great Fire of 1904 missed and the Salvation Army never misses, is the city's only evidence of nightlife. Every city has its equivalent. It is a twenty-minute walk along a string of pornographic bookstores, flophouses, penny arcades, tattoo parlors, surplus stores, restaurants, and strip joints. It is also a street of sounds: horns being bruised by heavy fingers, the lewd swishing on a drum, and a slattern's hurt cry: "Ya cheap bum, ya, why doncha come up with somethin', go for somethin', ya stiff." It is the street of the Gorilla Woman and Blaze Starr and transient strippers who arrive and depart about as often as the flophouse sheets are changed, a street where if you have it, they'll get it, and if you don't, well, "this ain't the Walters Art Gallery, champ." A street, just a G-string away from City Hall and police headquarters, where the cops will go blind if you lay a roll of bologna on them.

Yet the city—just as it is not certain whether it wants to be in the North or South—can't make up its mind about the Block. The street is infamous to some and a landmark to others. "Why," they say, "everybody from all over the world talks about the Block."

It is also being talked about in Baltimore. The Block was again prominent in the city's latest examination of its police department. In a six-hundred-page report of findings and recommendations, the International Association of Chiefs of Police raked the city's police department. The report found the city's meter maids surly, the horse patrol archaic, inefficient, and odiferous, and the pedestrian injury and fatality rate the worst in the nation. It is also implied that the police—poeleece to Baltimoreans—are not very bright. A number of times, it seems, they decided that citizens had died of natural causes, only to find later that the bodies they had sent to the morgue had fatal knife wounds and gunshot holes. The report did not get any better as it went on, but the citizens remained unflappable.

Still, despite its Keystone Cop police department and its insufferable torpor, you can *belong* and *almost* go back to Baltimore, where few genuine scandals occur, where nobody reads (at least not the *Sun;* the "best unread" newspaper in the country has a circulation of only 184,000). A city where the numbers business grosses $10 million annually and a big operator, who gets a big share of the take, gets caught—like some untutored back-alley purse snatcher—taking a fifty-cent play over the phone. A city whose Society is one of the most exclusive in the country and where all the money is clutched by a few tight-fisted hands. A city of factory workers who take their politics in the bars from lightweights whose political philosophy stops at Boss Tweed and Huey Long. A city that Alabama's Governor Wallace knocked over as if it were some Boys' Club amateur. A city where you can breathe a lot less polluted air than you do in

New York and see much more than 25 percent of a day's sun-light, and where you never have to worry about featherbedding jackhammer jockeys chopping up the street outside your win-dow at midnight. You can belong and almost go back to the city because there is order to life there, and a certain security to life there. Still you can't really go back, because it was (even though you were unaware of it then) and is a Harry Langdon kind of town, and if you have ever seen Langdon in a movie, you have to feel sad.

Besides, Uncle is gone now, and much of the section in which he lived is gone, too; the young people have all grown and left for their barbecue pits and slices of green lawn, and now only the old stay firmly on. Uncle, who used to sell produce from a horse-drawn wagon in the alleys and side streets of East Baltimore, checked out one day in an alley—right in the mid-dle of one of his typical arguments with a housewife who claimed his hard crabs were too light and his cabbage heads were too small. He lived all his life in East Baltimore, in the Highland-town and Canton sections, and he used to say, "Sonny, these people round here are the most civilized people, and this is the most civilized living in the world. They don't wanna hurt any-body, and they don't wanna be hurt. They just wanna be left alone. And if you wanna know this town, you better know these people here."

Uncle knew his town and knew his section and the people who are left. People who make sure their life insurance is never overdue, people who work hard and can be quite impatient with dreamers. People who live in blocks of row houses—red brick trimmed with white lines, window screens with pastoral scenes painted on them—that are fronted by white marble steps. Women who scrub the steps and sweep their patch of pavement. Men who go to the corner bar and buy kettles and pitchers of beer and then go home and drink it in the kitchen. People who sit on the steps on hot summer nights and in the kitchen during winter; their parlors, as they call them, once were used only for wakes and weddings. People who will listen to a Governor Wallace because he speaks to them about everything they have always feared—change, disorder, and intrusion.

"Sonny, change will come here, too," said Uncle one day by a pier, while the nephew stared vacantly at a freighter crawling through the water and wondered where it came from, where it was going, and if he would ever go. "The young will leave," he said, "and the old will stay. But the young can't leave it completely. They take a lot of the life with them, and the life here in East Balamer is a lot like the way Balamer is.

"You can't help lovin' this town," he finally said, "but you never know why. It's kinda like bein' in love with a certain kind of woman, maybe one with a broken nose. She may not be the prettiest or the most attractive, but she's real." He then jerked the reins in his hands, and the horse and wagon eased away from the pier.

2 To The Brink—
and Beyond

(NIAGARA FALLS)

Sports Illustrated
July 12, 1971

Major Lloyd Hill was not a real major. He did not mind being called "the Major," but he appreciated it being made perfectly clear that he was not a real major. It was not because he was not fond of officers. He just preferred his old rank of private in World War II; by some circuitous reasoning he believed it to be more individual. "I could have become a real major," he would say quickly, admitting that he often pondered the sound of Major Major Lloyd Hill. He said he would have become a real major had he not ingloriously dropped a case of ammunition on his big toe, which later led to the Major being separated from his right leg; the incident irritated him. He really had wanted to be gassed like his father, Old Red, a private who had wanted to be a major in World War I.

It was a soft, cool day on the Canadian side of Niagara Falls, almost soundless except for the sullen roar of the white, mean waters below and the Major's voice. He had been trapped

amid the ghosts of some lost regiment or other, but now seemed
to be emerging with a wistful lament of never having had the
chance to become a "crack mercenary" in Africa. It was suggested to the Major that his military past did not seem perti-
nent; whereupon, a bit struck by such irreverence, he said he was
only trying to show the spirit and backbone behind the saga of
the Hills of Niagara. He then moved on to the subject for which
he was best known: Niagara mania, and how to invest $1,000,
draw three hundred thousand people, and then kill yourself by
going over Niagara Falls in a barrel—presuming they ever
found a piece of you to prove that you were killed.

The Major was not just a mere historian or weaver of tales
about the Niagara and its deadliness. He was the last of a leg-
endary clan that believed the river to be its own, a people drawn
to the Falls for over half a century by its rage and beauty. It
went much deeper than peculiar fascination. It had been a fatal
obsession, one that was visible in the eyes of the Major's old, old
mother, who sat and rocked from dawn to dusk, listening to the
hypnotic thunder of the Falls. The obsession also could be heard
in the words of the Major, who spoke of the Niagara as if it were
flesh and blood, a beckoning enchantress who embraced you
and then dissolved into a toothless witch begging for another life.
"We have been generous to her," said the Major, pointing to a
copper plaque that read:

> The Hills of Niagara
> William (Red) Hill Sr.
> William (Red) Hill Jr.
> Norman Hill
> Major Hill
> Wesley Hill

The plaque spoke plainly—next to the first three names were crosses: these were the dead. Following the Major's and Wesley's names were horseshoes, for the lucky and alive. Wesley planned to stay that way, and he restricted his river fever to hunting and fishing. The Major was of a different disposition. Sometime in the next few months, on a day (as some say) suitable for dying, or a day when he felt the police were ripe for deception—for they have always viewed the Hills as a public menace—the Major would discard his crutches and be strapped into a contraption far up the Niagara. It might be a barrel, some sort of capsule, surely something worthy of so consummate a death wish. Its nomenclature aside, the object would measure five feet in width and seven feet in length. It would be made of stainless steel with an inner casing of one-eighth of an inch and an outer casing of one-sixteenth of an inch; there would be four to six inches between the casings and the interior would be packed with Styrofoam.

The Major was ecstatic as he probed deeper into the esoterica of his invention. His mother just shook her head, never missing a rock. She was very sick, but she had seen too often the river spit back her men, seen too much of Niagara death not to be still torn by the wolflike madness that continued to trail her family. She knew what the bodies looked like with their backs snapped as easily as if they had been dry twigs, and she knew what they looked like after they had been trapped behind the force of 25 million tons of water an hour and had run out of oxygen. "I'll be strapped inside in a standard parachute harness," continued the Major, "and I'll ride in a sitting position. I want to go straight over the middle. I figure when I hit, the capsule will plunge fifty feet underwater, and I'll come back to the surface two hundred feet downstream." The creaking of the rocker was suddenly the only sound in the room.

"All my life," said Mrs. Hill, still facing the window, "all I ever had was that river. It took my men, and I never want to see it again."

"Mom's been the main one to suffer," said the Major. "She never could understand the way it was with us and the river."

"All I ever had was the worry," said Mrs. Hill. "Just nights walking the floor. Two weeks after Wesley was born in 1930 they rolled my husband's barrel past my window. And I wrapped the baby up and carried him down to the river in my arms. It was so cold that day. I stood down by the whirlpool, and I watched Red's barrel be stuck there for six hours. I passed out three times. One time a doctor caught my baby falling out of my arms."

"We made eleven barrel runs in all," said the Major.

"Eleven too many," said Mrs. Hill, still looking out the window as the first signs of evening moved across her face. "I tried, I did. I tried to talk them out of it. But they never listened. The morning Red Jr. went over, he walked out of the house and I pleaded with him, right up until a big car scooped him up and took him away. I went and said a prayer. Then I went down to watch him come over. I've seen every trip every one of them made. But when I saw his barrel come over, I screamed. It was already ripped open. I knew he wasn't in it."

"He'd been thrown out in the upper rapids," said the Major, "before he ever got to the Falls."

"He knew," said Mrs. Hill. "He knew it was going to happen."

"We all knew," said the Major. "He didn't want people to think he was a coward if he waited to put in a metal lining."

"So . . . a dead hero," said the mother.

"Better than a dead coward," said the Major.

"Once you're dead, who cares?" said the mother, turning to look at her son, who at fifty-two and with one leg and a neck injury would not even let her die in peace.

The painful neck, which often had to be supported by a brace, came from one of the Major's five trips (more than any other man in Niagara history) through the various Niagara rapids. Even after you knew every whip of the water, every biting tooth of rock just under the surface, the possibility of death or severe hurt was hardly diminished. "No matter how much you know," said the Major, "it's never enough. The one thing you must never do is panic. You have to control your breathing and the movement of your body. Get all tense and stiff, and it will break every bone you've got. You go through those lower rapids, you know, at a speed of one and half miles in one and a half minutes—until you hit the whirlpool." It was in the whirlpool, a monstrous freak of nature, that the Major had come closest to being rubbed out. He was trapped there underwater for an hour. He did not know how far down he was, except that it was as if he were lost in some eerie dimension of the universe, and the sound of the water was like a million fiddle strings.

Long before that incident, in 1950, the Major had taken a crack at the Horseshoe Falls, which is on the Canadian side and the only one that is ever tried; the American Falls attracts only amateur suicides. It was the year before Red Jr.'s death when the Major climbed into a ten-foot stainless-steel barrel and began his rush down the upper rapids toward the precipice of the Falls like a Ping-Pong ball caught in a violent wind. Hundreds of thousands encrusted the river's shores. The Major was two hundred yards from the edge when the current propelled him to shore, and while disparate voices hawked souvenirs of barrelmania nearby, he was pulled out unconscious. He had suffered a bad concussion and his body was horribly bruised. The barrel was freed, and it went over the Falls like a riderless horse. The thought of that empty barrel still stalked the Major's dreams.

"A curse," said the Major's mother. "That's all it's ever been. All life ever meant to any of 'em was conquering that river. They *didn't* conquer it. That river will run forever."

The king of river rats, a man who knew the Niagara's every mood, Old Red Hill, the Major's father, would not have tolerated such mysticism from his widow, even though he knew that the Falls, with its ghostly veil of mist and macabre drone, could draw persons on the edge of insanity to their death. Could draw them, and then at some godless hour Old Red would hear the knock on his door and know that it meant another lost soul floating somewhere beneath the dark river. Often, intuitively, he did not wait for a knock, and in the middle of the night he would awaken and start dressing, and his wife would ask him where he was going, and he would say quietly, "To work." Work for Old Red meant another body. It was as if the river had called out to him, and, as Mrs. Hill noted, "He was never wrong."

It was said at the warped bars in the river saloons that Old Red had some dark pact with the Niagara. If so, one ancient riverman remarked, it was a bloody poor one, for the day never dawned that Old Red did not have to scratch for a dollar. His payment for retrieving bodies was meager, but it was unlikely that he even considered the money. He viewed himself, apparently, as a self-appointed sentinel of the river. Over the years he pulled nearly two hundred corpses out of the river, and nobody in Canada ("or on this planet," said the Major) had ever saved more lives: twenty-eight people from the river and thousands of wild birds trapped on the ice. The Canadian government awarded him four medals, which he liked to wear on Sunday.

It was obvious the old man could never satiate his appetite for heroism, and if the real connoisseur of heroes is the one who pursues death, that was Old Red. But the old man was not as expert on stripping clean the gullibility of tourists, though he and his family partially survived from them after he shot the rapids three times. He painted one of his barrels red and decorated it with an advertisement for himself in bold yellow letters— SAVED A GIRL FROM A BURNING HOUSE 1896. TAKEN OUT OF THE NIAGARA 177 BODIES. ONLY MAN IN WORLD WHO CAN WEAR 4 LIFE SAVING MEDALS. SNIPER IN 75TH BATT. WORLD WAR. GASSED. WOUNDED—and displayed the barrel in the family's souvenir shop. Old Red lived to die in bed. They said he died from the effects of having been gassed, but his widow, as well as those in the dim, hidden saloons who talked of him, believed that "he was too sick to run the river, and he died because he couldn't."

The old man left only a $420 insurance policy, despite the fact he had been a desultory smuggler during Prohibition. His sons, though, did not need money to confront the river. The old man had given them his instinct, his fierce independence, and his lust for the heroic moment. They were a hard lot, especially Red Jr., a brazen smuggler who was contemptuous of any law that came between him and the river. He lived purely for and off the Niagara, and his special haunt was the deep basin below the Falls, an otherworldly place with sheets of white spray and mad eddies filled with hundred-pound sturgeon, tenacious bass, marauding gar, and giant lamprey eels. That was his sanctuary from creeping reality and restriction, and that would be where they would one day find parts of his body.

As the Major told it, when his father was dying, he made Red Jr. promise that he would one day go over the Falls in a barrel; the old man should have saved his breath. The idea had always burned in his eldest son's mind, and long after his father had died and he himself had escaped death several times while shooting the rapids, Red Jr. one day glowered over mugs of ale and said, "I'm through waiting. This shooting the rapids has been practice stuff. I'm going over the Falls. Not in a barrel or a ball or a cylinder. I've given it a lot of study. I'm going over in rubber inner tubes. I'm as good a man as my father was. Now it's time to prove I'm a better one." The inner tubes, he thought, being light and buoyant, would not be dragged under and hammered down by the water. "It's the tons of water pounding you down that does the damage," he said.

"But even if that does work," said a friend, Bud Sinclair, "you can't fall one hundred and sixty-five feet without being seriously injured or killed. Give this suicide up and grow old and fat drinking ale."

"No, I've got it all figured," said Red. "The inflated inner tubes will act as a cushion when I hit. The long and wide inner tubes will be like shock absorbers. I won't go deep, and that way I'll miss the rocks down there that are the real danger."

"You're crazy," said Sinclair.

"Maybe so," said Red. "But you've got to admit that if I go through with it, I'm a better man than my father."

"If your father was still alive," said his friend, "he'd disown you for a fool."

"My old man would go over with me," said Red.

Probably three hundred thousand people lined the Niagara by noon on the day Red Hill Jr. chose to die. Far away, upriver, Red lounged calmly in a place of secrecy sipping an ale until someone ran in and shouted, "Somebody's tipped off the law!" "Use the decoy," Red said. A man with red hair and built like Hill slipped out of the room, and the rest waited. Bud Sinclair recalls the moment: "Downstairs, there were sudden shouts. A door closed, and there was a great commotion of grinding car gears and slamming car doors, and then sirens began wailing.

Hill waited for the sirens to fade, and then he got up swinging the football helmet he was going to wear. 'Let's go,' he said. I tried once more to argue him out of it. I said, 'Don't be a fool, Red.' He said, 'Not a chance. See you down below when they haul me out.'" The last thing he did was flip a coin. "Heads I win, tails I lose," he said wryly. He turned his palm up, looked at the coin, and then shrugged. It was a long time before they found what was left of Red Hill Jr.

"Just plain suicide," says Sinclair. "You don't have to know the river to know that. But Hill had to do it. He couldn't stop himself. He was driven by an urge that was bigger than himself, bigger than Niagara. If he'd succeeded, it would have proved nothing. Losing like he did proved nothing, either. Except that maybe Red was a brave but tormented and foolish man."

The death of Red was traumatic to his brother Norman, and he tried to flee the river and all its madness. He began to see the river in his dreams, shaped like the vast shadow of some prehistoric animal. He took a job out of town as a steeplejack. He found it dull and slowly made his way back to the river, where a power plant was under construction, and hired on. His second day of work, a year after Red's death, he was killed. A stone three inches in diameter dropped from three hundred feet above and crushed his skull.

"Maybe the first man who ever saw the Falls had the right idea," said the Major. "I think his name was Hennepin, a priest. He fell down on his knees in prayer, they say."

That was in 1678. By 1882 Oscar Wilde noted, "Every American bride is taken there, and the sight must be of the earliest, if not the keenest, disappointments in American married life." He added that it would be much more interesting if the Falls ran backward. Already the place had become a reservoir of fakery and relentless enterprise; it was here that Indian chiefs "from Ireland" peddled white pebbles and promoted them as "congealed Niagara spray." In 1859 a Frenchman named the Great Blondin became an international figure by walking a thirteen-hundred-foot cable stretched high above the Niagara gorge. For two seasons Blondin performed on the cable, and millions gawked at what he did. In the middle of the rope he somersaulted, prepared a French dish (which he washed down with a bottle of champagne raised from below), and crossed the cable blindfolded. He once had a narrow escape while carrying his manager on his back; it seems some gamblers had been careless with a knife on a guy rope. To the amazement of all, Blondin succeeded in doing what no one thought possible. He left the Falls with his life—and a fortune. He also left behind him an atmosphere that would hover above the Falls for decades like a mammoth dark-winged bird, and he created an allure that would often lead men along trails of deep irony.

Annie Edson Taylor was the first to try the Falls. In 1901 she was teaching grade school in Bay City, Michigan, when she suddenly announced to her students, "I'll go over Niagara Falls. Nobody has ever done that!" A few days later she headed east, a homely woman of forty-three intent on making money honestly and quickly. Upon her arrival at Niagara Falls, she went to a cooper by the name of Bocenchia and gave him her design for a barrel. It was to weigh 165 pounds, the same as her weight. Why did she need such a peculiar barrel? she was asked. "I'm going to ride it over Niagara Falls," she is said to have replied as she made her exit from the shop.

Annie got her barrel and, in it, dropped over the falls. For some time she was trapped behind the cataract before the barrel was ejected. When she was extricated, she was bleeding from the ears and her face was cut. "Nobody ought ever do that again," she said dazedly to the men who fished out the barrel.

That was the last of Annie's good fortune. The money she expected to draw from theater crowds never came. One reason was that she was boring and matronly, and audiences could not associate her with her deed. Even worse, according to one tale, she was seduced by a flimflam man who stole her barrel and shipped it West. He followed, stopping only long enough to romance a dance-hall girl and entice her to pose as Annie. With the real barrel and a pretty woman, he lived sumptuously ever after. As for the barrelless Annie, she died in Niagara Falls, a confused and lonely woman who wandered the streets selling autographed postcards and giving solitary orations about her feat.

An Englishman named Bobby Leach was the next one over the Falls, ten years after Annie Taylor. "If a woman schoolteacher can do it," he kept repeating, "I can do it." Tired of hearing him, friends pressured him into building a barrel. One July day Leach was cajoled into setting out in it. It was Old Red Hill who reached him first after he had made the plunge. Leach was alive, but barely; his kneecaps were broken, his jaw crushed, and he had a brain concussion that resulted in punch-drunkenness later in his life. Leach spent six months in the hospital, and when he was released, he toured the world with his barrel. In New Zealand, while limping down a street, he fell and broke his leg. He had slipped on an orange peel. That was the end of Bobby Leach. He contracted gangrene and died.

Next, an English barber and a Greek cook were drawn to the Falls. The barber, one Charles Stephens, could not stand barbering. He walked around town wearing a yachting cap and medals he claimed to have won for his daring; he said that he had often put his head in the mouths of lions. Just before he went over the Falls, he cabled his wife and eleven kids in Bristol, "Feat accomplished." Coming over the Falls, his barrel reared up straight and hung on the brink for twenty seconds.

That was the last anybody ever saw of Charles. All Old Red could find was a stave from the barrel and an arm with a tattoo on it requesting FORGET ME NOT. After Stephens, the Greek cook, George Stathakis, arrived on the scene, and the first thing he did was hire Old Red as his assistant.

Stathakis, a bachelor with a cadaverous face and body, said his reason for attempting the Falls was purely a search for truth. This seemed to correspond with his behavior back home; when not cooking, he would sit in the company of a 150-pound turtle named Sonny and compose metaphysical writings. "I plan to detach my mind philosophically," said Stathakis of his trip, "and store away each emotion for future reference." Looking at the cook's barrel, Old Red thought of the future, too. He requested the presence of two doctors and an undertaker. Stathakis's barrel, with Sonny aboard, came over the Falls and was caught behind the cataract. The man and turtle were imprisoned for fourteen hours. Stathakis died of suffocation, and the notebooks he had taken along were empty. The turtle survived. Old Red claimed the turtle and the barrel and exhibited them in front of the house. He made $150.

After Stathakis, three beat the Falls—a French Canadian named Jean Lussier, a mysterious Negro from New York City who called himself Nathan Boya, and a seven-year-old boy in a life jacket who was swept over accidentally. Lussier made it in 1928 in a huge ball. "I not so much as dent a fingernail," said Lussier, who lived afterward in Niagara, alone and impoverished. "The photographers, they want to show blood on my face. So I daub on red paint. But the trip over Niagara, she was nothing. I do it again, by damn!"

Boya came out of nowhere to ride the Falls in 1961 in what he called a Plunge-O-Sphere. It had a twelve-hundred-pound steel framework covered with seven layers of rubber and was equipped with seven canisters of oxygen. Only the police, shocked as if they were watching some creature rise from the river, and some old rivermen saw him do it. Boya turned down an invitation to appear on *The Ed Sullivan Show* and refused offers of money and exposure. Boya was not even his real name; he was believed to be one William Fitzgerald from Queens, New York. When he was pulled out of the river, all he said to the police was "Talk to my attorney. I've just integrated the Falls." He paid a $100 fine in a Niagara court—long ago it became a misdemeanor to go over the Falls—and disappeared, never to be seen or heard from again.

For a decade after, Niagara Falls sat quietly, encapsulated in the largess of its thousands of honeymooners who promenaded through town wearing new clothes and nervous grins or sat in their hotels sipping a complimentary cocktail consisting of rye, cranberry juice, and kümmel. Many never looked at the Falls, spending their public moments wandering through Ripley's, with its Lincoln Memorial made of pennies and its bicycle made of matchsticks, or searching the hundreds of shops for curios, such as the statuettes of a pregnant girl stamped with the line I SHOULD HAVE DANCED ALL NIGHT. Here and there were remnants of the madness that made the town famous: a barrel, a date, a name—all that was left of those many dead dreams.

The Major was seldom seen amid the imbroglio of bad taste. He stayed near the river, prowling it and plotting the return of the Hills. Besides, he and the law in town were not compatible. Once he had been involved in an altercation with a policeman, and the Major had turned the man upside down, taken his gun, and thrown it into a passing garbage truck. Another incident occurred when the Major, while sitting in a saloon, had said he could stop time. A debate ensued, and the Major, by way of what he considered a brilliant demonstration, jimmied his way into a funeral parlor and stole its big clock. It was a while before the Major could return to the bar, one where he liked to spend his nights over a few glasses of Captain Morgan rum.

On those nights he would often be quiet as he sat, either thinking or scribbling bad verse about the Falls like "If Old Red, my dad, could see / Just how his life's affected me." But he would become animated on the subject of guns and smoke and battle. He seldom spoke of himself, except to curse that case of ammunition. He would restrict his talk to his father, whom "they couldn't even kill with a ton of gas." It was only when a friend became too playful and accused the Major of pretending to be a real major that he would move toward a wall, drop his crutches, and throw up his guard. He then would go home and not be seen for a long time.

The Major had not been much in view for a few weeks, but he was proceeding with his plans for going over the Falls this September. He had raised the money for his barrel, and it was in production. He was also working with a Canadian television network on a documentary about himself and all the other Hills. Then on Monday, June 14, the same day old Jean Lussier suddenly died, the Major, for his own sake, was picked up by the police in downtown Niagara and taken to jail. He was drunk, and he had been shouting incoherently on the streets about Lussier and of how the river would never get Major Lloyd Hill. The following morning, when he was to be released, they found the Major dead of "natural causes." There was talk of cremating him and scattering his ashes out over the Falls, but nothing came of it. He was buried quietly, the last of the river Hills, and there were many who thought he would never have gone over the Falls because in his heart and mind and soul the river had long ago beaten him. He was in the end, they say, like one of the weary loons he occasionally rescued. They light above the rapids and are quickly dragged down to them. They cannot take off like smaller birds, and soon their necks drop listlessly into the water and they drown. It was not the way he wanted to die, not the way a Hill should die.

3 All the Best

(GEORGE BEST)

Sports Illustrated
March 27, 1972

Few men in games ever express the temper and rhythm of their times to the point of becoming the embodiment of a social climate. It is not only a matter of authentic genius; there is also a pure accident, a collision between a man and his age, and today only three men would seem to qualify as more than statuary passed in our race to crush boredom: El Cordobés, the bold vagabond from Andalusia who spoke in the bullring for an unshackled Spain; Muhammad Ali, whose courage spoke for sanity; and finally George Best, who *is*.

Just who George Best is accounts for volumes of opinion and thesis, agreeing only that he is the most gifted soccer player in Great Britain, that he has tippled his way through half of England's import of Russian vodka, that he has a Faroukian collection of girls, that he is—God willing—an outside wager to reach the age of thirty. He is one of the few figures, perhaps the last, of mythological dimension in the history of English soccer. A man of only twenty-five whose appeal is so vast, so hypnotic, he is daily matter for talk from Parliament to Soho, a source of vicarious pleasure and pique for millions. "Why, why do we make so much fuss over him?" muses an English critic, fearful that George Best dwarfs the game itself and dims its sanctity.

"George Best is an endless job," says his agent Ken Stanley. "We've a full-time staff of six people working continually on Georgie." The work includes handling roughly two thousand letters a week from every part of the world and the control of maybe one of the largest fan worships ever founded. "A lot of people don't like the fan club," says Stanley, "but it makes sense. If George gave everyone what they want, his mailing costs would run to ten thousand pounds. The club helps cut the costs. And we never asked anyone to join, people begged us to form it—fifteen thousand of them." By the time he is thirty, says Stanley, George Best will be worth a fortune, so extraordinary is the power of his name, attached to everything from eggs to men's shorts.

Going by train to Manchester, the besooted, deadly austere city north of London where Best reigns like a prodigal prince, one tries to put him in some perspective from the convenient valley of ignorance. Less dramatic than Ali, closer to El Cordobés, Best seems at first to be simply another totem in the current cult of image that can hardly bear much more traffic— another of those who are sold like the latest aberration in fashion, surface rebels who are trendily precocious and craftily practical, all of those free-form souls who have now become as prosaic as the crew cuts who adorned the Eisenhower era, the backlash of which may have visited upon us this even more boring species.

But George Best is a soccer player. Sung about in music halls, fought over in pubs, the game has always been the primary release for the working class. The cloth-cap tides eventually swept it to the top of the English sport and forged themselves, for one brief moment each week, into a new community. "All brothers together," wrote J. B. Priestley, "for...not only had you escaped from the clanking machinery of this lesser life, from work, wages, rent, doles, sick pay, insurance cards, nagging wives, ailing children, bad bosses...but you had escaped with most of your mates and your neighbors, with half the town, and there you were, cheering together...swopping judgments like lords of the earth, having pushed your way through a turnstile into another and altogether more splendid kind of life...."

For decades soccer clubs harvested the fanaticism and religiosity of the men from the mills and factories and fed on the abundant talent that came from them. Niggardly to their players, rigid in their demand for absolute servitude, the clubs thrived and stood contemptuous and aghast at periodic suggestions that they adopt a more liberal spirit. "I used to look at those crowds," recalls Jimmy Logie, a star in the 1950s, "and think I was the only star who earned less than the people watching me." Peonage ended early in the sixties, but it was not until Best came from Ireland, out of a council house in Belfast, that a new era became personalized.

To calibrate the rise of George Best, his impact on a generation, go back to what was commonly known in 1965 as Swinging London. Harold Wilson was talking about a classless New Britain. The King's Road in Chelsea, with its lovely girls from every corner of the earth, its mélange of Cockney burglars and escapist aristocrats, its air heavy with the scent of a New Day, was the first center of what would later be called social revolution. Even the old, gray *Tatler* sensed the surrounding decomposition, and its owners reorganized in an attempt at a journal that might appeal to England's "new aristocracy." But the grubby absolute of soccer remained as so much else was slipping past, though nobody on the King's Road—the sybaritic, the searchers for any old high—talked of a game so rooted in another time.

Then came George Best. For the first time, in a nation just as team conscious as America, a single presence seemed to dominate the stage; from the appearance of the players to the style of the game itself, things would never be the same again. Even though now he seems one of many, it is sheer nonsense to group Best with his imitators. He was an original, he was to soccer what the Beatles were to music out of Liverpool, what Carnaby Street was to fashion. He not only brought a new genius to the game, he transformed it into entertainment, a word some officials still cannot abide.

But George Best did not create himself, did not sit down one day at Old Trafford and say, "I think I will be different." It was the mood of the people that made him, and he moved upon it like a bottle on the sea, sometimes smoothly, often turbulently. Expressing that mood more and more with each new day of his young life, he became, and is, the epitome of the hero, meaning that he is what we are not, that he is unlike anything or anyone who trudges through our environment. It is a time of romantic longing, and few have satisfied it more than George Best. He is now the ultimate hero of the working class, which gorges itself on pieces of him every Saturday afternoon, and a flesh-and-blood fantasy to English soccer's growing new audience, the young and the beautiful and the hip who cannot distinguish between reality and role, to whom everything is a scene out of a movie ("like a scene out of *Casablanca*, damn it...you know, with a fan on the ceiling in this Moroccan bar").

Not even in the tweedy isolation of Blossoms Lane up in Manchester, where Best owns a house and often broods these days, can he shut out the hysteria, evade the reach of those who want to be near him. "It was once quiet in Blossoms Lane," says a woman on a nearby farm. "Now the place has become a Sunday drive-out, a main stop for tour coaches, and cars are passing up and down all hours with people just gaping out and teenagers stomping all over my lovely garden hoping for a glimpse of him." One of the men who worked on the house says, "It was a public monument before the roof went up. On Sundays you could not park for the sightseers and girls who came out to watch the work. Why, when we advertised for general laborers, the replies were five times the normal. Forty instead of the expected eight! Best was always Georgie to the workmen. I can see him now, sitting on a wall during the tea breaks having a cup from a laborer's brew can."

Quiet and running colors, the late-October day up on Blossoms Lane seemed far removed from the shadow of the Irish war, but there it was, like shrapnel in your cornflakes. Police rimmed the Best house, not because another girl had recently thumbed her way to his house to present her dreamings at his front door but because his life had been threatened a week before, and now a woman had reported that two men had rung her bell, asking for Best's address. One of them, she said, had a gun.

As he opened the door, having peeked through the window and waved to the police, the lunacy of Ulster was etched deeply on the face of George Best, and rightly so: when it comes to Ulster, birth and blood are not gainsaid by altering one's geography. "The Protestants are getting more Protestant," says Best, "and the Catholics more Catholic. Even the wildest rumors are believed over there. They're saying I gave Ian Paisley three thousand dollars to help finance one of his churches. Imagine anything more ridiculous. But that's the kind of thing that can get you shot. It's so horrible, and there seems no way out." He guides his visitors through the great windowed house, which cost him £40,000 and is replete with the gadgetry and comfort and—to some—the ostentation of sudden success: a mammoth color television and stereo that disappears by remote control, a large wine rack, a sunken tub that looks like an empty lake, a game room from which he once threw a pool cue through the window in a moment of lonely rage.

Now, walking from window to window, he pauses to comment, "If a sniper wanted to do a job on you, he couldn't pick a better place." He adds that it was not really injury, as had been claimed, that prevented him from playing for Ireland. He says he has been told that if he goes there, he will never make it back to England. He appears agitated; the deep-set, blue eyes with the half-inch lashes that are forever being mentioned on women's pages are empty, the face, with its pall of a beard, grows darker in the dying light. It is not existence on the precipice of danger that bothers him so much but danger's intrusiveness, its coming at a time when he was performing as no other British player before him, all with a zest and joy that critics once contended had been doused by his fame.

"You know," he says, "I still find a special thrill in playing with goalposts with nets. When we are training at Old Trafford and there are no nets, I feel like going in a huff and refusing to practice. I still get a special charge when the ball makes that whirring noise as it hits the nets." The phone has beeped constantly. Most of the time he has left it to his answering service, but he can scarcely bear to do this, for the phone offers escape from his isolation, though it means, more often than not, idle and constipated exchange with a girlfriend; he is not glib, on the phone or off it. Then it is his mother who calls, and his response to her is cool and tinged slightly with bravado, as if he hopes his manner will allay her fears, quiet her roiled emotions, the

anxieties about him that have impaired her health since the day
he left home for Manchester when he was fifteen. He puts down
the phone, sighs, and shakes his head.

"My sister," he says. "She got shot in the leg coming out of a
dance. Not badly, but bad enough. And she got shot because she
is my sister."

Night falls, and Best directs the conversation toward less
sinister matters: a note from Harold Wilson commending him
on a spectacular goal, a letter from a close girlfriend who pleads
with him to turn and chase whatever it is that he is running
from—and would he refrain from kicking down her door at all
hours of the morning because the next time he does, her neighbor says she will have her police dog attach one of his lovely
legs. "I used to joke that my ambition was to be a millionaire,"
he says, veering from his personal straits to his fiscal condition.
"Now it's not so much a joke. I'll be disappointed if I'm not near
it by the time I'm thirty. Then I'm going to breeze. I've had Manchester. It's like Peyton Place. Everybody knows what everybody else is doing. I don't know if I could ever live anywhere in
this country after I've finished. I thought Switzerland was great,
but when I went there, I found it was too perfect, too beautiful,
just too much."

Though a common condition in youth, the restiveness,
the urge to be somewhere other than where one is, seems almost
chronic in Best. His sudden flights are seldom signaled. He will
be in his villa in Majorca, and he will fly back to London to get
a haircut. He will be up in Manchester and will suddenly make
a three-hour drive to London for dinner. His father recalls answering a knock late one night at the house in Belfast. "There
he was, Georgie," he says, "standing on the doorstep wearing
one of those Honolulu shirts and old suede shoes, no shave, and
he's askin' for two quid for the taxi. Then he runs upstairs,

picks up the twin girls and his little brother out of bed, and brings them down and plays with them for a couple of hours. The next mornin', dawn hardly up, he catches a plane back to Manchester."

Best walks his guests to the door, and he appears reluctant to say good-bye. "To tell you the truth, I'd like to go into town and have a drink with you, but the police won't let me out of this place. I'm glad I've had someone to talk to. I think I'll get a bird over here. You know, some bloke in London would rip me for saying that. Like they always do, he'd write I was not serious about my work. Well, I know I would be a far better player if I became obsessed with the game as some fellows are. It just so happens that the way I'm made—and, let's face it, the way I look has a lot to do with it—takes me into many other things in life. I get on very well with birds, and I'm not one to fight against that. I like to enjoy myself, to get pleasure out of the money I'm making."

He smiles and then says, "If I had been born ugly, you'd never have heard of Pelé. As it is, it just wouldn't be possible, you see, for me to live like a monk to suit the demands of the game. I'd go mad. I know I burn the candle at both ends and drink too much, but I love the game and work hard at it. I don't kid myself that I give it absolutely everything I could. When you ask me if I consider myself the best player in the world, the answer is no. But I'm sure I could be. When I'm right at my sharpest, I feel I can do anything with the ball whatever the opposition. All I'm saying is that I could never narrow my life down to the point where the only thing that mattered was the game. No one knows how it feels to be me. I…"

His voice trails off, and then one of the police hollers out of the dark, "You're a fine target, standin' there in the light, Georgie. You'll catch a cold, too."

How strange it all still must seem to Best, that house, the
police out in front of it, a life so frightfully remote from his gray
smoke of an existence in Belfast: the front doors of the houses
painted the same; scrawny privet hedges; ragged kids in the
streets in the winter light, trying to dribble with balls made of
binding rags; the streams of men, their breath on the air, hands
deep in their pockets, returning from the shipyard where his father worked. "Every night after lessons we played football until
bedtime, using the streetlamps as floodlights. Who cared how
little money we all had? I never wanted pocket money. Only the
game counted. We lived for Saturday afternoons when we would
bundle our boots into schoolbags and dash off for the local bus to
the pitch."

He was fifteen—"just a speck of a body"—when Bob Bishop
first saw him. Bishop was the Irish scout for Manchester United,
and he wired back to United, "I think I have found a genius."
The scout went to the Best house and found the genius out
front in the dark dancing with a tennis ball; he invited him to
spend two weeks in Manchester. "When he arrived," says Mrs.
Mary Fullaway, who was his landlady for years and would become another mother to him, "all I remember is this little head
looking out of the car window, and I recall saying to myself,
'Well, he'll never make a footballer!'" The next night Best fled
back to Belfast. "I felt I didn't belong," he says. "I was very homesick. When I got home, my father was furious. He felt that I had
thrown away a chance of a lifetime. I'm sure he felt like whack-
ing me. Yet my mother understood. She put her arm around me
and said, 'Never mind, Son.'"

Best returned to United, which found him odd jobs, and
when he was seventeen, the club signed him. Four months later
he was in his first match; it was to be one of the most memorable
debuts in British soccer. He brought the dribble back into the

game, a lost art that had faded with Stanley Matthews and Len Shackleton and become obsolete with the genesis of the versatile player of the midsixties. "The memory that Best left in my mind after that game," recalls one critic, "was of frailty animated into intensely personal enterprise." Quickly, Best became firmly entrenched among the elite of the game, his innovation and instinct exploding into the sort of virtuosity that defied the pedestrian language of soccer. "I've never liked tactics," says Best. "Tactics bore me." The fans steadily came to agree with him, and few will ever forget the pass he once made for a United goal; like a street urchin, with mud crusting his wet, black mane, Best made the pass with a stockinged foot while holding his boot high in the air.

That sort of acrobatic plainly excites Best. He sometimes imagines himself in a Cup Final at Wembley before the Queen with millions watching on television. He imagines Manchester leading by two goals with twenty minutes left; the team is invincible, so he says, "It is time to show off." First a long kick from the goalkeeper balloons down the field, and he traps it against the turf with his backside. "Can you hear the roar!" he says. "The cheek of it! A player so in control he can bring a ball under his spell by sitting on it. But I haven't finished." The crowd bays crazily. "They want more," he says. "I sweep past the left flank of the defense bouncing the ball on my thighs and never letting it touch the ground. Listen to that crowd," he suggests. "Then the final stroke. A center across the face of the opposition goal. Forget about the laws of balance, I fly into a headstand and volley the ball into the foot of the net with my feet. God, can you hear them!" Impossible? "No, I've done all these things in practice, and I've kept the ball off the ground in a lengthy dribble against West Ham."

Any talk of individualism, or of Best, personal or otherwise, usually invites comment on Sir Stanley Matthews, who was knighted for what he did on a soccer field. Matthews was a dour figure who typified the working class of the thirties, a part of England that could not have related to the glamour of any era and never thought of clawing its way out of anonymity, a silent horde that lived daily with dole and debt. By his every feature, Matthews was one of them. He had high cheekbones, pale lips, an unemotional face that seemed never to have known youth; if you were going to paint the face of Stanley Matthews, it would be the classic worker's face. He never smoked, never drank, and two sentences back-to-back were a speech for him. Thrift directed his personal life, and hard work wrought a career of tempered steel. Until 1965, Stanley Matthews was an inexorable force of drama and dignity across the terraces of British stadiums.

"In a sense," remembers one fan, "Matthews's clinging to his playing days was very like the manner in which he played individual matches. When he moved with the ball, shuffling, leaning, edging ever closer to the defender, he was always the man teetering on the very brink of disaster, and we waited breathlessly to see whether this time he would fall or whether yet again he would come swaying back at the last possible moment to run on clear and free. We'll never know how he would have fared today against these faster, lighter, more tenacious defenders. Some think he would not have done well. Maybe, but if I were going to pick an all-time international team, I'd have Matthews, at thirty-five, on my right wing and George Best [actually also a winger] at inside right, and invite the opposition to find the ball."

No quality of perception is required to say that Best and Matthews would be an attack for the ages, even though the only thing they would have in common would be their immense prestige and spare bodies. Unlike Matthews's, Best's face implies that he would crumple in the presence of a hard day's work. It is a face, one thinks, that would bring a snicker from a workingman; surely he could not impute to it the stuff of heroism. But in England today as elsewhere, the worker, like those who play on King's Road, wants his share. The prolix cliché now used to define his times is, after all, "the revolution of rising expectations," and more than ever he resents the grinding monotony of so much of his work, the obscurity of it all, the cloddish debasement of his being. He is as restless, as disconnected, as any kid with a knapsack and a thumb on his way to London. Whatever it is out there they are expecting, he wants some of it, too, and through George Best he has a piece of today.

For all of his elastic appeal, the pop idolatry that seems to distract from his fathomless talent, it is only the Best on the pitch that is genuinely stirring. Out there, searching for space in which to start his long, truly beautiful dribbles, he offers the constant promise of the incredible. "If I had the whole of Britain to choose from," says Sir Alf Ramsey, manager of the English soccer team, "instead of just England, the only non-English player I would pick for my team would be George Best." Sir Matt Busby, a director of United, says that he would not put a price on him, but "in straight cash we'd need a million for him." Busby believes the knife-edged drama of Best taking a ball so close to an opponent to beat him defies imitation. "He is possibly the greatest player on the ball I have ever seen," says Busby. Danny Blanchflower, once one of the stars in Britain, says, "Matthews was, let's face it, a supreme dribbler who would tax even the most ruthless, sophisticated defenses of today. But he was primarily a provider. Tom Finney was perhaps a better all-rounder than Matthews. But George Best gets my vote. He's a master of control and manipulation, a superb combination of creator and finisher, and he can play anywhere along the line. But more than the others he seems to have a wider, more appreciative eye for any situation. He seldom passes to a colleague in a poor position. He is prepared to carry the responsibility himself. Best, it seems to me, makes a greater appeal to the senses.

"His movements are quicker, lighter, more balletic. He offers the greater surprise to the mind and the eye. Though you could do nothing about it, you usually knew how Matthews would beat you. In those terms, he was more predictable to the audience. Best, I feel, has the more refined, unexpected range. And with it all there is his utter disregard of physical danger. Just think of his ability to beat all of the giants in the game while in the air. He has timing and balance in his feet and ice in his veins. But I doubt if he will ever play as long as Matthews. George is one of the most closely marked players I have ever seen. Hatchet men track his every stride, and he takes terrible punishment."

Evidence of the violence dealt to Best is visible after every match. His shoulders are black-and-blue and his heel tendons and fragile ankles show the impact of persistent boots. A scar runs across the ridge of his right brow; there is another on his left knee. The right knee has hardly any cartilage. The pain absorbed, the pressure of being hounded, and his own quick temper keep Best in constant trouble with officials; the fact that he plays for United does not promote coolness, either. The club, one of the most magnetic in Europe, is no stranger to bad conduct, and its fans are famous for their misbehavior. They are not enamored of London teams, and one of their songs goes, "Oh, we kicked him where he lives and we kicked him in the head. Bleedin' old Cockney . . . he's dead." Such a team and fans are dry tinder to Best's inflammatory petulance, and the results seem forever splashed blackly across the tops of English papers.

"He's a temperamental player," says referee Eric Jennings, who was caught by some mud Best threw. "No one else can take the ball off him. If things go wrong, he gets upset. I think it's his nationality."

"I don't ask for special consideration for George," says Busby, "but in some respects he deserves it. I am convinced that some opponents have gone out to hurt him. He takes some knocks long after the ball is gone. No one in the game takes as much stick as George and probably no one ever has."

Of more concern to Busby, his current manager, Frank O'Farrell, and the press—the latter sympathetic most of the time—is the personal comportment of Best. His lapses range from numerous nightclub incidents and romantic entanglements to motoring infractions and serious breaches of training. Always there is a girl who eventually sells her story of George to one of the papers, which usually titillates the masses with headlines like "One Dance and George Ruins My Romance," "George Best the Lover...by the Girl He Planned to Wed." One of his more publicized entanglements was with a Danish girl named Eva Haraldsted: he invited her to spend a week in England, and she stayed on to sue him for breach of promise. "I finally settled it with her," says George. "I gave her some money, and she used it to get a nose job."

Eva says, "George was gentle, he was kind, he made me feel that he was the only man who mattered. When George wanted something, money was no object. Why, when my clean clothes ran out—remember I had brought only enough for a week—he gave me a blank check to go and buy some more. One of our first differences was when he picked up some spareribs with his fingers to chew them, and I said, 'George, that's not very nice.' I wish I had kept my mouth shut. He hated me to defy or contradict him, especially when other people were present. On the way back in the dining car, after a game, one of his friends offered me a cigarette. George said, 'She doesn't smoke.' I didn't, but I took the cigarette just to let George know I had a mind of my own. He didn't speak to me the rest of the journey.

"He had a fear of breaking a leg, and he told me the trainers of the other teams always shouted, 'Go for his legs!' He also had a thing about his image as a nice guy, and he would not leave a card game if he was winning. He likes to stay until he had lost. The George Best I knew was simply sensitive and kind. But his pet hate remained. He couldn't stand for me to argue with him in public. Once when I did, he told the papers the following day that we were through. I asked him why and he said, 'Because I feel I can't remain faithful to you.'"

Another girl suggests that going out with Best "is a bit like being on a jet plane, piloted by a blindfolded Jekyll and Hyde." She says that a girl with Best is in a situation in which she has little or no control, and that above all she must have a complete disregard for human logic. "I was watching a movie with him once, and suddenly my name was flashed on the screen. There was an urgent message for me at the manager's office. I made a mad dash up the aisle, thinking of every serious thing I could imagine. The manager calmly handed me the envelope. I opened it nervously, and what do you think it says? 'I Love You, G.'" A more concise assessment of Best comes from still another girl: "Sometimes he's an Irish navvy, sometimes he's Cary Grant, but mostly he's himself, quiet, withdrawn, rarely speaking. We used to have some beautiful silences together."

The pursuit of girls, often as carefully studied as the invasion of Normandy, seems to have finally treed Best himself; that is, if girls are what motivates his truancy from training. His first brush with United came a little more than a year ago. He missed a team train back to Manchester and went off to London instead. There, with half of Fleet Street banging on his door, he was found with an actress. Busby suspended him for a fortnight.

The episode was not generally laughed off as a typical Best escapade. The press and the public, to say nothing of his team and his friends, were by this time distinctly concerned about George. "I was so bloody mixed up," he tried to explain, "that I just wanted to get away for a few days. I just wanted some peace and quiet. In the end I panicked. I didn't know what the hell to do. I only wanted some breathing space. I'm so nervy now I even look over my shoulder to see if anyone is following me or watching me. I would be lying if I said I didn't like all the fuss when I first started. I did. But suddenly it's all gone sour. Every move I make is magnified. Even my house gets it. They come and look at it and say it looks like a public lavatory. That's unkind."

A subsequent and similar flouting of training appears to have brought the full wrath of United down upon him, even that of the players who revere him. Best had not been playing to form, and United seemed sadly mediocre. "He'd been part of the decline," said one player, "and he should have been training all week to help us put it right." But Best had disappeared again. At first it was thought that, fearing for the safety of his family, he had returned to Belfast, but when Frank O'Farrell went there to see if he could help, he learned George had not been home in months. O'Farrell returned to Manchester in a graveyard mood. A week later Best proved to have taken off for London again; the script varied principally in that the girl this time was not an actress but the current Miss Great Britain.

When O'Farrell finally had a private talk with Best, he emerged saying, "I think he is a lonely boy, a very lonely boy."

But then he dropped his ax. He fined Best two weeks' pay, ordered him to train with the regular team in the morning and
with the juniors every afternoon for a week, and told him he
must forfeit his day off for five weeks. He then cut at the root of
Best's life, demanding that he move out of his house and back
into digs with Mrs. Fullaway. All single players are required to
live in boardinghouses, but Best had been an exception.

A headline in one of the next day's papers read, "Best Must
Leave Home." Another said, "The Best Sentence." Beneath it
was an article by Mrs. Fullaway entitled "I've Kept the Room
Ready…for My Little Boy Lodger." "Don't feel sorry for the
wee boy," says Pat Crerand, George's closest friend on United.
"What he needs is a good kick in the arse. If Georgie keeps going on, he will not last much longer than another two or three
years. He has not got the same respect for football that he once
had." Says another, "George needs help. He's got to find out
who his friends are. People are getting famous just by being
seen with him. There are too many people saying, 'Come on,
George, have one more for the road.'" Dave Sadler, who once
lived with Best in digs, says, "Sure, I lived with him, but I don't
know him. I've not scratched the surface of him." The beauty
queen Best had been seeing during his absence from United
could only say, "How can he court me now?"

The question is surely of small concern these days to Best,
who has become, to the stranger studying him, a curious, incomprehensible little man, instead of the cardboard figure revealing only a mania for girls and nocturnal wanderlust. Now
there are glimpses of a hidden self, a self whipped by the compulsions of his youth and times, a Black Irish insistence on self-
destruction. To the student of Best, they indicate much more
than a caricature—and a future that could find him done in by
his image. The race with his façade has left him lonely and con-

fused, a small animal caught in a headlight. "My life controls me," he complains. "But I want to be in control of my life." Maybe that is what he was saying the day a girl he had been seeing stopped by to pick him up. He was gone, leaving only a note on his door. It read, "Nobody knows my name."

4 No Place in the Shade

(COOL PAPA BELL)

Sports Illustrated
August 20, 1973

In the language of jazz, the word "gig" is an evening of work, sometimes sour, sometimes sweet, take the gig as it comes, for who knows when the next will be. It means bread and butter first, but a whole lot of things have always seemed to ride with the word: drifting blue light, the bouquet from leftover drinks, spells of odd dialogue, and most of all a sense of pain and limbo. For more than anything the word means *black*, down-and-out black, leavin'-home black, what-ya-gonna-do-when-ya-git-there black, tired-of-choppin'-cotton-gonna-find-me-a-place-in-de-shade black.

Big shade fell coolly only on a few. It never got to James Thomas Bell, or Cool Papa Bell as he was known in Negro baseball, that lost caravan that followed the sun. Other blacks, some of them musicians who worked jazz up from the South, would feel the touch of fame or once in a while have thought that their names meant something to people outside their own. But if you were black and played baseball, well, look for your

name only in the lineup before each game, or else you might
not even see it there if you kept on leanin' and dreamin'.

Black baseball was a stone-hard gig. Unlike jazz, it had no
white intellectuals to hymn it, no slumming aristocracy to taste
it. It was three games a day, sometimes in three different towns
miles apart. It was the heat and fumes and bounces from buses
that moved your stomach up to your throat, and it was greasy
meals at flypapered diners at 3:00 a.m. and uniforms that were
seldom off your back. "We slept with 'em on sometimes," says
Papa, "but there never was 'nough sleep. We got so we could sleep
standin' up or catch a nod in the dugout."

Only a half-mad seer—not any of the blacks who worked
the open prairies and hidden ballyards in each big city—could
have envisioned what would happen one day. The players knew
a black man would cross the color line that was first drawn by
the sudden hate of Cap Anson back in 1883, yet no one was fool
enough to think that some bright, scented day way off among
the gods of Cooperstown they would hear their past blared out
across the field and would know that who they were and what
they did would never be invisible again.

When that time comes for Papa Bell—quite possibly the
next Hall of Fame vote—few will comprehend what he did
during all those gone summers. The mass audience will not be
able to relate to him, to assemble an image of him, to measure
him against his peers, as they do a white player. The old ones
like Papa have no past. They were minstrels, separated from
record books, left as the flower in Gray's "Elegy" to "waste its
sweetness on the desert air." Comparisons will have to do: Josh
Gibson, the Babe Ruth of the blacks; Buck Leonard, the Lou
Gehrig of his game; and Cool Papa Bell—who was he?

A comparison will be hard to find for Papa. His friend Tweed,
whom Papa calls *the* Black Historian, a title most agreeable to

Tweed, says you have to go all the way back to Willie Keeler for Papa's likeness. Papa's way was cerebral, improvisational; he was the master of the little things, the nuances that are the ambrosia of baseball for those who care to understand the game. Power is stark, power shocks, it is the stuff of immortality, but Papa's jewel-like skills were the meat of shoptalk for twenty-eight winters.

Arthritic and weary, Papa quit the circuit twenty-three years ago at age forty-seven, ending a career that began in 1922. During that time he had been the essence of black baseball, which had a panache all its own. It was an intimate game: the extra base, the drag bunt; a game of daring instinct, rather than one from a hidebound book. Some might say it lacked discipline, but if so, it can also be said that never has baseball been played more artfully, or more joyously. "Before a game," says Papa, "one of our big old pitchers, he'd say, 'Jist git me a coupla runs, that's all.' You see, we played tricky ball, thinkin' all the time: we git a run, they got to git two to beatcha. Right?"

The yellow pages of Tweed's scrapbook don't tell much about the way it was, and they don't reveal much about Papa, either; box scores never explain. They can't chart the speed of Papa Bell. "Papa Bell," says Satchel Paige, "why he was so fast he could turn out the light and jump in bed before the room got dark!" Others also embellish: he could hit a hard ground ball through the box and get hit with the ball as he slid into second; he was as so fast he once stole two bases on the same pitch. "People kin sure talk it, can't they?" says Papa.

Papa says he did steal two bases on one pitch, which was a pitchout. "The catcher, why he was so surprised the way I was runnin' that he just held the ball," says Papa. "I ask him later what he doin' holdin' the ball, and he say he didn't know, 'cept he *never* seen a man run like that before in his life." It is also a reliable fact that once in Chicago, on a mushy field, he circled the bases in 13.1 seconds, two-fifths faster than Evar Swanson's major league record. "On a dry field," he says. "I once done it in twelve seconds flat."

Papa could run all right and he could hit and field as well. He played a shallow center field, even more so than Willie Mays when he broke in. "It doesn't matter where he plays," Pie Traynor once said. "He can go a country mile for a ball." As a hitter Bell had distance, but mainly he strove to hit the ball into holes; he could hit a ball through the hole in a fence, or drag a bunt as if it were on a string in his hand. Bell never hit below .308, and on one occasion when he was hitting .390 on the last day of the season, he gave his title up; he was forty-three at the time.

"Jackie Robinson had just signed with the Dodgers, and Monte Irvin was our best young player," says Papa. "I gave up my title so Monte would have a better chance at the majors. That was the way we thought then. We'd do anythin' to git a player up there. In the final two games of the season, a doubleheader, I still needed a few times at bat. I was short of times at bat to qualify for the title. I got two hits in the first game and sat out the second game. The fans were mad, but they didn't know what we were trying to do. After the season I was supposed to git the two hundred dollars for the title anyway, but my owner, he say, 'Well, look, Cool, Irvin won it, didn't he?' They wouldn't give me the two hundred dollars. Baseball was never much for me makin' money."

Papa earned $90 a month his first year back in 1922. He would never make more than $450 a month, although his ability was such that later he would be ranked on Jackie Robinson's all-time team in the same outfield with Henry Aaron and Willie Mays. Bill Veeck, who also saw Bell play, puts him right up there with Tris Speaker, Willie Mays, and Joe DiMaggio. "Cool

Papa was one of the most magical players I've ever seen," says Veeck.

The money never bothered Papa; it was a game, a summer away from the packinghouse. "'Cept one time," adds Papa, "when one team told me to pay my expenses from St. Louis to Memphis. They'd give it back to me, they said. I git there, and they say no. Owner of the club was a dentist. I say to 'em I didn't come down here 'cause I got a toothache. So I went back home. Owners are owners, whether they blue or green."

Papa spent the winters in the packinghouse until he learned of places like Havana and Veracruz and Ciudad Trujillo, which competitively sought players from the Negro League. He will never forget that winter in Ciudad Trujillo. It was in 1937, he thinks, when Trujillo was in political trouble. He had to distract people, and there was no better way to do that than to give them a pennant. First, Trujillo had his agents all but kidnap Satchel Paige from a New Orleans hotel. Then he used Paige to recruit the edge in talent from the States: namely, Papa Bell and Josh Gibson, who, along with Orlando Cepeda, the storied father of the current Cepeda, gave the dictator a pat hand.

The look of that lineup did not ease Trujillo's anxiety. "He wanted us to stay in pajamas," says Papa, "and all our meals were served to us in our rooms, and guards circled our living quarters." Thousands would show up at the park just to watch Trujillo's club work out, and with each game tension grew. "We all knew the situation was serious, but it wasn't until later that we heard how bad it was," says Papa. "We found out that as far as Trujillo was concerned, we either won or we were going to lose big. That means he was going to kill us." They never did meet Trujillo. They saw him only in his convertible in the streets, all cold and white in that suit of his that seemed to shimmer in the hot sun. "A very frightenin' man," says Papa.

Trujillo got his pennant and his election. A picture of Papa's, taken near a large stream, shows the team celebrating; the dictator had sent them out of the city—along with their fares home and many cases of beer. It had been a hard buck, but then again it had never been easy, whether it was down in Santo Domingo or back up with the St. Louis Stars or the Pittsburgh Crawfords or the Homestead Grays or the Chicago American Giants. East or West, North or South, it was always the same; no shade anywhere as the bus rattled along, way down in Egypt land.

Papa took the bumps better than most. Some, like Josh Gibson, died too young; some got lost to the nights. *Coolpapa*, as his name is pronounced by those who came from the South as he did, well, Coolpapa, he just "went on movin' on." That was the way his mother taught him back in Starkville, Mississippi, where he was born in 1903; look, listen, and never pounce, those were her words, and all of them spelled survival. Work, too, was another word, and Papa says, "If I didn't know anythin', I knew how to work."

Long days in the sun and well after the night slipped across the cotton fields, all that Papa and his friends could talk about was "going off." Papa says, "One day some boy would be there along with us, and then he'd be gone. 'Where'd he go?' I'd ask. 'Why, that boy, he done gone off!' someone'd say. Next you'd see that fella, why, he'd be back home with a hat on and big, bright suit and shiny shoes and a jingle in his pocket." They would talk of the great cities and what they would have when they, too, went off, and only sometimes they would hear about baseball. An old, well-traveled trainman used to sit under a tree with them on Sundays and tell them of the stars he had seen.

"Why, there's this here Walter Johnson," the trainman would say. "He kin strike out anybody who picks up a bat!"

"Is that right?" Papa would ask.

"Sure enough, boy. You'd think I'd lie? Then there is two old boys named Ty Cobb and Honus Wagner. Well, they don't miss a ball and they never strike out!"

"Never miss a ball?" gasped Papa. "Never strike out? Is that right?"

"I'm tellin' ya, boy. I've been to the cities and I know!"

"Well, mmmm, mmmm." Papa would shake his head. "Only one thing botherin' me. What happen when this here Walter Johnson is pitchin', and these other two boys are battin'?"

"Y'all go on!" the old man would yell, jumping up. "Y'all leave me alone. I'm not talkin' anymore. Don't none of ya believe. I should know. I've been to the cities!"

By sixteen Papa was up North in St. Louis with several of his brothers and sisters, who were already in the packinghouse. "Didn't want to know 'bout ball then," says Papa. "Jist wanted to work like a man." His brother suggested he play ball on Sundays. "James," he said, "you a natural. You throw that knuckleball, and there ain't nobody going to hit it." Soon he was getting $20 to pitch, until finally he was facing the lethal St. Louis Stars of the Negro National League. "They were a tough club," says Papa. "And mean! They had a fella named Steel Arm Dicky. Used to make moonshine as mean as he was on the side. His boss killed him when he began to believe Steel Arm weren't turnin' in all the profits."

Bell impressed the Stars, and they asked him to join them. "All our players were major leaguers," says Papa. "Didn't have the bench to be as good like them for a whole season. We only carried fourteen, fifteen players. But over a short series we could have taken the big leaguers. That October, I recall, we played the Detroit Tigers three games and won two of them. But old Cobb wasn't with them, 'cause twelve years before a black team whipped him pretty good, and he wouldn't play against blacks anymore.

Baseball was all you thought of then. Always thinkin' how to do things another way. Curve a ball on a three-two bunt-and-run in the first innin'. That's how we beat big-league teams. Not that we had the best men, but we outguessed them in short series. It's a guessing game. There's a lot of unwritten baseball, ya know."

The Stars folded under the Depression. Papa hit the road. An outfielder now, he was even more in demand. He finally began the last phase of his career with the Washington Homestead Grays; with Josh Gibson and Buck Leonard and Bell, it was one of the most powerful clubs in the black league's history, or anybody's history for that matter. "I was 'bout forty-five then," says Papa. "Kinda sick. Had arthritis and was so stiff I couldn't run at times. They used to have to put me in a hot tub. I had to git good and warm before I could move." Yet, he had enough left to convince Jackie Robinson that he should never try to make it as a shortstop.

"It was all over the place that Jackie was going to sign with the Dodgers," says Papa. "All us old fellows didn't think he could make it at short. He couldn't go to his right too good. He'd give it a backhand and then plant his right leg and throw. He always had to take two extra steps. We was worried. He miss this chance, and who knows when we'd git another chance? You know they turned him down in Boston. So I made up my mind to try and show him he should try for another spot in the infield. One night I must've knocked couple hundred ground balls to his right, and I beat the throw to first every time. Jackie smiled. He got the message. He played a lot of games in the majors, only one of 'em at short."

Papa was named to manage the Kansas City Monarchs' B team in 1948, the agreement being that he would get one-third of the sale price for any player who was developed by him and sold to the majors. He had two prospects in mind for the Browns. "But the Browns," says Papa, shaking his head, "didn't want them. I then went to the Cardinals, and they say they don't care, either, and I think to myself, 'My, if they don't want these boys, they don't want *nobody*.'" The Monarchs eventually sold the pair: Ernie Banks and Elston Howard. "I didn't get anything," says Papa. "They said I didn't have a contract. They gave me a basket of fruit! Baseball was never much for me makin' money."

Life began all over for Papa. He took a job at the city hall in St. Louis as a custodian and then a night watchman. For the next twenty-two years the routine was the same, and only now and then could he go to a Cardinal game. He would pay his way in and sit there in the sun with his lunch long before the game began; to those around him who wondered about him, he was just a Mr. Bell, a watchman. He'd watch those games intently, looking for tiny flaws like a diamond cutter. He never said much to anyone, but then one day he was asked by some Dodgers to help Maury Wills. "He could run," he says. "I wanted to help." He waited for Wills at the players' gate and introduced himself quietly.

"Maybe you heard of me," Papa said, "maybe not. It don't matter. But I'd like to help you."

Wills just looked at him, as Papa became uneasy.

"When you're on base," said Papa, "get those hitters of yours to stand deep in the box. That way the catcher, he got to back up. That way you goin' to git an extra step all the time."

"I hadn't thought of that," said Wills, who went on to steal 104 bases.

"Well"—Papa smiled—"that's the kind of ball we played in our league. Be seein' you, Mr. Wills. Didn't mean to bother you."

After that year Papa seldom went to the ballpark anymore. He had become a sick man, and when he walked, his arthritic left side seemed to be frozen. It was just his job now. In the afternoons he would walk up to the corner and see what the people were up to or sit silently in his living room turning the pages of his books of pictures: all the old faces with the blank eyes; all those many different, baggy uniforms. There is one picture with his wife, Clarabelle, on a bench in Havana, she with a bright new dress on, he with a white suit on, and if you look at that picture hard enough, it is if you can hear some faraway white-suit, bright-dress music.

Nights were spent at city hall, making his rounds, listening to the sound of radio baseball by the big window, or just the sound of the hours when winter mornings moved across the window. When it was icy, he would wait for the old people to come and he would help them up the steps. Often, say about 3:00 a.m., he would be looking out the window, out across the park where the bums would be sleeping, their wine bottles as sentries, and he'd wait for their march on the hall. They would come up those steps and place their faces up against the window next to his face and beg to be let in where it was warm.

"We're citizens, old Bell, let us in," they would yell.

"I know," Papa would say.

"It's cold out here," they would say.

"I know," he would answer.

"No, you don't, you…" And Papa would just look away, thinking how cold it was outside, listening to all that racket going on out there, trying to think of all the things that would leave him indifferent to those wretched figures. Then it would be that he sometimes would think of baseball, the small things he missed about it, things that would pop into his mind for no reason: a certain glove, the feel of a ball and bat, a buttoning of a shirt, the sunlight. "You try to git that game out of your mind," he says, "but it never leaves ya. Somethin' about it never leaves ya."

Papa Bell is seventy now. He lives on Dickson Street in

North St. Louis, a neighborhood under siege: vacant, crumbling houses, bars where you could get your throat cut if you ever walked in the wrong way, packs of sky-high dudes looking for a score. They have picked on Papa's house a couple of times, so now when he feels something in the air, hears a rustle outside of his door, he will go to the front window and sit there for long hours with a shotgun and pistol in his lap. "They don't mess with Papa anymore," says his friend Tweed, looking over at Papa sitting in his city hall retirement chair. "It's a reclinin' one," says Tweed. "Show 'im how it reclines, Papa."

Now the two of them, Black Historian Tweed and Papa, who sits in his chair like a busted old jazz musician, torn around the edges but straight with dignity, spend much time together in Papa's living room. They mull over old box scores, over all the clippings in Tweed's portable archives. They try to bring continuity of performance to a man's record that began when nobody cared. They argue, they fuss over a figure here, they assemble pictures to be signed for people who write and say that they hear he will be going into the Hall of Fame; the days are sweet.

"Can't believe it," says Tweed. "Kin you, Papa? Papa Bell in de Hall of Fame. The fastest man who ever played the game."

"Ain't happened yet," cautions Papa, adjusting his tall and lean figure in his chair.

"Tell me, Papa," says Tweed. "How's it goin' feel? De Hall of Fame...mmmm, mmmm."

"Knew a fella blowed the horn once," says Papa. "He told me. He say, 'Ya got to take de gigs as dey come.'"

5 Why Ain't I in the Hall?

(HACK WILSON)

Sports Illustrated
April 11, 1977

I've been dead just about thirty years now, since November 23, 1948, to be exact. I didn't much like the idea at the time, but what can a man expect who abused himself so badly? Now, having long ago gotten used to my present state, I look back and see a lot of mercy behind the moment. F. Scott Fitzgerald, that writer fella, whose own end came several years before mine, told me I was a fool for being so grateful; he's still mad as a hornet. "I had so much left in me," he shouts. And I say, "Yeah, but you should've thought of that when you were working double time in all those Paris joints." I could have kicked myself for saying that, because he's such a soft, gentle guy, and besides, look who's talking.

Maybe Fitz has got a point, about his death, that is, not mine. Mine came at the right time. I was miserable, having been cut off from the only world I ever knew—sunlit ballyards with that smell that all had, the feel of a good piece of wood in your hands and the sweat pouring out of you. Maybe you miss a couple of pitches, and the crowds in those stands that seemed to be pushed up so close to you would begin to roar until, waiting for one more swing, the sound was like one of them Chicago elevateds bearing down on you hard. And suddenly, there the ball was, with its tail snaking up and down, its newness and speed making this hissing noise. In the time it takes for one heartbeat, I would have *all* of that white. Sometimes. I never knew a better feeling in all my life. It was like finally getting to an itch in the middle of your back. So what could come after that, after I'd finally ruined it all, after all those protectors of the game's sacredness who would never forgive or let me forget? Where was I going in the year of '48 on that damp day in Baltimore? Oh, I had been dead inside for so long, and publicly forgotten for more than ten years. My name was gone like a click, and nobody remembered me much, except some barroom historian when they were sweeping out a joint before the sun broke.

My name was Hack Wilson. Baseball was my game. I really don't know what I'm doing here talking like this. It's never been my style. You could put my ego under a swaybacked ant. Well, maybe that was my trouble, among other things. I never spoke up much for myself. And I don't want it to sound like I'm pleading now, but right is right. I've waited for some reporter to come along—oh, how I've waited—to give me my due, to bring to life the man who drove in 190* runs one year (Babe says that's one record they ain't *never* going to get) and hit more home runs in one season—fifty-six—than anyone else ever has in the Na-

---

* Major League Baseball commissioner Bud Selig credited Hack Wilson with an extra RBI on June 21, 1999. Researchers discovered that an RBI that Wilson had recorded in the second game of a doubleheader between the Cubs and the Cincinnati Reds on July 28, 1930, was inadvertently awarded to his teammate Charlie Grimm. Wilson's single season RBI record now officially stands at 191.

tional League. But they all act like I died owing money to their grandfathers. The only time my name ever comes up is when somebody looks like he might get near the RBI record—if the season was eighty games longer. That's all I come down to: some lines in a record book. Yet, I guess I can understand these new reporters. Putting together someone's life who's been dead for thirty years is like a man chasing his hat in a high wind. Pretty soon he sees himself chasing the hat, which is blowing farther and farther away, and begins to feel stupid and lets the hat go. He says to himself, "Who gives a damn, anyway?"

My trouble is that nobody even thinks about chasing the hat. I'm not news. I'm not even a good feature story. None of the guys still alive, like Waite Hoyt or Freddie Lindstrom or Charlie Grimm (see how long a man can live when he keeps his life in order?), knew me well enough to put me together. Sure, I was one of the boys, but nobody knew who I was or how I felt. They used to laugh me off; I was a very funny man to them. Hell, half the time I didn't know what I was about. Ballplayers didn't sit around and think about themselves much in those days. And all the stories done on me at the time, they were like a beer without a head. The writers could've done better. It wasn't that they didn't know something about me. I used to drink with some of them, lend them money, and laugh with them long into the night. I was a good talker. Toward the end, though, I stopped talking to most of them. I got sick of the way they made me look in print. Like a jungle boy, some creature who'd dropped into Wrigley Field from a tree. I was their creation, I guess they thought. It wasn't even a good creation. Not like Babe Ruth. They laid it on thick for Babe. I could've used some of his New York writers.

So as baseball opens another season, I think it's about time I said my piece. I've sat back with everything bottled up inside and watched what's been going on for a good while now, and I think I deserve my due. Babe says I got it coming. I belong in the Hall of Fame. There! I've said it. Never thought I could ask anybody for anything, and I'm not really asking now. I just want them committee members to take a look at Hack Wilson again. It's one thing being dead, you see, but it's another being ignored. I must confess I never gave much thought to the Hall of Fame until lately. Awards never meant nothing to me; it's how a man works at his trade that counts, what he does with the tools he has. But over the years I've seen a lot of curious players being put into the Hall. I'm not going to name any names. And I'm not going to compare myself with more modern players. Those arguments are never settled. I hear them all the time. Old men tell me broads aren't beautiful anymore because they haven't any meat on them. Some even claim the weather is lousier than it used to be. They talk as if no rain never fell when they were kids.

You can't move people around in time. I mean you can't say things like Grover Alexander was a better pitcher than that wonderful case out in Deetroit now. What's his name— Feederich? Alex's got the figures, that's all I know. And so have I. You can't blow away the figures. My figures, the way I see it, put me in the Hall. Take those 190 RBIs in 1930. Lou Gehrig got 184 in '31, but that's the closest anyone's come. Just think about those 190. How often you have to hit in the clutch, how often the ball has to been hit cleanly somewhere. You need some luck, but it's never a fluke when you bat around those kinds of runs. I was a player of flesh and blood, too. I mean I made people love me or hate me. Or laugh. But I never influenced my age, if that's what being immortal is about. What's immortality, anyway? Look at history. Kings and generals seem to work by themselves, as if their battles were fought without armies. Guys who can tell you all about Babe's sixty home runs can't name most of the other regulars on his team. Who were the guys who blocked for Red Grange? Who caught Johnny Vander Meer's two straight no-hitters? I feel like one of these questions now. Who's the guy who drove in 190 runs? Hell, I wasn't no supernumerary or whatever you call them. I wasn't no valet to the famous. I *was* famous. I left my personal stamp on the game.

They called me Caliban, who, if you don't know, is this savage and crooked-shaped slave out of Shakespeare. I didn't know what they meant at first, but then I caught on after a couple of years and I didn't like it much. I'd like to have a buck for every name I was called. When I think back to it, I'm glad I don't have to look at that shape anymore. I had an eighteen-inch neck, sixteen-inch biceps, and weighed sometimes as much as 230 pounds—and I stood only five feet six inches high. My legs were ridiculous stubs that bowed like an ape's. I must have had the smallest feet—size four and a half—next to Tom Thumb and small, very small, and delicate hands. I couldn't hold a regular bat; I had to have one with a reedlike handle that I would whip out at those high, outside pitches. Many of my drives went to right and right-center. That takes strength. All my power was up in my shoulders, my upper torso. When I came up, no uniform could be stretched to fit me. I was a mess then, but later on, you would've called me a sawed-off Babe Ruth.

Half the time, I looked like I'd been rolling in a coal bin. I didn't invent the belly slide, but I sure did use it more than others. I could run, even though sometimes my mind might be elsewhere. Old John McGraw saw me thrown out at second one time on a single, and he roared, "Wilson, did you ever hear of speed?" "Sure," I said, "that's what pays off in horse races, isn't it?" So there I'd be with ridges of dirt on me and an overlay of tobacco juice, running with my head down and my cap flying off, showing everybody my bowl haircut; I went to better barbers later. McGraw demanded I at least get a shave. The pride of the Giants, he said, was at stake. "I can't shave," I told Mac. "I got some kind of skin itch. The razor only makes it worse." "Holy God in heaven," McGraw yelled. "Don't tell me you're lousy, too!" McGraw grew impatient with me, particularly after I had a brawl with one of his outfielders, Jimmy O'Connell. Mac was told about it the next day. "O'Connell's down," the guy told him. "Wilson's just knocked him over the piano. O'Connell's up! Oof! Wilson just socked him back over the piano. Jimmy's getting up again!" The guy was telling the story so well that Mac became afraid that O'Connell might get hurt. "Jimmy," Mac howled, "for the love of Mike, shove the piano over on top of him!" Mac finally built a doghouse for me.

Don't get me wrong. I don't think I'm one of those immortals history is always serving up. They can deal around me. I had a good fan who raised ten kids on a factory worker's pay, giving all of them schooling and character. That's immortal! It's just that I've been getting heated up of late. The Babe, you see, keeps needling me about not being in the Hall of Fame, and I got to admit I'm starting to feel desperate. All I want to do is be remembered. Now, it looks like I got one more chance to make it. That's if the Baseball Writers' Association has anything to say about it. They made a proposal to the Veterans Committee that it should start picking two players a year who failed to make the Hall in the fifteen years they were eligible. These two players would be on the ballot with everyone else. They'd be well publicized as "second-chance" candidates. If they didn't make it this time, they'd never make it. Here's where it gets sticky. The second-chance candidates would be limited to those playing after World War II. The Association wants the book closed on the rest of us. So it goes.

You can see why I'm getting edgy. I don't know why it's come down to this. I think in the past some of the writers thought I didn't play long enough. How long is long? I played twelve years in the majors, had six great years. How many big years did that Sandy Koufax have? I'll tell you. He had six, and he got in the Hall the first year he could. And his big records—all them strikeouts and all them no-hitters—most have been tied or broke by now. This ain't no slur on Koufax. Just making a point.

Then, there was all the mistakes I made in the 1929 World Series. That didn't help any. I think old Bill Terry, who's a committee member and managed the Giants, told them it was a bum rap. But the worst break came after my career. Bob Broeg, the St. Louis writer, will tell you. "My assumption," Broeg says, "is that a lot of writers back then held Wilson's short career and personal behavior against him." Now, there it is out in the open, and that's a nice and fair man giving it straight. My behavior. What behavior? Did I steal from anybody? Who did I ever hurt by being mean? Didn't I always give my club a day's work for a day's pay? I sure wish I had the Babe's writers. He didn't need them. I did. Look at him, he's over there laughing his butt off.

Yeah, well, I've been coming close to the Hall lately. I understand I missed by one vote this year. And from the voting, it looks like a lot of these young fellas playing today have made them guys on the committee think twice about bad old Hack; the players out there now make me look downright saintly. Broeg, who's also on the committee, says there's been other things working against me. "We only get to elect two players a year," he says. "We also feel obliged to look into the pioneers of baseball. It's an obligation to the historians. So that leaves us with just one more player. This year we put Joe Sewell in. Human nature being what it is, you know, Sewell, who is alive, can ap-

preciate it now. It's a matter, I guess, of human frailty. I don't
necessarily adhere to that view, but some others may have."
Okay, I'm not human anymore, you can have that. But history!
What's more historical than those RBIs and my fifty-six home
runs? I broke my tail that year, even though half the time I was
hungover. Few players have ever had a year like I did in 1930.

I don't recall how they came, they just came. Nobody made
much over RBIs back then. They just wanted to see the big
poke. The Elgin Watch Company gave me a watch for each
home run—my friends had a lot of watches—so I can't say I
didn't know what time it was in some speakeasy at three in the
morning. But just recently a gent by the name of Emil H. Rothe
of Chicago came up with a breakdown of those RBIs. He says
only twenty-three of my fifty-six homers were with the bases
empty. But my other homers drove in forty-one teammates, so
altogether my homers accounted for ninety-seven of my RBIs.
None of the homers were hit with the bases loaded. Singles
added forty-eight more RBIs, doubles picked up twenty-six,
and triples brought home five. I got eight more on sacrifice
flies, four on fielder's choices, and I walked twice with the bases
full. That Rothe should've been one of my writers. Kind of boring, yeah, but that's the kind of stuff I could use now. It keeps
people's eyes trained on the serious side of a man. It shows them
I wasn't all play. But my Chicago writers, they just kept hound-
ing old man Veeck, William Veeck Sr., boss of the club: "Where
was Wilson last night? Look at him, must of drank up all of Al
Capone's bad booze!"

"I don't know where he's been," the old man used to say.
"All I know is that he never comes to the park from the same
direction twice."

Veeck was Dutch. I was what they call Pennsylvania Dutch.
I was born Lewis Robert Wilson in Ellwood City, Pennsylva-

nia, a little town on the western border of the state. I don't know how the name Hack came about when I started playing in the majors. Maybe it was because it looks as if my body had been hacked away. I was a sight, I know that. My father was a hammerman in the steel mills. My mother died young. We moved to the other end of the state, to Chester, near Philadelphia, and I started working when I was fourteen as a printer's devil, then on the railroad. At seventeen, I already weighed 160, and baseball was in my bones. I finally hooked on with Martinsburg, West Virginia, in the Blue Ridge League. After a couple of years I was sold to Portsmouth, Virginia. In 1923 I hit .388 there. The owner, Frank D. Lawrence, said he was going to sell me to the majors where I belonged. He wanted $10,000 for me. The scout for the Giants went back to McGraw and said, "I wouldn't give ten cents for him. He looks like he's standing in a puddle." There were a few days left in the draft, so Frank D. Lawrence went up to New York to see McGraw. He was up against a tough poker player in McGraw.

"Look, Mr. Mac," Lawrence said, "let's get down to business. I know you want Wilson."

"What do you want for him?" said Mac, laughing.

"I want twenty-five thousand dollars," said the owner.

"You want twenty-five thousand dollars for a bush leaguer?" shouted Mac, hitting the ceiling.

"You'll never regret it," said Lawrence.

"They tell me he's too fat," said McGraw.

"That isn't fat, Mr. Mac," the owner answered. "That's iron. He's the strongest man in baseball."

Well, Lawrence made McGraw a proposition. He would sell me for $5,000 if McGraw would pay him $1,000 for every point I was hitting over .300 by May 15 the next season. If I was under .300, then the deal would close at the original five grand.

McGraw was impressed. He always liked the give-and-take of deals. But he backed off and gave the owner $11,000 for me. He saved a lot of money. By May 15, 1924, I was hitting .371. Mac saved himself $65,000.

I played 107 games that season, but only 62 the following year before—I've never been able to get to the bottom of it—McGraw sent me down to Toledo. He later said he lost me in a clerical error, that somebody fell asleep and the Giants forgot to exercise their option. Can you imagine Mac ever making a mistake like that? "Best thing that ever happened to you, kid," Babe is over there saying. "New York wasn't big enough for both you and me."

I was picked by the Cubs in the fall draft, and that would be my making and my undoing. The Cubs were made for me. I loved Joe McCarthy, the manager, who took a lot of heat because of me. I don't know what to say about the old man William Wrigley. His son, P.K., who still has the club, knew me back then. The only thing P.K. remembers is that I was strong and used to help load trunks for road trips. How do you like that, the way I played for his old man?

Oh, it was something to be a star in the twenties. The whole country went on a binge after World War I, and I was right in the middle of it. Chicago was an open city; anything went. I wasn't wearing any more of those cheap, loud, checkered suits, a little too tight for me, like the $17.50 job McGraw first saw me in. I was wearing silk shirts, big silk ties with flowers on them, and beautifully cut double-breasted suits. But the clothes didn't help me much. I'd always look like a bulldog coming out of a blanket. Worse than that after a long night in the speakeasies. I was crazy about speakeasies. They were romantic places. As soon as you walked in, you were a special person in a special group. The places had an unreal feeling to them. The women looked more beautiful. Everybody shook your hand. The years were wild. There was something in the air. Athletes, well, they had become important. The writers later called it the Golden Age of Sports. I used to like the neighborhood bars on the North Side, too, and sometimes I'd go over to Al Capone's club. That got me into trouble. Capone came out to the park one day, and I went over to greet him. Later, Judge Landis, the commissioner back then, called me on the carpet. He was real fired up. "What are you doing talking to that gangster?" he asked. I said, "Well, Judge, I go over to his place, so why shouldn't he come to mine?"

Joe McCarthy, he had to be a saint to put up with me, what with the press and the moralists yapping at his heels. But I seldom let him down. He's ninety now, and he says to this day, "No tougher player ever lived than Hack Wilson. We didn't have any superstar status in his days, but if there had been, he'd've had it." Joe never had any bed checks. If a guy was ready to play, that was it. Still, he didn't want me to think I was fooling him. He'd always ask to see the matchbooks in my pocket so he could see where I'd been the night before. He'd play me on those terrible hot days when I could barely crawl. On one day like that, I hit two homers right off, and Joe came up to me—I'm ready to be put out of my misery—saying, "You go in now, take a shower. I don't want you to miss your rounds tonight." Joe tried hard to reform me. He even tried a little experiment on me in the clubhouse, calling me over and setting up two glasses, one full of water and one full of gin.

"See this here, Wilson," he said. "Watch what I do here. Watch closely." He pulled out a worm and dropped it into the glass of water. The worm just wiggled around.

"Now," he went on, "look at this." He pulled out another worm and dropped it into the glass of gin. The worm dropped to the bottom. Dead.

"Now, what does that go to show you?" he said quietly. "That worm's dead, Wilson. Does that mean anything to you?"

"Sure, Skip," I said. "It just goes to show you that if you drink, you'll never have any worms."

I went right on belting down a glass of gin before warming up. I wasn't hurting Joe. I was hurting myself in the long run, sure. But I was loyal to Joe. I wanted to please him, and when I didn't, he'd be there shaking his head, saying, "Don't you like me, Hack? Don't you want to play for me? You're letting me down."

That would put me on my knees just about, and I'd be nearly crying inside. I only let him down once real bad. It was in the '29 Series against the A's, who had Lefty Grove, Al Simmons, and Jimmy Foxx. That was one of the best teams ever— and so were we. We had Pat Malone, Kiki Cuyler, Charlie Grimm, Gabby Hartnett, Rogers Hornsby, and Riggs Stephenson. They beat us, and I helped them do it. We were leading 8–0 in one game, and there was a long fly ball hit to me in center field with the bases loaded. I looked up. I couldn't see it. I began to panic. Where was the damn thing? I never did find it. Then another fly. The same thing! My mistakes opened the door for the A's to win the game and the Series. I was the first guy to hit .400 in a Series and be the goat. McCarthy was heartbroken. He still hadn't gotten over it by spring training. I was out in left shagging the balls, and some kid came up to Joe and pestered him for a ball. The kid kept after him, until Joe, getting a little annoyed, turned to him and said, "Son, do you see that fat fella out there in the outfield?" The boy nodded. "Well," said Joe, "you just stand behind him, and you'll get more baseballs than you know what to do with."

They called me Sunny Boy Hack after the '29 Series. The fans turned on me. They thought I'd been drunk during the Series. The press fed the fire. I became a cartoon character. Joe was under pressure. I'd go into the stands after the fans, but I couldn't take on the whole city. I'd go into a saloon, and the ones who used to drink to me would turn away. It was hell. I began to drink more, if that was possible, and the trainer, Andy Lotshaw, would try to slap me awake on the rubbing table. Bill Veeck, son of William Sr., used to follow me around when he was a kid. He remembers, "One day Andy had Hack sobering up in one of those big, high old tubs. In the tub with Hack was a fifty-pound cake of ice. Well, what would you do if a fifty-pound cake of ice jumped into your bathtub with you? You'd try to jump out, right? Hack's body was blue. Every time Hack's head would bob up, Andy would shove it back down under the water, and the cake of ice would come bobbing up. It was a fascinating sight, watching them both in perfect rhythm: first Hack's head, then the ice, the head, then the ice. That day Hack Wilson hit three home runs for the first and only time in his life. I still can't believe it."

To tell you the truth, I can't believe 1930 myself. I may have needed a compass to find home plate, but I hit fifty-six homers, seven more than Ruth, drove in those 190 runs, produced 280 of the 998 the Cubs scored, and became the Most Valuable Player. But I was feeling it inside. One night I woke up on a road trip, sweating and screaming, "Get out! Get out! They're after me!" My pal Pat Malone grabbed me by my nightshirt just in time. I was on the windowsill. There wasn't much iron in me anymore. With four games to go, they fired Joe McCarthy and made Rogers Hornsby player-manager. That was the beginning of the end for me. The next year was awful; Hornsby was on me all the time, looking for an excuse to get rid of me. He wanted to be the big man. He resented me. He was a selfish guy who'd get his own way or bust. It was all right for him to play horses and chase women, but I was some kind of a bum. The guy was like a cop. You couldn't read the paper or smoke in the clubhouse. You were lucky if you got to read your mail. You came in and sat like a monkey on a chair. No laughing or playing around. He ran the place like a Sunday school. Besides that, he took the bat out of my hands on those 2-0 and 3-1 pitches I used to feast on. I had to take a lot of cripple pitches. He eventually suspended and fined me.

That season Hornsby hit me with $6,000 in fines, and I couldn't afford it. I was making upwards of $40,000, but gambling and bad investments had taken care of most of it. I had a bad year in '31. Only 13 homers, a .261 average, and 61 RBIs. The Cubs sold me to the Cardinals, who moved me on to Brooklyn. I wasn't happy. One day Joe Judge, one of my teammates, found me sprawled in front of my locker, empty bottles all around me. "My God," he said, "they'll fire you for this. They want you out there to hit. I'll clean up the mess." After the game, they all came in and saw the bottles in the trash can and just laughed. It didn't matter. The fat man, you see, had clubbed one out of the park. But who was I kidding? There wouldn't be many more. Soon Casey Stengel, who had a sense of humor, became manager, and the incident occurred that summed everything up. Even now, I don't know whether to cry or laugh. We were playing in Philadelphia in their little bandbox. Boom-Boom Beck was pitching for us. Now, there was a pitcher with a perfect name. The hits off him used to make a boom sound against the fence. It wasn't any different against the Phillies this time.

Hits kept clattering off that tin fence in Baker Bowl. The noise was enough to make you deaf. My ears were ringing. My tongue was hanging down to my knees in the hot right-field sun. Finally, Stengel comes out to relieve Boom-Boom of his pain. But Boom-Boom doesn't think he's in pain. He keeps jumping up and down and waving his arms, and I figure I'll take a breather in the shade. Then, suddenly, I hear this terrible noise from that tin fence again. Off I go, chasing the ball. I run it down, wheel, and make a beautiful throw to second base. The whole place is in an uproar. I'm asking myself what's going on, and now I see what happened. Boom-Boom, you see, wouldn't leave the game without one more boom. He had turned and heaved the ball right off the fence. I was stunned. Later Stengel said, "Wilson, let me tell you, you never made a better throw in your life. It was right on the money—but it was a bank holi-day." It was good for a laugh, but I couldn't laugh anymore. The rest was downhill. I drifted around on some semipro teams after the Dodgers and the Phillies let me go. In a little while I was forgotten. Veterans Committees forgot me. Nobody wrote my life story. The Hall of Fame was closed. I was baseball's shame.

I lived with my wife and my son, Bobby, in Martinsburg for a time, but I got restless. I spent a lot of time chasing around and fighting people in my pool hall. Sometimes I wouldn't come home for days. My poor wife divorced me in 1938, two years before she died. And I feel bad that my son scarcely remem-bers me except as a public figure. He's a fifty-one-year-old elementary-school principal, a book reader, a bachelor, as dif-ferent from me as night and day. Now that the Jaycees have be-gun a drive to get me into the Hall, Bobby is trying to help. But for years he wouldn't even talk about me, and I can't say I blame him.

I went back to Chicago and ran a couple of saloons, then ended up in Baltimore during the war. I got lost there. None of the baseball men there knew I was in town, and I never went to the minor league games. It hurt too much inside. I stayed to

myself, eating my heart out. I used to kid myself that if I had
to do it again, I wouldn't change a thing. Deep down, I knew
better. It's all there one minute—then it's gone. Don't ever let
no ballplayer tell you he don't miss the game, the crowds, the
light on you all the time. It's painful to break away. I ended
up getting a job at a swimming pool, then in the public parks. I
used to get the baseball diamonds ready for the kids to play
on. You know, running the foul stripes down the lines, raking
the infield. Now and then, I'd get one of them kids aside and try
to teach him how to handle a bat. I'd spend the nights in those
dark, little neighborhood bars that reminded me of Chicago. I'd
sit for hours over glasses of beer, sometimes till they closed. I
used to do a lot of thinking in those bars. About the way it'd
been.

I thought back to when I was a kid, and how they never let
me forget I was ugly. The other kids would ask me what tree I
lived in. They'd tell me not to step on my tail. At first, I couldn't
fix the creeps, but later I sure did square it. I guess I was what
you might call a natural man. Maybe, as the writers always said,
I was primitive, too. If you got personal with me, you only had
one choice: fight. Once, when I was young and had a job cleaning
out spittoons in a saloon, a guy hollered, "Hey, freakie, come on
over here!" I almost broke his neck with a headlock. I knew I
was ugly. I didn't need anybody to tell me.

I didn't bring much respectability to the Cubs, but I brought
a million or more fans into the park for them every year. The
headlines, though, used to turn the stiff necks even stiffer: "Raid
on Beer Flat Nets Hack." "Wilson Terrorizes Fan in Stands."
"Railway Depot Brawl Brings Riot Squad—Hack's in the
Middle Again." The last was the time when me and Pat Malone
nearly cleaned out the whole Cincinnati team over something

that happened in a game. The fat man could hit with either hand. With the kick of thirty mules.

The thoughts would go on, adding up to nothing, but adding up to everything, it seemed, after a few beers. Before I was thirty, I'd been in enough trouble for a gang of sailors. The Anti-Saloon League wanted me declared a menace to society. One of its officials once came up to me, then ran out screaming when I stuck an electric buzzer under her petticoat. Judge Landis was always on me, especially after he showed up for one of our games and saw me play a line drive into an inside-the-park homer. "The old man's raving," they told me. "He's going to throw the book at you. He thinks you're drunk." I went to see him the next day, and there he was, pointing his bony finger at me and telling me what he's going to do. I let him finish. Then I said, "How much of the game did you see?"

"I left," said the Judge, "directly after your disgraceful exhibition. Don't lie, Wilson. I know you were the under the influence."

"Well, if I was," I shot back, "how come I doubled in the seventh and homered in the ninth?"

But nothing could stop me then, not even the Judge. The fans rolled into Wrigley Field, and old man Wrigley's eyes gleamed over all the money his team was making. "We'll have a bodyguard on Wilson," he ordered, thinking about protecting his gate receipts. The guard stuck with me for two days. I introduced him to a waitress who, he later claimed, spiked his drink and put him on a bus to Keokuk, Iowa. He was right. In all, I must have been fined something like $20,000 during my career. I wasn't proud of the way I'd been, sitting there in a saloon and thinking back. I was paying for it now. Alone. An old, old man at only forty-eight. Barely able to afford a beer, since I quit the park system. People used to say I would die friendless and penniless. I did. I remember the day well.

It was cold and damp, nothing special about it. I remember having passed a Chinese restaurant, advertising full-course meals for a buck. I didn't like Chinese food, but I made a mental note to get in on that. All I had to my name was a dollar. I thought of all those $10 tips I used to pass out. So here I was just about broke, threading my way back to my room as the lights were going out in the bars all over town. That was always the loneliest time for me. I finally got to the top of the stairs of my rooming house. Then I seemed to lose my balance. They found me later at the bottom of the stairs and took me to the hospital. I died there. A pulmonary condition complicated by internal injuries, they called it. They couldn't find anybody who knew me. The rumors began to spread that I died in the gutter. I guess a lot of people started to collect their bets. Nobody claimed my body for two days. There was no money for a funeral.

Then all the boys from the bars passed the cup, and they come up with enough pennies and dimes to buy me a burial suit. The Elks Club members back in Martinsburg were hurt by the publicity, and they drove up in a long line of cars and took my body back to where it all began so long ago. I *belonged* to somebody. I was one of them. They laid it on good there. None of the baseball big shots showed up. My son, Bobby, wasn't there, either. That's all right, some people don't like funerals. Joe McCarthy came down later and dedicated a fancy ten-foot-high granite stone for me. It sits in Rosedale Cemetery on a nice slope between some Canadian elms and arborvitae bushes. The stone has a couple of crossed bats and a ball sitting on a bed of leaves, with an Alpha on one side and an Omega on the other.

Pretty fancy, I'd say. The inscription reads ONE OF BASEBALL'S IMMORTALS, LEWIS R. "HACK" WILSON, APRIL 26, 1900—NOV. 23, 1948, RESTS HERE. Hundreds of old Blue Ridge League fans stood in the rain at the burial. And many of them cried.

The fans never forgot Hack Wilson. Only baseball did.

PART FOUR

GIGS

1 A Hurdler in Inner Space

(EDWIN MOSES)

Esquire
June 1988

Odd, he was thinking, how a streak leans on you, twists you, turns you, can overwhelm the most finely tuned psychology designed to protect you from its vast intrusions. He was stretched out on a bed in a dark Madrid hotel room, listening to the horn of Miles Davis make brooding runs that seemed to fall off sharply and start to probe all over again. Before a race, the horn on the tape deck was always there, the notes like loyal guides directing him toward a mood—aggressive, calm—whatever he needed to carry him through those moments of pure physical fury that, if they were not getting more physical, were becoming more furious. But he wasn't getting anything from Miles's horn today, his mind was just out there floating, unable to hook into any kind of thought pattern, and he regretted that he hadn't brought along one of his physics books.

Edwin Moses smiled as he opened the curtains, letting in the piercing light of the Spanish sky. Question: What do you do to concentrate? Answer: Get down with Miles Davis and in

with the particles and waves. But few reporters ever wanted to
know about this, all they wanted to know about these days was
the streak, that quick surface strike into the public imagination,
or *the thing,* as he privately began to think of it. Strange, he thought
now, the way any prolonged assault on perfection begins to sur-
round itself with so much collective psychic energy that it can
implode, scattering character far from its center. The psychological effects of slumps have always been known to athletes,
sensed by fans; slumps disassemble, crush the will, change a man.
But streaks bring joy, ennoble, are the mammon of the godmak-
ers. Yeah, he had to smile, but try lugging this mutha around for
nine years, nine months, and nine days.

The numbers were always with him. Just the other day he
saw a long line of black-cowled nuns moving into a church; he
instantly turned them into a metaphor for the streak. The same
with the birds in the sky, or jets waiting to take off; any unbro-
ken line, and there was the quick flash of the streak through his
mind. Winning, he finally had to admit, was becoming too desperate a matter; the very thought of winning or losing was perilous in the hurdles; only the pure act itself, four hundred meters
of instinctual reaction, must dominate the mind. He was eager
to feel the surface under his spikes now, to retreat into the still-
ness, that splendid void that he has always found in the hard
geometry of the chalked, measured distances; yeah, a streak
can lean on a man, all right.

And what a record it is: two Olympic gold
medals, two world championships, and the streak—107 straight
victories in a sport where the margin for error barely exists. For
twelve years (the average career is three to five years) he has attacked the 400 intermediate hurdles with the kind of vigor and
Pegasus form that would have been the stuff of sports-page son-

nets in another age. He has been the epitome of what the French call the *idée fixe*; the man cannot be diverted from his vision. Before Moses came along, 48 seconds could not be broken; he's broken it twenty-seven times, run eighteen of the nineteen fastest times on record, among them the world mark of 47.2. Says Danny Harris, his most fierce competitor, "In Europe, they'd pay to watch him run by himself." They already have in Taiwan— five thousand of them. Dick Hill, senior associate athletic director at the University of Louisville, says, "You want the Olympic attitude, what it should be but seldom is. It's Edwin Moses. Body and motion is my discipline. He's the most remarkable athlete of the twentieth century. Perfection."

Maybe that's the trouble. Ultimately, perfection seems to alienate more than it ever endears, especially those who are closer to the heat. When there wasn't any money around in big-time track, who cared if everybody thought Moses was the King of Siam. But when the checks started to be written, Moses was the big horse in the gate. "Oh, yeah," says a friend, "and he gets all the oats. It's money, jealousy that's behind any knocks on him. What else could it be? For an image hustler, he's a helluva hermit." The friend strikes a revealing note. If you look around the floating, sad-comic opera of celebrities trying to sell themselves, where is Edwin Moses? From afar, without buying into the whole Olympic brag of the ideal, and without Moses uttering a word, it is not hard to have the innocent hunch that here might be the last warrior, the seeker of excellence for its own sake, the one who decides that if his performance is not electric enough, then forget about the Jockey underwear. He might as well be an apparition. You don't see him on TV exchanging banalities with Johnny Carson; in fact, you never see him anywhere except when he folds himself into the starting blocks and goes to work.

Isn't that right, Edwin? "I wouldn't know about that," he says. Let's try again. Doesn't it seem you're the most available public figure on the landscape. "You think so?" he asks. When's the next plane out of here? you wonder. He is walking on a beach in Southern California, not far from his home. The ocean is placid, the beach empty. He often runs here in the morning, or he comes to watch the birds. They calm him, and the sight of a pelican will draw his undivided attention. "Hey, look at that," he says abruptly, "a pelican." The observation startles; the silence had become a roar. "You never see much of them anymore," he says. "People have been catching them. They cut off their beaks. People." Go on, but he drops the beaks, his voice trailing off with a hint of bewilderment. The winter light catches his tinted glasses. The glasses have been a personal trademark, projecting mystery, a threatening insouciance. Andre Phillips, a top hurdler, got him right: "I first saw him on TV. The Montreal Olympics. I was just a kid. There he was, hood up and glasses. The dude had come out of nowhere and there he was and you still couldn't see him. No face. Like a ghost. *Theee* ghost. He was there, but he wasn't. Hands off. Alone. Cool. I really threw myself into the hurdles after looking at him."

Better hurry, then, before he disappears right in front of you. What about the streak, Edwin? The ending of the streak in Spain was supposed to have devastated him (though it's hard to see him devastated by anything right now). The suggestion is that since the loss to Danny Harris he can't be around mirrors; all he can see in them is a human being. Wait a minute, this guy walking on the beach, two thousand feet deep into silence? One would have a better chance of finding a black pearl in the sand than locating an ego of that dimension. "I lost," he says. "It was a race, and I lost." But then, suddenly, he is putting you there in Madrid, hardly a man still running a finger over scar tissue.

The monotone is gone, the words are carrying colors as he re-creates the June night six months before: the way he felt before the race in his hotel room, the sound of Miles's horn; the ping-pong thoughts about the psychology of humping a streak up the mountain each time out; the sky looking as if it had been torn from a canvas in the Prado. And finally the explosive start of Harris out of the blocks, and how he hadn't had a plan for that possibility (extremely unlike him), then the cataract *swoosh* of sound from the crowd, the knifelike inner wince of recognition that it was all over. Unthinkingly, he continued his famed victory lap around the track, and the Spanish, who have a nose for drama, filled the stadium with the chant *Torero! Torero!* "Something extraordinary was gone," he says. But, he adds, slipping now into low gear, "it was a race, that's all. I lost. One shouldn't make too much of it."

The great electronic beast began to chomp: Moses Beaten. In France, a boyhood friend, Dr. Archie Mays, walked toward a newsstand with a certain feeling of unease. Headlines in five different languages looked back at him. Mays says, "When you're close to someone, you pick up on things. All those years, he never once talked about the streak. He had it locked up tight inside himself, and who knows what it was or wasn't doing to him? And you began to take it for granted that he would win. When he ran, it was like he was teaching little boys. But early last year, I sensed something was wrong. He didn't seem like he was all asses and elbows as he got ready. He's a walking closet of scraps of paper, with plans jotted down for his training. He always pulled them out and showed me. Not last year. He seemed de-tached. There was a sense of an edge lost." One look at Moses in Spain, and Danny Harris was sure of it. He says now, "The pressure had gotten to him, and I knew. Hesitancy. Very tentative. He didn't look like he wanted to take off his warm-up suit.

Didn't want to run. He can say all he wants that the streak wasn't eating him up, that he didn't feel any pressure, but I know better. Once, I was on one, just fourteen straight. It's a terrific feeling, what more with nine years of never losing! It's like an important possession. You don't even want to think of parting with it. But it gets to you. Everybody's gunning for you. You're mind won't let you alone."

Athletes will admit to anything before acknowledging the erosive damage of pressure. There's already enough vulnerability to go around in the percentages, and in the instant exposure as soon as you put on the gear. If they talk about pressure at all, they will direct you to the guy in the other lane, or sometimes look at you as if you've just discovered a weak limb on their family tree. But pressure is the big cat in their lives; the idea is to keep it caged and sedated. No one has ever been better at that than Moses, yet his loss in Spain loosed a wave of speculation that the royal robes might have become a trifle frayed. After all, he was crowding age thirty-three, the hair was going fast, gray was snaking around the temples, and who knows what private doubts were hidden behind those eyes, the eyes you never see? "It seems that everybody wants to rush me off the stage," says Moses, "but they just have to wait." They call him the King of Sticks on the circuit, and sometimes he gets the impression from the huge crowds that he should dutifully surrender his head for the sake of historical continuity. "It's love and hate now," he says. "But I have to be dealt with. I concede nothing—not even to age." As if to etch it indelibly in the track world's consciousness, he came back after Spain to crush the field, including Harris, in Paris and Berlin, and won his second world title in Rome in what many consider the most dramatic race ever, a victory over Harris by just a billow of his jersey— two hundredths of a second.

Now as he leans on a pier and looks out, he seems, for some reason, like an old friend, somebody you'd ask for very personal advice. He disarms, neutralizes the desire for taut penetration, makes asking him questions that you would not want asked about yourself seem like oafish intrusion. Yet it would be a mistake to think that he will ever hunker down and give you a tour of his life. "Nobody gets into Edwin's world," says Danny Harris. Above all else—his easy charm, his proclivity for being civil at all times—this is an interior man, friendly with the desert quiet within himself. When he does try to come out of his interior, he's like a carpenter with language, building staircases that come to a sudden halt. He drops his tools and says to himself, "Hold it, this might lead somewhere I don't want to go." His pal Archie Mays says, "Language is a big thing to him. Not only his own. He can hear hostility and deception. He's not about to walk into anyone's backyard knowing there's a pit bull out there. People can become afraid of his reserve, his demeanor. He's got a lot of faces, Edwin. The Business Face. The Track Face. They're all real. The Understanding Face and the Angry Face." Like? "When those eyes just come out over the glasses."

The glasses are being lowered now, and the eyes are moving out like two freight trains. The incident on Sunset Boulevard has been gently introduced. If you have an once of sensitivity, this is the kind of moment when you wonder why you didn't become a bricklayer. The snippet of celluloid from three years ago is filling his mind, the images must sear: the Olympic Hero and the Street Hooker; Moses in his immaculate white suit leaving the jailhouse, the vacuity of his face; the impeccability of a whole persona at this moment irrevocably compromised; the runner stumbles. The hooker cop had approached him at a red light, he joked with her about price, then hit the gas when the light changed. A block away he was surrounded like Public

Enemy No. 1. Price had been mentioned, and that was enough for the cops; the Olympic license plate also lit them up. Once in court, he was quickly found innocent, an apparent victim of cops too eager to affirm their status as a special squad. Publicly, he had become more raw meat for a morally ascendant society, with an increasingly hair-trigger tendency to impose moral absolutes—on others. The notorious tabloids of France couldn't even get worked up about it, except to cluck. Well, there go the Americans again with their heroes, back to Hawthorne and giving out scarlet letters. But with serious portraiture in mind, you can't avoid the misfortune, it is vital. How did a man like Edwin Moses respond to being staked out in the media sun, how far did it drive him into his interior and what did he find there, how did he hold on to what he was all about? The Hollywood incident had hurt him badly—and it still does. His eyes flash, and then he turns back to the car.

Moses shows up the next afternoon to see his physical therapist, Ken Yoshino. He looks tired, says he was wired up last night, didn't get much rest. "I began classwork toward an MBA last night," he explains. "It's exciting." Says Mays, "He's a searcher. Athletes get in trouble when they quit and find emptiness. Edwin will just go on another search." He's already got a BS in physics, a BA in business. All the world's a classroom. He's become an expert scuba diver, had a pilot's license. Pursuits that lengthen the distance between him and people? He ponders: "Could be. I never thought of it that way." He can also spend a lot of time photographing birds; an egret can put him into a trance. So can biology books; if he had his way, every hotel room would have a *Merck Manual* of symptoms instead of a Bible. Right now, he has a back pain.

Yoshino examines the point of the twinge. Edwin is on his

belly, wearing just shorts. Besides those eyes and that winning, rascally gap between his teeth that contradicts a sometimes grave profile, the longness of his body captivates; the legs mute the rest of his six feet two inches. Yoshino points to his prize corpus. "God made him one of the most efficient machines on earth," he says. "Body fat. Negative. Diet? You ever watch him eat?" Yes, and it's painful; he looks as if he's dining at the Borgias. "He even carries his own water in the back of his car. Look at his legs. Most athletes have an eight percent discrepancy in leg strength, he's got only two percent. Gives him an even foot strike, continuous drive. The guy's a Vienna symphony of physical harmony." What about aging? "His back pops where it never used to. There's an unstable section in there. But man-to-man, he can win for the next two years."

Later, intimations of track mortality are given quick dispatch. Entering his home over Newport Bay, Moses says, "I can't even bear to think of quitting the hurdles. I'm not going anywhere. But it's too bad you can't be like a musician and go until you can't blow anymore." The house is lined with books, strewn with memorabilia that chart his rise from a skinny college kid at Morehouse College to the covers of world magazines. He produces one, an Italian fashion number: no glasses, the gap in the teeth, big smile. "See how warm I can be?" he says. The European atmosphere for track, he says, is like an NFL title game. "But I don't care much for the crowds," he adds. "You're up for grabs. After I ran in the LA Olympics, the fans outside were in a feeding frenzy. They nearly ripped off my clothes. I felt in real danger." He talks fondly of his appeal in Europe—and why not? It's his power base, but it wasn't always so; Edwin Moses has taken world track from the dark ages to the marquee.

He runs fifteen to seventeen meets a year, getting $30,000 or more for each trip out. He won't crunch the numbers, but it's

clear that the figure puts him in the area of a half million annually; shaved down, that comes to about thirty grand. He
breaks in, "For every minute I actually run. Say around ten minutes of work a year. But it was hard politics getting here." Back in
the early days, world track was a back room with a little guy and
a satchel, where two things were sure to happen: they cheated
you out of your money and made you feel like a Third World
indigent—without brains. An imperious cartel of promoters
seemed impenetrable. After the '84 Olympics, Moses went
head-to-head with the cartel. He was vilified in Europe. But if
you are in track promotion, how do you announce that you
can't afford Edwin Moses? He aimed his mystique and his new
manager, Gordon Baskin, at the walls of the cartel. Baskin is an
ex-banker who knows the location of the throat. He didn't need
the job; Moses was an adventure. The cartel came down in a
heap. You can still hear a lone scream accusing Moses of wrecking world track.

The other noise is from the athletes themselves. The bottom dogs have trouble with the vision of the plutocrat in their
midst. Even with the bigger checks and heightened image, they
resist his efforts to unify them for the future. "Not a union," he
says. "Just hard diplomacy and staying together in our efforts.
The cartel may be down, but not out." As one doubter says, "Why
should Godzilla care about the mice?" He is both respected and
suspect among other athletes. He's admired for what he's done
and for his sincere willingness to render counsel to anyone who
seeks him out. But some of the suspicion rears over the streak; to
preserve it, Moses ducked tough competition, took a powder after the LA Olympics. "Ridiculous," he says. "All my contracts
are signed before the season. Besides, if they wanted me so bad,
why didn't they come after me?" Says Harris, "I didn't hook up
with him once until Spain. Only Edwin knows if he was ducking

me." Why didn't he enter wherever Moses was scheduled? "They lock you out," he says. "Edwin pulls the strings in Europe. He runs the show. You dance his dance."

This amuses Moses, bringing forth one of his chuckles. "I guess they think I'm the cartel now," he says. "The biggest psych job ever. Andre Phillips and Harris actually making people believe that I was trying to duck them." A rare glimpse of his pride as he says, "Look at the skeletons I've left behind. I've been through generations of hurdlers. I'll be retiring a few more before I'm done." The sudden, high acidity among hurdlers is unusual. They are not given to the volatility of sprinters. Sprinters are emotional, joyous, social, apt to exchange confidences. Hurdlers seem solitary, brooding, wary sentinels of their secrets, their state of mind. They work in a mist, full of tiny pulsations of mental signals. Watch them just before a race: all eyes, no breathing, their cerebral gears shut down, just that camera grinding in their minds. "Edwin takes the film," says Dick Hill, "to a level where we can't see. If his critics could tune in to the visualization that he has of himself, they'd take off their spikes and get a job."

Moses pops a tape into the VCR, and as the images come into focus, he chuckles: "There you are—Edwin Moses the radical." The tape shows him winning the gold medal in the '76 Olympics. The face is solemn, that of a school kid tired of giving answers to everyone in class. The modest Afro fills out a small head, the dark glasses are already paramount to the look, but what's that bobbing around the neck? A leather-thong necklace? An ornament of dissidence? Doesn't say much, either; there's menace here, all right. "They typed me right off," he says. "They didn't care that the glasses were prescription. I still can't see. I have to struggle through serious optical fatigue. The rawhide-cord necklace was a gift from a college roommate. No symbolism." Lloyd Walker, an Olympic coach, discovered him as a hurdler just months before Montreal. "He was a natural," says Walker. "I watched him crush the drills, went to Europe, and said, 'You are all coming in second.'" The '76 Olympics didn't do anything for him, Moses says, suddenly blacking out the tape. "I was forgotten instantly. Who knows? Maybe everybody did buy into me as a black terrorist in embryo."

What about the tape of his loss in Spain? "I have one here someplace, but can't find it." He pauses. "Maybe I'll never find it." Instead, he inserts a sort of lab tape done for Kodak, Edwin Moses at a thousand frames per second, bare chested, the body encrusted with beeping gadgets that monitor his physiology. His style is murderously fluent, the aura is primal. He loves talking about the technical subtleties, the seconds between hurdles (3.1 to 4.8 toward the end), the intricacies of his ascent over thirty-six-inch-high "enemies," and the descent that sends three thousand pounds of pressure slamming into his joints. "It's in a way like taking off and landing a jet on an aircraft carrier," he says. "You have to have the right thrust up, get up, and have the right glide slope coming down, with very little runway to deal with. You don't have time to think. You have to know. Thinking can be costly. For the hurdles, you have to be a little crazy. You have to run hard, you're going to be tired all the time. You're going way beyond what the body was designed for. On every single hurdle. Just to try for it is a physical nightmare."

Moses is the de Sade of preparation, sadistic with his body. When he's through flogging himself, he takes all the readouts from his monitoring devices and lets his computations speak to him. "Physically," says Hill, "you always know what to expect from Edwin Moses. The big variable is what's in his head. He's always got five, six plans ready for any way the race shapes up. His head is the scary part." Moses says he's an athlete only when he races; the rest of the time he's an artist putting together a canvas, the race merely "the act of writing my signature." He thinks now of the pain, saying, "The pain can make you scream. You can't stand, sit, walk for long. It travels up the back of your legs to your head." Says Iowa State coach Steve Lynn, "I don't know how he does it. All that boredom of isolation, the hurt for so many years. There'll never be another Edwin." Harris agrees, "You won't catch me going over the sticks when I'm thirty. Something special about that man on the inside."

"All right, Edwin, what's on the inside?"

"Not all that much," he says, fiddling with his lunch. "You'd be surprised.

"I think about a lot of things, but not much about myself. Only on the edges. I haven't had much time for serious introspection."

"Money?"

"I count it. I'm not into ostentation."

"Reincarnation?"

He laughs.

"How about fame?"

"I don't need to be famous."

"Ducking the opposition?"

"Think about it," he says. "What for? They're good for business. Long time ago, I inquired what it would take for me to make the hurdles a big event. The answer was TV and people who look like they can beat you. I like the hot guns. They put focus on the event."

"The perfect race?"

"I keep searching for it. Could be in the coming Olympics. If the weather's right, I could crack into forty-six for a new world record. But it's tough. You need help. The others force you to the limit. It's like calling a board meeting, and you hope that every member is going to contribute loudly. It doesn't happen that often. I think the board will convene with serious, very serious intentions in Seoul."

"Power?"

"To be able to function," he says. "Not to use over other people."

"Is there life in the universe?"

"I believe in the possibility of aliens." He chuckles. "You're leading me somewhere."

"Sunset Boulevard?"

"I thought so," he says, grimacing.

The Moses firmness doesn't wobble in the face of breezy familiarity. He sighs, deliberates over the $100,000 misunderstanding; that's what it cost him in legal fees to defend himself against a crummy misdemeanor. In the realm of commercial endorsements, he was suddenly in limbo. He was under siege. His wife got one call from a reporter asking, "How can you continue to enhance his career after this?" Being married to him was never easy, if only because of the distance there between what he feels and what he shows. Myrella never wavered, and their marriage has struck deep roots since. "Yeah"—Archie Mays laughs—"he'll even kiss her on the check in public now. He's not as tightly wrapped up about marriage. The stupid incident in Hollywood hit a profound chord in him. And made him very vulnerable. He wasn't used to that kind of feeling." Or, as Moses says, he felt the sharp edge of "the randomness of things, of life, how it can shift on you and you're helpless." He will make a single observation on the incident: "Far in the back of my house, sometimes late at night, when I was trying to sleep, you could hear a coyote pack tearing apart a kill. That sound told you all there was about the way I felt."

Mays says, "Let me put it this way. Take the area of business. You can't hype the guy, he'll throw off the fat and go for the meat. He goes at himself the same way. Celebrity bores him. Manipulator of perception? All he's out to control is his space. Personal dignity is what matters to him. Period. He guards it like a wolf. Dignity. That's why I think when I look at Edwin." Dick Hill, though, sees a hurdling machine. "I can't look at him to this day without thinking about when he was up against Andre Phillips. Edwin was beaten. No question. Andre shot by him after eight, and it was all over. Then Moses went deep down. Maybe it does have to do with dignity. Moses keyed on the tenth hurdle, attacked the track. And bam! Andre's eyes went to the ground. He was questioning, and Moses was gone. With one move, he was the beautiful composite of what we try to teach at the Olympic Training Center. Fight. Concentration. Mind-set. Body control. A kinesthetic sense of awareness of all combinations. It was awesome. *He* is awesome."

But *awesome* won't do, neither will *superstar*. Indiscriminate use in the eighties has driven both descriptions into the Woolworth bin. The late critic Kenneth Tynan coined two designations that would fit Moses. One of them he called *s'imposer:* the talent for imposing, asserting authority on a given field of work, saying, "Inside this field, you will defer to me." The other term—more visual—is *high definition performance*. It communicates authenticity (not celebrity), transmits the essence of one's talent to an audience with economy, grace, no apparent effort, and absolute, hard-edge clarity of outline. Edwin Moses is an HDP; anything less misses the man as well as his work. Chisel it in under the bust, remember it when the camera pans the chute in Seoul and comes in tight on those eyes.

2 Brando

Esquire
November 1989

How civilized the fame game was then, a timid, furtive glimpse for the observer, the observed cordoned off by a dreamlike distance of respect. Worship knew its place; so did greatness. It was caught sharply once by a young American student as he sighted Flaubert suddenly passing his table, their gazes meeting, his eyes like bits of faded blue sky, the huge body looming down, then gone, a magnificent ship of achievement receding in the sunlight like a mirage, leaving behind forever a face, the smell of afternoon wine, and mystery unscarred by any attempt at aggressive familiarity. How easily devotion and curiosity were sated. All that was asked of, say, a Shelley was his ballet of lines, never mind that he was a conniving weasel, an evangelist of free love, a brooder in private about his lack of noisy attention. The exposed colossus was to be the meat of the next century.

No wiser or more wounded authority on that subject exists than Marlon Brando, the tortured exemplar in the age of perfected mythomania. The fame game seems to have eaten him alive, crunched and munched him into a brand-name mythological mush (so many conflicting tales, so many refractions from the light of grinding axes) that repels him, created a dark lore that has fascinated for nearly five decades. The tranquil, public haze that gathered over the likes of Shelley and Flaubert is all he ever seems to have desired, the work dwarfing fraudulent celebrity, the work speaking for the man. To that end, he has gone to dramatic lengths, from playing the imp or the fool when treed for interviews, to coiling into a merciless critic of himself, of the twisted values of the business that spawned him, and of the society that honors him; from the isolation and hermetic gloom of his Beverly Hills remove, to his primitive self-internment in the South Seas.

No matter how inaccessible or contemptuous he is, no matter what he says, nothing seems to diminish the gravity of his name, the wonder, ever since he stood beneath a balcony in *A Streetcar Named Desire*, an animal in pain, and screamed from the bottom of his being, *Stellllaaa!* Now, after nearly ten years of chosen estrangement—he seems to use disaffection and distance the way other actors use a false nose—Brando is back to work on the legend again in two films: *A Dry White Season*, as a South African lawyer for a ten-minute turn well below his price, and the soon-to-be-released *The Freshman*, in which he plays a Mafia chieftain who crosses paths with a college student (Matthew Broderick) in New York. His choice of these films is instructive.

The South African lawyer appeals to his genuine, almost clinical rage toward injustice. Give him a script and he'll examine it like a medieval archivist, blowing away the dust of nonsense, looking for villains and saints that correspond to his life views, for themes that illuminate the polished grubbiness of the world. To the ordinary, unobfuscating mind, *The Godfather* was about people shooting other people all over town, turning blood into marinara sauce, and at its best a well-observed anthropology of a subculture. But to Brando, the Mafia was a metaphor for corporate thuggery in America, Don Corleone the archetype of the man in the Oval Office: humanity masking the capacity for evil. *The Freshman* would appear to be Brando-proof, free of darkling mirrors, a lap for the money, something that touches the whimsy in him. Except: the director, Andrew Bergman, also wrote *The In-Laws,* Brando's all-time favorite film, a threepenny opera about the CIA, the one monolith he despises more than Hollywood and the goonlike media.

But after ten years of absence, it is remarkable that there remains any demand for Brando, and it would be understandable if there were none; he has always carried a lot of unkempt industry baggage. The war stories have traveled down the decades, sure anathema to the new industry, which is sensitive more than ever to a poltergeist loose in their profit line; the very mention of Brando's name has been known to cause four-star heartburn. The legend, then, the talent, cannot be denied? Would that it were so, but the new executives—who bring to film all the passion they would to a bar of soap—have no patience with historical memory, abominate the heirloom name, except at the Academy Awards, when they gush with soulful treacle. Instant, disposable legends (how many will be around ten, even five years from now?) lashed to flashy, empty vehicles and aimed at the new audience inform the ruling interests; true giants belong to college film festivals, to the art-house-movie rats who like to debate the stylistic quiver of a lip into deep revelation.

To the executive mind, Brando might as well be coming back from the dead, doing the Lazarus turn for posterity.

Lengthy careers of a singular cut don't alchemize with the new audience. Orson Welles wasn't allowed to work for years for many reasons, among them his film sensibility. The same for the great director Elia Kazan, and now Robert Altman. John Huston stayed in action because he was the consummate politician—legend had the powerful Ray Stark clearing the brush for him. Talent needs content, a story and characters to match it, components that are vague to an audience that expects ten-car pileups, orgiastic violence, technological feasts for the eye, and comic-book zaps for story, a trend well under way when Brando took a powder. To this audience—say, under forty, certainly under thirty—the Brando name can't mean much; some fat guy, maybe, sitting around and eating breadfruit on an island.

If they remember him at all, it might be as Jor-El in *Superman*, to his critics a cynical grab for the money ($3 million for several minutes); to the more sympathetic, his effort, perhaps, to catch the new wave, to keep active until the right property showed up. Both views are probably correct; Brando can never be accused of simplicity of motive. If he cared at all—and that can never be certain—the experience had to be unsettling, this glimpse of the possible fate ahead, the actor as harlequin on the make, the queasy recognition that he was doomed to be an Easter Island statue in a cheesy shopping mall. That, of course, grants him a pride to which he has never spoken, a passion for excellence to which he has never admitted, not even at the start of his career, when he disassembled the craft of acting, cleaved at the baroque, when he filled the screen with a ragged, mean diction and projected a humanness stripped of artifice and pretense, flesh and blood all over the place, a soul bared for once, and wriggling in a gauze of light.

The magic is central to the lure of Brando, especially to

those over forty, some of whom met him for the first time in *The Godfather* and *Last Tango in Paris*, others who were there when it began, all of them waiting for the voltage to hiss and crack one more time. To his older followers, he has always cast a wider net in his roles; the very life of the times ran through him. Like a sudden slap to the face, he seemed to put young males in touch with their maleness, to replace tentativeness with a code, however primordial. After his performance as the dominating baby-beast Stanley Kowalski in *Streetcar*, urban centers and colleges were filled with young men in torn T-shirts who vowed never to be a pushover for any woman. In *The Wild One*, he presaged a coming era of rebellion and psychic unrest, made the leather jacket a symbol, and flooded the highways with motorcycles. What was he rebelling against? His character replies, "What have you got?" In *On the Waterfront*, he struck a resonating twang in many men with a heartbreaker to his double-crossing brother, Charley, lines that are still repeated: *I coulda had class, I coulda been a contender*, an impeccable thrust to the heart of being a man, to all those futures out there in the dark sure to be glutted with dream robbers like union boss Johnny Friendly; the massive scar tissue awaits, can you handle it and move ahead with dignity?

And the stories, the lore lived up to the screen identity: there was a long-standing intimation that he could never answer a curtain call during *Streetcar*'s long Broadway run unless he could produce an erection. "The Slob," *Time* called the image. Brando didn't fancy the label much. Yet, offscreen, his behavior obliged. He hated the feel of new clothes, so he borrowed his agent's old suits; most of the time he was in jeans, adding to his brute sexuality. He was boorish at parties, with crude put-ons. When a woman columnist finally met him, she said, "Why, you look like everyone else." He looked at her, then walked away and stood on his head. The first words he said to a Chicago publicist, getting off the train with a pet raccoon on his shoulder, were "Where can I get Russell fucked?" Was he out to startle, to *be* the celluloid image (quite doubtful), or was it all just an exterior behind which he could hide and probe for a true self that could cope? The quest, along with shrouding depression, led him into ten-year therapy with Bela Mittleman, and after the psychoanalyst died, he still seemed adrift. With resignation, he once confided, "All I want to be is normally insane."

There are people who, when they cease to shock us, cease to interest us. Brando no longer shocks, yet he continues to be of perennial interest, some of it because of what he did on film, some of it because he resists definition, and maybe mostly because he rejects, by his style of living and his attitudes, much of what we are about as a nation and people. He seems to have glided into the realm of folk mystery, the kind that fires attempts at solution.

When he first came along, there were just lazy gossip columnists and press agents, all like a swarm of mice nibbling at him. Now there are zoom lenses, photographers dangling from helicopters, an editorial derangement overdosing on the star shot or interview, and guys who would hack through a jungle for a chance to discover what he reads in the bathroom. As he returns to public view, how disgusting it must be to him, how cornered and exposed he must feel, with tiers of insensate cameras whirring and recording the decay of a face and body that stopped women's hearts and made men squirm over their genetic shortchange, showing what happened finally to Kowalski, Terry Malloy, the smirking, cocksure Johnny on his cycle, revealing to the star-greedy world raw evidence of how ephemeral and mortal even the gods are; Brando lumbering about, hair whitened,

face melting, and carrying three hundred pounds; Brando gorg-
ing on crab legs, the butter dripping from his chin like rain-
drops. He never understood the attitude of the late Harold
Clurman, whom Brando knew on Broadway. "What an adventure, life," he was fond of saying. "What fun, this flop." The flop
part devoured Brando; the fun of fame, money, women, and his
talent was impenetrable.

Brando has always disparaged the specialness
of acting, equating it with some mindless reflex and an ordinariness common to all humans. Duty, art, that's simply ethe-
real piffle for a dronish exercise that is no more romantic than
drilling teeth. It is an outlook directly at odds with the holy
cosmos of theater and movies; a fire hose on the power of illusion, a deterrent to the tunnel-vision ambition that feeds the
tradition. But this attitude has not been rare among actors, particularly Spencer Tracy and Richard Burton. Tracy factored
out acting to knowing your lines and not knocking over the coffee table. He thought it an immature calling, and when Brando's
wife Anna Kashfi sought his advice, he told her, "Don't fret
about it. Acting doesn't require brainpower. Look at your husband." Burton thought the craft diminished the man into fop
and pined for the beery, bloody Welsh rugby fields that had
forged him, where a man's sense of himself could be made pal-
pable. What a paltry ambition, acting, Brando told an interviewer,
then asked, "How come you always ask questions about acting?
What else you got?"

Stella Adler, the grande dame of acting scholarship, was the
first influence on Brando's career, in 1943. Irrepressible, dominant, she knew how to fill a room. Her approach was to allow an
actor to free the irrational in himself. An actor must contend with
words, bring imagination to them. Ever since, Brando has used

words as keys with which to enter the deep center of a character. Some have thought that he is incapable of remembering lines; they are printed on cards around the set, even on the foreheads of other actors. Odd, for a mind that can quote obscure passages of Shakespeare without effort. Quite simply—and to him like so much about society's writ of life itself—the discipline of line rote reduces him to a mechanism, imprisons whatever mood or energy he wants to fire out. He needs a lot of room. Adler gave it to him first, and he's fought with every stentorian director who's tried to put his talent in irons. It was Adler's contention that she taught him nothing, that she "just opened the door, and he walked through it." She added, "He lives the life of an actor twenty-four hours a day. If he is talking to you, he will absorb everything about you, your smile, the way your teeth grow."

By an infinite number of perceptions he seems to form tacit conclusions about the fate of a picture, about what amount of creativity it deserves. He can disappear from the screen or at-tempt to commit visual suicide, as he did in *The Missouri Breaks,* trying to con with a pathetic accent, dancing a jig on credibility when he turns the character of a western killer into a dippy, overweight drag queen. He's walked through a lot of films; so did the titan Olivier, but none of them stuck to him, nobody counted. Being an earnest technician, the gallant professional who doesn't let the side down, never figures in the mix. As Burton said of himself, Brando cannot pander to a project; it works or it doesn't. But even Burton, who admired Brando, said that "I [wish I] could take him in my teeth and shake enthusi-asm into him." Above all else a reverential man of the classic stage, he thought that Brando ruined many performances by underarticulation.

The history of his interaction with his peers doesn't fit the Brando who disdains his work, minimizes its import. Such a man would be above the fray, would not care enough to respond to the threat of competition. But actors, whipsawed emotionally from day one, are poised on the edge of envy all their lives. They are sensitized to the tiniest slight, can turn any incident into a contest of wills. Even so, the idea of those of huge stature childishly mucking about competitively would seem to be too trivial, a fiction devised by the press. In diaries, Burton enlightens on the subject, how the compulsion to win, always there on the inside, is driven from the outside, too. A friend back in Wales asks him, "What do you think of this Brando boy?" Burton replies, "Very good, very good indeed." The friend draws close and says, "But, Rich, can you beat him?" For all his protestations, Brando played the star business like everyone else. His antennae shot up in the arena; it was just that his method of offense (rattling other actors, turning sets into chaos, playing mind games with directors) was more opaque.

Eddie Jaffe, a press agent, of all people, sees much more. Jaffe and Brando were close in the early days, even shared the same psychoanalyst. "All his actions," says Jaffe, "what made him, drives him, or cripples him, come from a monumental, dark lack of self-esteem." It began early and was locked up forever in his mind when he told his coarse father that he wanted to be an actor. "What?" asked the father. "Look in the mirror! Who would hire a yokel like you?"

To Brando, authority, any kind, unbalances him. Brando was in awe of Charlie Chaplin, until he worked for him in *A Countess from Hong Kong*. Brando has never claimed to be handy with comedy, a deficiency he often regretted when he would endlessly watch Laurel and Hardy films; he thought he would learn from the great Charlie. Instead, Chaplin manacled him with punctilious direction, burdened him with minutiae. But it was more than that, Brando related later. "He was a mean man,

Chaplin. Sadistic. He humiliated, insulted his son [Sydney, who
had a small part]." It infuriated Brando, and when Chaplin tried
the same thing with him, Brando told him where he could stick
his movie, frame by frame, adding, "Don't you *ever* speak to me
in that tone of voice." Chaplin, he said, was a remarkable talent
but a monster of a man.

By then, Hollywood was coming to the same judgment
about Marlon Brando. *Countess* was near the end of a long line of
ten failures, not only at the box office. There had been aesthetic
collapse in his unengaged work. And though all stars make
horrendous choices of films (instincts are not infallible, you
have to trust others eventually), the constant yelp of Brando's
dogs quelled the roar of his mystique. He had become a hack, a
turbulent hack at that. In Hollywood, genius is equated to
money rung up: a place run by cultural swine. His ex-wife Anna
Kashfi says Brando had noted this from the first, saying that you
could defecate on their rugs out there if the price was right;
now his career was in slithers. He spurned a retreat to the stage
(unlike Burton and Olivier); theater required a grueling attention span, high-octane commitment; he surely hadn't forgotten
how *Streetcar* had ravished his psyche. As it was, he drifted,
leaving behind much animus but a vast indelibility, a model for
future actors. As director Lewis Milestone observed, every
punk extra with a couple of lines wanted to do and be a Brando.

It has been conjectured over the years that
Brando threw himself so intensely into the role of Stanley
Kowalski that he became him, a trampler of other people's feelings, with a porcine sex drive in relentless snuffle. The latter
appealed instantly to men (if that was murder one, then most
of them would rise for conviction), and women sensed a freeing
sexuality in him, a feral quality that recognized no constraints.

Back then sex was a murmur bound with restraints and a rigid exterior of decorum. All the great screen lovers were feathery, rakish threats, perfumed, ample with technique and conscious of sexuality's exterior. Brando was sweat, jungle demands, and there were no rules, only a room and a bed; a kitchen table would do. And he had no conscience; look what he did to haunted, fragile Vivien Leigh in *Streetcar.* Kowalski was a reality transplant that never let Brando alone.

"I hated him," said Brando. "People have asked me if I'm really Kowalski. Why, he's the antithesis of me. Kowalski is a man without any sensitivity, without any morality but his own."

There is no reason—except for his swirling love life off-screen and some volatile testimony from an ex-wife—not to take him at his word. He has spent his whole life running from "The Slob" tag. The first thing he said after he became a star was "Now I have to educate myself." Since then, he has pursued Eastern religions, read philosophers from Lao-tzu to Schopenhauer to the point of eyestrain, his single goal being to try to understand himself and human beings, to find The Truth from somebody "you think is not a bullshitter," somebody who has the eyes of a saint and the perceptions of a ghost. He's never gone along with Stella Adler, who liked to quote to him, "Don't try to know who thou art. Long hath this idea tormented thee." Those who have been close to him say that much from the search eludes him, that he is a man going at an iceberg with a pick, the chips flying up brilliantly to him but never forming a unified whole.

Whatever the depth of his intellect, there is a special, pure, childlike wonder in Brando. He does not want to be what Kowalski communicates, that "we are here for one, terrible, gnashing, stomping moment, and that's all." He wants to make sense of things, never more evident than when he used to camp out at night while shooting *The Missouri Breaks.* With the Montana sky ablaze and banging, he sat in the dark, quietly intense and fingering a computer, timing the lightning strikes, which were enough, he said, to make him feel religious. This side has been shown only rarely. Mostly, he has condescended to inquiry with baiting and a weird, oblique gamesmanship. One of the few interviews of any length was with Truman Capote. The writer first met him in a deserted theater. *Streetcar* was in rehearsal, and the young Brando was asleep onstage, on his chest an open book, *Basic Writings of Sigmund Freud.* He was in denim pants and a white T-shirt, and Capote instantly saw the sexuality. He wrote, "It was as if a stranger's head had been attached to the brawny body, as in certain counterfeit photographs. For this face was very untough, superimposing as it did an almost angelic refinement and gentleness." He went on to talk about his aquiline nose and full lips that had a relaxed, sensual expression. Years later, Capote wrote him off as a dummy. "Maybe," joked Brando, "because I got my nose broken."

Brando was passionate about boxing, and before *On the Waterfront* he spent days studying the middleweight Rocky Graziano. During the run of *Streetcar,* he liked to spar backstage, hence the broken nose. He was not only pleased at how he got it, he was elated that it made his face more interesting. The producer Irene Selznick agreed: "I honestly think the broken nose made his fortune as far as the movies go. It gave him sex appeal. Previously, he had been too beautiful." It was an appeal that he dismissed. Women, he said, never stared at him when he walked by. If they did, it was the movie-star gawk.

"You've got to have love," he told Capote. "What other reason is there for living? That has been my main trouble. My inability to love anyone." He didn't seem to stop long enough to find out; he had harem taste. And he leaned toward dark, dusky women, usually foreign or of foreign extraction. Light-skinned women, he told Kashfi, derailed him sexually, explaining, "My mother was blond, you see." The Eurasian beauty France Nuyen was one of the few famous women he romanced. Brando drove her so wild that her weight soared and she lost a role in a movie. Another, so frustrated, put a voodoo doll on his lawn. Another attempted suicide, anything to retain his attention. He tried to understand the impermanence of love: "Nothing lasts for more than a little while. You could love a girl so much you could cut your stomach open. A year later you never want to see her again." He sought beauty, but was more drawn to lives of odd content. "He was talking to me one day," remembers Eddie Jaffe, "and he said excitedly that he had just met the most beautiful woman ever. Wow, I thought, he'd had some beauties. I asked him why. And he said, 'She's had the saddest life I've ever heard.'"

Kashfi attributes this preference to Brando's need to feel superior to women. Their marriage produced one boy, Devi. He supposedly never lived with Movita, a Mexican actress, yet it was a legal union on paper that gave him another boy, Miko. Since then, he's had a Tahitian wife, who recently sounded rather impatient with him. But it was the marriage to Kashfi that was a nightmare. According to her, it was rife with violence, torment, kinky sexual compulsions (his, of course), and free-fall neurosis.

In her book, she accused him of being a "clumsy seducer" and a sexual hog, a man who all but lit candles to his penis. Some of her nonsex observations are very revealing, if you can believe them, but when it comes to a man and a woman in their bed, or a battle for child custody, it is best to seek a neutrality of judgment. Besides, what did she expect when he first showed up to court her dressed as a Good Humor man, white shirt, pants, shoes, and rode around Hollywood in a convertible with a trick arrow sticking out of his head. To her credit, she dismissed most of the premarital tales she had heard. But she thought he was capable of bizarre constructions; he relished the yarns when she asked.

And who wouldn't believe anything after *Last Tango in Paris?* Here was Kowalski with an education and emotionally vanquished. The critic Pauline Kael correctly called it a stupendous film breakthrough. The director, Bernardo Bertolucci, had wrung Brando dry; he hadn't been guided, slyly coerced into a performance like this, since the days of Elia Kazan.

The film is centered in a vacant apartment, an asylum of crushing fears, of bad memories. An ex-boxer and actor-rebel, Paul (Brando) is an aging reject of society, with the harpoons of life exposing torn emotional flesh. All his life he has been in search of love; now he wants a reality he can understand: no names, no identities, detonated sex without love. "You see," he says to Jeanne (Maria Schneider), "we're going to forget everything we knew. All the people, wherever we lived. Everything outside this place is bullshit." He overwhelms her, pummels her sexually into a mere body, sodomizing her and forcing her to recite a declaration against love and society. Watching one scene, Brando's dresser said, "Something's up, he's taking this seriously." An actor friend, Christian Marquand, was astounded: "Forty years of Brando's life experiences went into the film. It is Brando talking about himself, being himself. His relations with his mother, father, children, lovers, friends—all come out in this performance." At the end of the shoot, an exhausted Brando said, "I will never go through this again."

With his career inert in the late sixties, Brando spent all of his time on a Tahitian atoll he had purchased. He was attracted to the lassitude and openness of the society, to the purity of life, and no doubt to the beautiful women, unimpaired psychologically. There is a lot of Rousseau in him, a back-to-nature idealism that drives him to want to remake the world. It would be startling if Brando had not read him, for much of his social thinking echoes Rousseau's view that "man's breath was fatal to his fellow men." On his island of Tetiaroa—*tetia* meaning "standing alone" and *roa* meaning "far away"—it was as if Brando were going about putting Rousseau's meditations into action. When he wasn't walking naked in the moonlight, he worked like a slave trying to effect a utopia. He poured millions into the environment, threw himself into a myriad of scientific experiments aimed at creating a simple, highly functional society free of Western values.

The sixties were also a propitious time for Brando's instinct for social redress. He campaigned hard for the civil rights movement, fought for the Black Panthers, and championed his favorite cause, the plight of the American Indian. Wrongly, critics saw his activities as a device to revive a failing career. His compassion for bottom dogs went way back. Once, when he had his own film company, he was in a funk over the Chinese, and one of his partners shouted, "Stop worrying about eight hundred and fifty million Chinese! Worry about us, two Jews—your partners." He agreed later to do the film called *Burn!* with Gillo Pontecorvo. Shooting took place in the heat of Colombia, and he was quickly at odds with the Italian, the way he treated blacks, who got half the pay of whites and were given slumlike living facilities. "I want to kill Gillo," he was heard saying. "I really want to kill him." Questioned why, Brando raged, "Because he has no fucking feelings for people."

Going into the seventies, Brando moved out of semi-exile and into one of the most protean runs of his career. By now, there was a whole new atmosphere in Hollywood, charged by filmmakers and actors who had grown up on his films. He had always had the adulation of younger actors. James Dean used to follow Brando around like a shadow; he was tepid about Dean, even jarred by his wildness, and he told him that he was "mentally disturbed and should go into analysis." Jack Nicholson said Brando was a heroic figure to him. When he moved out of Hollywood, right next door to Brando, he still stared with awe at his neighbor. "No telling," he said, "how many people were trying to emulate his timing, his style." When Brando walked onto the set of *The Godfather,* Al Pacino lost his composure. He was in a daze, his face white and his hands shaking. "What's the matter, Al?" an executive asked. "They want you in there. Go on." Pacino said, "You don't understand. Have you any idea what it is for me to be doing a scene with *him?* I sat in theaters when I was a kid just watching him.... He's God, man." Coppola had been vindicated after Paramount studio chief Robert Evans questioned his judgment in wanting to hire Brando. "I'm surprised at you, Francis," said Evans, shaking his head, filled with visions of chaos and a destroyed budget. Not on firm ground himself, the young Coppola pleaded, "You don't know what an effect he'll have, you don't understand his mystical relationship to actors."

Robert Mitchum rightly observed some time back that no one ever did a film *with* Brando. "He'll take you to hell in a dogsled," said Lewis Milestone. But these new directors seemed to enter a cobwebbed room of Brando's mind, they jostled his imagination and creativity. "When people deal with him honestly," said the late director-actor John Cassavetes, "there's no one better—ask any actor." Whatever it was, Coppola freed the giant in Brando with Don Corleone and did it again later as he pulled out the tenebrous, lost reflections of Colonel Kurtz, in a dim, shadowed cave dwelling at the end of *Apocalypse Now.* A master of improvisation, Bertolucci had Brando right in his gunsight, won his enthusiasm by encouraging him to shape scenes in *Last Tango*. "An angel as a man," said Bertolucci, "a monster as an actor. He is like one of those figures of the painter Francis Bacon who show on their faces all that is happening in their guts."

So with two new films, Brando is back, slowly closing the circle of his career. Who is Marlon Brando? Is he Kowalski of *Streetcar*, the rebel in *The Wild One*, the lost Paul in *Tango*? Who will he be next, as he feels his way toward the events of aging and death, fumbling for a serenity that has seldom been there in his life?

Extraordinarily, and emblematic of his disarrayed genius, parts of a self-portrait can be found in most of his films; no actor has thrown himself so naked to our voyeurism. Anna Kashfi says his whole life has been this: "Here I am—don't look at me." On film, at his very best, he has had nowhere to hide. And you can ponder what gnarled, semiblinking neuron in his brain has motivated Brando to turn himself into a three-hundred-pound remove from a former self; the apogee of narcissism turned like a knife inward. Striking looks and fame made him feel like a geek; growing ugly closes the case out, seals off affection with a releasing finality. As for his work, a powerful argument can be made that he has been the greatest American actor of this century—the single one who will survive well into the next. As Nicholson says, "The man does scorch the earth, right? I mean, for two hundred miles in any direction. Not much leavin's." And when Marlon Brando is gone, a wind will gust around an empty throne and sway the heavy curtains on the wall.

3 Jerry Glanville's Unbuckled Ego

Esquire
October 1990

Pro football coaches work in a business of hysterical attention, of fierce expectations and instant, unmerciful answers. Football is sky-to-earth lightning, the kind that streaks windows and seems to be looking for *you*. It's not like baseball, with rich texture and languid turns of plot and gathering nuances. Nor is it like basketball, where form holds like haze and sometimes seems like a performance lab for sneaker technology. Both can seem like far-flung nineteenth-century expeditions, epic in length but short on breakthrough dispatches. Not so with pro football; it's a mass Wagnerian catharsis, a weekly reaffirmation of some ancestral blood bond.

That observation is going to be too tame for Jerry Glanville, recently head coach of the Houston Oilers and now with the Atlanta Falcons. His verbal sketches of the game, his NFL dossier indicates, are free of any language that might obscure his "dirt-honest" views, mainly that pro football is about splintered

bones, spinning eyes, and the separation of consciousness, with
the heretical intent of disengaging a priapic opponent; in other
words, to deball and expunge the will of the man in front of
you. This is what tears the great stadium hordes from ordinary
humane instincts: the game macheted open to its mean-red raw-
ness. The old guard prefers to talk of sophisticated intricacy, of
physical chess—and not at all about Jerry Glanville, lover of fast
cars, $1,000 boots, and melancholy guitars, self-promoting hagi-
ographer of dead icons. And a bit more: the first rock 'n' roll
coach in history; scrawler of graffiti on league politesse; the ab-
errative, dark rogue-prince behind the mask of an impish
lounge comic.

"Is that all?" asks Glanville.

"Just perceptions."

He leans forward and whispers, "Could it be Satan?"

Glanville sits behind his desk in his signature wardrobe:
cross hanging around the neck, black pants and shirt, and a ton
of belt buckle, a setup that has made him as identifiable as Andrew "Dice" Clay, only a trifle less embattled. Oddly, he is rather
mute. He seems more like an Episcopalian bishop who has been
grappling with too many canonical problems. He had been hospitalized for pneumonia only two days before, and he is wafer
pale, his voice is weak, and he is somewhat disinclined to engage
in anything that might make him think. The light talk glides toward the public vise that is the coach's life. He backpedals,
seems to prefer measuring the gabby visitor, the depth or shal-
lowness of the encounter ahead.

Not yet realizing that elaboration of thought for him is stylistic crime, you tack to the left, rather than engage in mouth-
to-mouth resuscitation. You advance the idea that pro football
has become mere entertainment. Like rock concerts with cardboard rockers. Like movies that no longer transport to larger

meanings but strangulate on hype; the *show*, the brute sell as driving principle. Is pro football veering too close to being a pseudo-event, a synthetic arrangement, like Sugar Ray Leonard fights or presidential campaigns? Hasn't the game simply become a lavishly mounted gig for owners and players and television to frisk clean a national obsession? Recent strikes for the grabbing of the riches, for who controlled the *product*, said it loudly: the major collaborator—the fan—is crudely expendable.

Glanville sips from a glass of water, then moistens his lips. He might be slipping into gear. Football as a show? Football as something not real, less than the will to power and excellence, less than life itself? What true believer lets that sort of indictment slide? Then he goes blank, as if a teacher has made him wade through the heavy water of John Locke on human understanding. Or maybe he's personalizing it all, figuring he's being the target here for someone trying to bait him into self-incrimination. After all, the rumors are still in his ears that he has been hired by Atlanta because his visibility will help fill a new stadium.

He prowls around for a response, perhaps stalling to determine if this is an attack dog or just a fool. He's been known to read snoops quickly, segregating them into carriers of pesky dumbness, friendly fire, or malice with intent. He suddenly laughs, a mongrel expression that's half-squeal, half-cackle. For some reason, he's decided that he is being used as a ball of yarn for a playful kitten who wants to unspool his gaudy strands to get to the center of what he is about, perhaps one that will grow sharp teeth if he's not careful. "Hey, you had me going for a minute," he says. "But I'd have to be really dumb to think you're *that* dumb about football." He pauses. "You know, I really didn't want to do this piece. I gotta be careful of certain writers. Don't come across them often, but I can smell them." His nose sniffs deeply. "Tricky ones with serious intentions." This kind, he says, don't want your head, they want your soul. He much prefers TV people, and why not? He is an artisan with the twenty-second sound bite, and TV couldn't care less if there is any *there* there in Jerry Glanville. "I could be made of wood," he cracks. "Just give 'em a good, snappy line. I love it."

Rising from his desk, he walks to a small picture on the wall and points to it. "This is a shot of the twenty-eight NFL coaches taken every year. It's like a reunion of fighter pilots. Each year, the faces change. Three or four gone. Down in flames. That sound like a show to you? He draws closer, saying mockingly, *"A pseuuuudoevent?"* He shrugs, laughing off the desperate urgency about his work, dismissing the radioactive heat suspended over each game, made almost unbearable by fans who consider defeat a medieval pox or a mugging of their own selfworth. On Mondays after a sorry outcome, coaches sit like spent bullets on postmortem TV specials or radio talk shows, all but begging for fluttery, timid questions to hammer into credible alibis. Print reporters ferret for perpetrators. The atmosphere is no place for a porcelain ego.

Outside now, Glanville slowly walks around a lake near the Atlanta practice field. He wears a *High Plains Drifter* coat against the spring chill. "You'd have to take an ax to my ego," he assures. "Some might say it's out of control. I say it's healthy. This ain't a game for tin men, you gotta have a lotta lion in you." He cuts to stark imagery. "I know what fans feel because I feel the same thing. After every loss it's like a beer bottle having been whipped across my face." Does he forget easily? He is told of an anthropologist who once described the human mind as rat country. A twilit desert of neurons, where nothing is ever lost, just gathered up by mental rats. They wait in long shadows, the rats, the rememberers, the keepers of failures, of lost chances and personal incompleteness. "Rats, huh?" he says. "I understand that. I'm an authority on them rats."

NFL coaches are rarely out of stride with one another. They've always had certain chivalric imperatives—no public displays of ego or intramural sniping. And most of them go to work hearing the distant, call-to-arms trumpet heard in the movie *Patton;* the military metaphor fuels them. "They truly believe," says one general manager, "they are leading large men into large battles." Glanville is no different. But he departs from the collective by his use of unclubby rap and the way he seems to turn the fray into light opera, like when he started leaving tickets for long-dead stars. To some, the device revealed a man starving for attention. But when you look at his choice of subjects, they mirror aspects of Glanville himself. Elvis Presley: the first powerful threat to national propriety. James Dean: the anointed symbol of compulsive revolt. W. C. Fields: the humorist and slayer of the fake.

An official once asked Glanville to help him lower the decibels that were delaying a Houston game. "Hey, what can I do?" he replied. "They hate *me* more than you!" If ever he was more dead certain of that, it was in the final weeks of last season at Houston, a period that will not be lost in the memory of the fans or of Glanville, for all his deflecting humor; nerve endings were spitting like fallen electric lines all over town. "What is this!" he remembers thinking. "I felt like I was in that Sam Peckinpah movie, *Bring Me the Head of Alfredo Garcia.*" The mood was typical of the AFC Central Division. The air that wafts across these games is heavy with the smell of cordite; division play seems like those irrational struggles of Old Europe in which enemies forgot the reasoned political purpose for battle and settled into the letting of emotional blood. For Glanville, it was the perfect stage, especially those last weeks of '89, when a division championship was in his grasp.

Houston was always an outsider in the Central Division, geographically and in city character. Cincinnati, Cleveland, Pittsburgh—those places are about industrial soot, mist, and frozen tundra, a lingering respect for hard work, about staving off urban decay. Houston was oil, warmth, a city of the future. The Oilers had no work ethic, were clumsily managed; winning didn't seem to matter. Glanville's arrival changed that; he whipped the Oilers into two straight play-off shots. Heading into Cincinnati, they were 9-5 with two games to play; one more win and they had a division title. A reporter cornered Glanville one day with a question about Bengals coach Sam Wyche. "Well," said Jerry, "he's no hero of mine." He insists now that the rest of his answer was lopped off, that he said that no opposition coaches were heroes to him.

Wyche, known as a prickly, sensitive individual, given to by-the-book NFL decorum, was coldly purposeful against the Oilers on Sunday; he and the Bengals went after them as if they were sides of beef falling from a truck. In a burp, the Oilers were behind 31–0, then 45–zip well into the third period. Wyche then called for his infamous onside kick, recovered, and drove another stake into Glanville's heart. The last twenty-one seconds saw the market on infamy cornered. Wyche sent out his field-goal team. "I don't remember that score," says Glanville disingenuously. "So what, 61-7? All I can think of is my team calling time out. They're out there freezin', their butts badly kicked, and, hey! They call a time-out. Maybe they'll miss. That shows me something. The score? Who cares?" Wyche was going to make sure he did care. "Call me," he said, "if you find anyone who likes Glanville."

A week later, Houston lost to Cleveland. Backing into a

wild-card play-off spot, Glanville knew that he was up against it, that the town was in the mood to offer him a blindfold. "Maybe a chair, too," he says. His adversary was Chuck Noll, his most cherished heavy bag. Give him a chance, and he'll build a whole stand-up routine on Noll. "Can you imagine," he rasps, squinting, "being the last man on earth with Chuck Noll? Lookin' at that face? I had a face injury once. The doctors wanted to cut. The trouble was I'd never smile again. Just like Chuck Noll." Like Wyche, the Steelers' coach had trouble with every Oilers game being turned into a railroad wreck by an engineer who either worked with a pint in his hip pocket or was genuinely committable to preventive isolation. A piece of postgame film from 1987 animates much about their relationship. The ritualistic shaking of the hands takes place (the Steelers had been all but put in body bags), and Glanville is thinking, Isn't this big of him; but Noll won't let the hand go. "You tried to hurt us. Your guys coming over, jumping on people like that, you're going to get your ass in trouble." Jerry tried to free himself, and there's Noll croaking, "I'm serious!"

This one proved to be a game worthy of driven men. In the last minute, the Oilers, behind by a point, were one play from a winning field goal. Glanville called on Lorenzo White, the back he always called East-West, for his habit of running horizontally. White ran into trouble, tried to find room near the sidelines. "It's weird," Glanville recalls. "You stoop down. The place is like a wall of sound. The chills are up your back. But everything is soooo quiet. Sort of like a haunted house. The bodies are fallin' and flyin' in front of you in this awful slow motion. I can still see Rod Woodson's helmet heading like a bullet for the ball. Lorenzo's face screwed up for the hit. Right in front of our bench. The ball loose now, right in front of me. I want it! Hey, this is my career! Dive on it! Do something, you idiot!" The Steelers recovered and four plays later won it with a fifty-yard field goal. After the game, Glanville's son crawled up on his lap and cried. "I said a prayer," Glanville says, "to protect us from the evil I could feel in the air." Evil? "Hey, it was going to be a jungle out there."

Houston combusted after that loss, with Glanville being blamed for everything but the economic slump. There are some who wonder if the two losses may not have sent all sorts of rats scurrying in his attic. "He went strangely quiet after Cincinnati," says John McClain, a Houston beat reporter, "and acted weird after the play-off." Printouts of tactical felonies, of un-chained ego displays, were unfurled in the media; old, festering team disputes were explored. Glanville was using the team as an extension of his ego, first as an instrument of how tough he was, then as a showcase for his personality. He had to have a motif, all had to revolve around him, hence the black outfits, his preference in music, his talk about fast cars. General manager Mike Holovak, an old-school man, despised his black look, his hammy talk shows. He wasn't too fond of Glanville as a techni-cian either. The players were said to be split, too, with the of-fense complaining that the coach made their job more difficult because of his savage defensive orders. Always diplomatic, quar-terback Warren Moon was rumored to have no use for Jerry. At times, it seemed the whole city was polarized. "Glanville," says a Houston columnist, "insists on violating the cardinal rule of the game with his mouth: never give the other team incentive to beat you. He was gunned down here because of his cheap-shot mentality and his ego." Even now, the implication sets Glanville off. "That's Noll and Wyche," he says. "Chuck Noll was the most brutal coach in history. When he was on top, he had his players whip you like a hound. In the early eighties, they ground Warren Moon's head into the dirt, you needed a drill to get it out. When I took over, I made my men watch that film. I vowed Noll would never do it again. Now he just whines." He adds, "Ask Joe Namath if I'm a dirty coach. My old Detroit defense once sent him home packed in ice. But he was a man. We were just physical, he said, not dirty."

Glanville eventually asked for permission to talk to Atlanta. He recalls—after the Atlanta interview—talking to owner Bud Adams.

"They won't hire you," said Adams.

"No? Well, let's see," said Jerry.

"Stick it out here another year. You're too far out to get another job."

"If I can't, then I wasted twenty-six years."

Now forty-eight, Glanville has pulled the dogsled all his life. Inspection reveals a natural bottom-feeder, from any purview except his own, since his childhood. "Everybody had flags out for Eisenhower's birthday," he says. "I walked outside and thought they were for me." He was raised mainly in Detroit, mostly by his mother. Teachers bored him, truant officers chased him over fences, and he seemed destined to be near violence. Delivering newspapers, he was robbed by an older man and shot in the eye with a BB gun. Later, he got into an argument with an older brother, home from the navy, over who would sleep in the bed. The quarrel lasted five blocks, then ended with Jerry being cuffed to a parking meter by the police. He found some release in high school, where a coach liked to grin and point to him as "just a thug who lives to hit people."

A linebacker at Montana State, he was short, weighed 215, with a nineteen-inch neck, "like a fireplug with hair." He soon got homesick, returned to Detroit, and began work on a Chevrolet assembly line. If critics wonder why Glanville is Glanville, they can in part look at life on the line. It turns you into a zombie or compels you to seek color—"the edge"—forever. "That score?" says Glanville. "That wasn't humiliation. Sam Wyche never worked on an assembly line. Covered in oil from head to toe... You had to press a red light to go to the bathroom, and there were usually five lit up ahead of you." A Northern Michigan coach rescued him. One day he walked out and threw his badge at the plant. At Northern he played football and majored in psychology ("I memorized everything, never carried a book"), had his salivary glands crushed, got into an off-field punch-up with an ex-marine that hospitalized both of them. "I later tore up a knee," he says, "finished out scouting for the coach. He taught me to think in football."

Glanville was unloading sacks of flour when he got an assistant coaching job at a high school in Lima, Ohio. Sometime later, he got a call from Rollie Dotsch, the Northern coach. "I'm looking at your defensive films," he said. "You should be in a college job." Dotsch got Glanville a job as an assistant at Western Kentucky, where he got his master's and become a close pal of Joe Bugel's, now coach of the Cardinals. There wasn't much eating money; they lived on pizzas, drew game formations on cartons, and argued. One day, in full view of the players, they slugged it out over a fine point about the bump-and-run; they needed mops for the blood. The next year he was at Georgia Tech, under Bud Carson, now head coach of the Cleveland Browns. Before long, he found himself in charge of the Oilers' defense. He was named head coach with two games left in 1984. "I pulled a trick on the league," says Glanville. "The league hasn't recovered yet." At first, he wouldn't accept unless he was going to be retained for the next season. "Win the next two games," they said; he lost both. He's not certain why he was rehired. But Houston had always been a quixotic club.

"The Oilers were a joke," says Glanville. "Smack 'em in the mouth, pee on their pants, and they still wouldn't hit anybody." Defensively, he got right to the point; they were not going to be beaten by fifteen- and nineteen-play drives; they would be destroyed swiftly or not at all. To Glanville, defense was not cerebral; it was an exercise in cumulative punishment. Prop up a runner, and if there's no whistle, dice 'em and then serve. Houston, under Glanville, was no place for players who wanted to pull up a beach chair on the injury list. Other players could smell a faker; they began calling them lassies and searching for clues of fear in the opposition. "You sense it out there," says Glanville. "The receiver who short-arms the ball, the runner going out of bounds. I love to see that, then I know we're doing our work." Of course, some players didn't buy into him. Big Harvey Salem used to think Glanville was too inhumane, too cruel. He took to calling the coach Billy Jack. "I went to the movie," Glanville says. "No resemblance. I'd never take my boots off to kick somebody in the mouth." Tired of the complaints, Jerry moved Harvey's gear into a toilet stall and put his name over it.

Sports figures ferociously believe that they should be immune from critique, that their work should not be examined like that of actors or musicians. They act as if people aren't paying hard money to see them; support should be mindless, close to gratefulness. Glanville was a rich vein of quotes, accessible and blunt. A local press usually loves this style—and a target that doesn't move. But the Houston press stopped laughing early in 1986, when he lost eight in a row. His job was in jeopardy. His humor began to leak bitterness. "You can call him an asshole," says McClain. "He don't care. But never question his masculinity or say he doesn't know football." That's what Glanville thought the press was doing. He offered to engage a couple of columnists in the Astrodome. A year later, on his radio show, he wouldn't field any questions unless the caller had canceled his subscription to the *Houston Chronicle*. Wasn't that a mite ridiculous, maybe paranoid? He says, "I'm nothing if not ridiculous. Paranoid?" He then mimics Bogart in *The Caine Mutiny*, rattling imaginary steel balls in his hand, eyes frantic, and demanding, "Where's the strawberries? Who took the strawberries?" Right now, he's still smarting over an assistant who promised to join him in Atlanta, then backed out when the Oilers offered him an assistant-GM job. "He backed out for *that*?" he says. "For a job where you talk to yourself? We were close. He gave me his word. He's dead with me." To prove it, Jerry sent him a single black rose. "The Oilers," he says, "reported me to the league office."

"I feel welcome here," says Glanville, inhaling the cool Atlanta air. "The owner, Rankin Smith, says he wants me to be the coach until he dies. I gotta get him a nurse." Atlanta has long been known as a conservative, bloodless outfit, a team so perpetually adrift that fan interest has been spent. It has also had misfortune: drug problems, players killed in car wrecks. The team is a flat tire, and Glanville knows it. His star defensive player had said as much in a meeting earlier in the day. He was tired, he said, of being beat up; he wanted out. Glanville looked him squarely in the eye and pointed: "I didn't come here to be beat up. I don't know what we'll be, but nobody's going to work us over physically."

He may never be a front-office coach, but Glanville *is* a player's coach. He gets into their minds. "The modern player," he says, "is stronger and faster than ever. But there's nothing inside. A couple of bad games and they're ready to quit. The difference in winning is fractional. It's how you perceive yourself. Getting an identity." He doesn't care much for high-fiving hot dogs, or amateurish end-zone displays. He wants joyful "trained killers" who want to *splat*. His team meetings in Houston became bedlam, with film being backed up and run repeatedly at a true splat. "Like a window shade," he says, "being snapped up by a big wind. We liked admiring our work. We even roared when *we* got whacked." His dressing rooms startled more than one official. "We had big speakers blastin'," he says, "and we'd be up rockin' and rollin'. The joint vibrated. You could feel the energy in your fingertips."

Glanville suggests a ride in his black Corvette. The car jets down the highway. "Nothing good was ever accomplished at fifty-five," he says. "Unless you're still in first gear. I love muscle and acceleration." How does he get players to respond with such intensity in these days of wealth and pampering? "Coaches rap me," he says. "But they're hypocrites. They all want hellfire intensity." He laughs. "I don't know. Maybe I'm Satan. The dark prince, like you say. A weaver of spells." Most likely, the attitude is generated from his own rebelliousness. He convinces players that they are all High Plains Drifters, dustcoated and headed into a town that doesn't want them. The phrase "living on the dangerous edge" is their mantra by him. "The edge" can mean an insane tactic like using a safety blitz forty-six times in one game, or a state of mind that will not allow any outside dictums to stop them from being less than what Glanville wants. "On my clubs," he says, "you're gonna find the real in you, or you're gonna be gone."

Glanville's black ensemble is part of the attitude. "At first," he says, "it was a device for players to spot me on the sidelines. But I saw the press, the fans, seeing something else. Black was saying something about us." His scalpel wit conceals his hostility, yet deflates. Players pick up on his cheekiness. Whipping past an expensive housing area, he points and says, "Look at

that great house, and next door is a pink pickup. See it? Must be
Chuck Noll's." He then comments about Bill Walsh's having
been labeled a genius. "Walsh then called Sam Wyche a genius
and Wyche filled his house with mirrors," he says. "There are
no coaching geniuses. Of course, saying that is unholy as hell."
Glanville seems to have a need to create enemies, to bring the
game down to a fierce personal level, to wrest it away from
dull-eyed technocrats, many of whom doubt his sincerity. "My
wife," he says, laughing, "can tell you how real I am." Early in his
career, before the NFL, Glanville and his future wife, Brenda,
were on a highway after a rough loss. He was tensely quiet. Worried, Brenda said, "It's only a game, Jerry." He swerved to the
side, braked the car, jolting her forward. Eyes afire, he yelled, "If
you honestly believe that, then get out of my car! It's not *just* a
game! It's my life!"

Real is a word much used by Glanville. He scans his times
and sees detritus: disposable men, collapsing families, a national errancy. It vexed him recently to see his son eating lunch
in a school cafeteria, so he told him to start making his own. "A
small thing," he says, "but not to me." A real football play is a
blocked punt and recovery: it communicates massive will, a "close
to the bone" character. "Like one of our players who broke
the arm of one of our own and asked for the X-ray and cast so he'd
always remember. Like players with the attitude of our Dicky
Byrd. I always called him Puke. He said, 'Coach, do me a favor.
Don't call me Puke around my parents.' 'Okay,' I said. He said,
'Just call me Vomit.' A guy like this has to be on my team."

Is Glanville an anomaly in the NFL, or is he just the most
visible and reprehensible of a new cut of coach? Last season,
coaches were never more prominent, paining owners as well as
league officials. Browns owner Art Modell, for one, didn't like
their verbal brawling, their uncommon zest for attention. "We

never used to see them in the old days," says Ernie Accorsi, the Browns GM, "except when the ball went out of bounds." Now TV cameras stay on them, sensing drama. Big close-ups. The attention magnifies their passion and ego.

Accorsi says he never liked Glanville or his team's image. "But then you get to know him," he says, "and he's charming. I'd rather deal with him than guys who portray themselves as pinnacles of Christianity and stab you in the back. Jerry always comes at you from the front: I don't see a phony, I see a guy who can't believe he's dug out from a hole. All that fifties stuff is real with him. It's not an act."

Glanville's personality is rooted hopelessly in the fifties, a time for brutish engines like the '57 Chevy's, for outlaw hotrodding; when sex hid behind steamed car windows; a drawntogether time of work as religion, of last innocence: the creamy glow of Marilyn Monroe, the squint of James Dean, the pout of Elvis Presley. It wasn't an act when he kept an Elvis impersonator with him at practices or left tickets for the dead or cruised the Houston streets in his '50 Mercury, just like the one in *Rebel Without a Cause*. "Driving it is like being in a time warp," he says. The tickets "were for pure fun. Then it became more. Like I wanted to keep the memory alive. Then he ain't dead, right? Why would God put us here just to die? God doesn't tell bad jokes." For someone depicted and minimized as a Not Ready for Prime Time coach, he seems stuck back in time. Look over his office: no football memorabilia, just some prints of the Old West and a large, wistful poster of an art-deco movie house. Marilyn Monroe is selling tickets, Elvis grins in the saddle of a Harley-Davidson out front, and the marquee above reads GLANVILLE LIVES.

4 The Betrayal of Michael Levine

Esquire
March 1991

With eyes closed, no chop, and plenty of silk, Michael Levine plays late at night on his tenor sax, the counterpoint of distant car horns and sudden voices trading *muffugs* while passing beneath the open window. Curious, how the sound of a sax so easily fastens to a mood. In certain clubs, the sound sweats raw, drifting sex and imminent possibility. At a union-hall wedding there is a rough, hell-raising smirk to it. Here, the used-up quality of the notes, acoustically jailed, seems to isolate the mythology of the private dick: transient and alone in the wild urban ocean, a man with too much past freed only by dreamy, hour-of-the-wolf trips through "Stardust."

The film-noir cutout fits to a point, right down to the shabby one-roomer up here on Manhattan's West Side. Even without the plaintive horn, you can see a lot of boot marks on this man; the face has been somewhere. But very far from the celluloid rag shop of crime—commendations line his walls. For up to a year ago, when he retired, at age fifty, he was a high-voltage player in the preeminent social rot of our times—drugs. As an agent of the Drug Enforcement Administration, he had an international reputation for deceit. Now, free from bureaucratic irons, he is the chronicler of the tale—with a costly license. His marriage is gone. His close friends are dead. To sleep at night, he listens to tapes of falling rain.

Levine ran his fingers over the high-tech surface of a nine-millimeter Smith & Wesson. The feel reassured but made no promises. Problems at home had forced him to transfer to New York as a DEA group supervisor in October 1983, a post without the creative thrill of snaking manipulation, or the creeping menace of exposure. It was simply three or four raids a week by about ten men, their guns drawn in tight, dim hallways, all of them heaving breath, frozen before *The Door*. Here their impeccable design and technique always seemed a fool's conceit, reduced to a click of darkest chance.

Direct assault on crack houses was a mad, rote exercise for most agents. A spread of gloomy percentages awaited: doors booby-trapped with shotguns; all kinds of cutting-edge ordnance; African tree vipers (called three-steppers, meaning three steps and you're dead) loosed on the floor; designer attack dogs, kept hungry and mean, their vocal cords severed to ensure maximum startle. Dobermans would rip and tear, go up and down the body like a typewriter. A pit bull loosed among charging agents in a semidark room would fragment ingot nerves into leaping popcorn; shots were fired from every angle.

Levine flipped open a second gun, a .38, loaded it, then slipped it into his ankle holster. He leaned back and closed his eyes, filled his mind with an old talismanic image, that of a seven-foot, black warrior-god named Pedro Rocamora, assigned to him by a *macumbera* back in Argentina. He had gone to her to

placate a friend after he found a part of his jeans nailed to a wall
at home, slashed at the knees and surrounded by black symbols.
The old lady told him he would soon be shot in the head by
strangers. She would give him Pedro. "Got one with a better
name?" cracked Levine. "Pedro doesn't sound up to it."

But part of him had stopped laughing long ago. Several
weeks after the *macumbera*, DEA cables reported learning of a
$200,000 contract package for the head of *un judio trigueño* of Ar-
gentina. Not much was left of "the Dark Jew" now. All that cunning, point-blank energy, and success drifted like specks in the
DEA computer universe. Gone, too, was a clear and perfect belief,
as well as the need for superreality and the angry hunt. From
Buenos Aires to Panama to the roulette of the street raids, Pedro had gotten him out of some tight fits.

Soon, Levine and his men were moving toward their target.
A few weeks before, they had performed a raid with movie director, William Friedkin (*The French Connection*) on board for
close-up research. Up against some Rastafarians, Levine and his
partner watched shotgun pellets pass between them. Mike went
to check on Friedkin and found him understandably bellied to
the hall floor. "I love it!" said the director, looking up. "Yeah,"
said Mike, "why else would anybody do this shit?" Levine berated
himself later for behaving like a danger junkie, a burlesque figure. Those guys quickly vanish from the shelf.

In some neighborhoods of upper Manhattan, you can almost hear the cracking of marrow bones, as crowds of dealers
fling themselves at cars of buyers. Inside the buildings, too many
lost, young girls lie on beds, strung out from heroin, their pale
beauty trickling red down their necks; dazed, stranded wives
huddle with children fed and cleaned less than a crate of fighting cocks. Up here, agents like Levine dwelled on an old Yiddish
proverb: "If God lived here, they'd break his windows."

When he jumped out of the car at his end of a pincer movement on West 144th Street, Levine had staying alive on his mind more than ever; there were scores to be settled after all he'd seen. The air was filled with shouts of "Go! Go! Go!" He knifed into a prewar building, saw a door slam at the end of a shadowed hallway. A battering ram dropped the door, and Levine headed for a loud noise in a bedroom. With a gun in his hand, a guy was going out a window. Levine raced forward, only to watch him bounce two stories below, then come up running. Mike jumped—no bounce, just splat. He lay there in pain, feeling his back locking and ankle ballooning.

A row of blackbirds looked silently down on him from the top of the fence. He shut his eyes hard, then opened them. His focus was coming back, and he used the fence to slide halfway up to one foot. Then, out of the corner of his eye he saw a black streak, a kind of preternatural, no-sound laser focus, loosed from the basement by a dealer. Legs folded for the ascent, the Doberman was now close enough for him to see threads of saliva on its teeth. Levine fired, stunning it with a shoulder hit. He fired again, but the nine-millimeter jammed. He got another round in the chamber just in time for a second charge. The shot blew the Doberman's head off, and Levine's one leg buckled as he melted down the side of the fence. "Gee, Mike," shouted a rookie, looking down from the window. "Just like a jungle movie."

Limping up Broadway at twilight, weaving through mousy psychopaths and encamped dealers, Levine winces as he thinks back to his narrative of that last Harlem run. Though his aim was to attach a face to agents ("they're the lost legion"), to put some of their work in relief, he senses that he has come too close to the DEA's menu depiction of the drug war. "The jungle, the street war," he says, "plays well on TV. The DEA loves the jungle! But the war they don't want you to know about is out of a John le Carré novel." Levine's career would fit with cryptic snugness into such a novel: the driven, tight-visioned operative abandoned by the political whims of theatrically self-conscious superiors; the classic equation of intense belief confronted by hierarchical cynicism. The result produces someone like Michael Levine, now viewed by the DEA as its version of Philip Agee.

Agee, according to the CIA, gave up names in the field and put them in jeopardy. A stone-cold law-enforcement type, Levine would cut his throat before endangering colleagues. In some ways he's a Gordon Liddy without the institutional amorality and obsessive warrior display. Service to a code for him is paramount—until what is asked of the code becomes crazed, sophistic, and produces actions counter to reason and the general good. "Levine's no Agee," says a fellow agent. "Mike was the best we've ever had. He speaks for a lot of agents. I can't say any more, okay? You want me to get career cancer?"

Levine was and is a benchmark figure in DEA history. His successes were numerous, his style inescapable. Over a long career, he fired his gun maybe three times, and he had been in some tight spots. "Mike, you see," says another agent, tapping his head, "was all up here. Up against it, he'd use muscle. To use a gun was failure to him." He could speak peasant, street, or hidalgo Spanish without a stumble, could spin angel-hair castles of trickery. He's been a special-operations officer on the Southern Cone in Latin America; an undercover agent and a supervisor on then Vice President Bush's South Florida Task Force; an inspector of worldwide operations; and an instructor in undercover tactics and informant handling. When Robert Stutman, head of the DEA in New York, began his 1987 celebrity raids into the heart of the war, Levine was chosen to lead various senators and the likes of Dan Rather on newsy expeditions.

With a semilimp and three herniated disks, he ended his career after twenty-five years of service. At a ceremony, a DEA official said, "Of all people, Mike, who would've bet *you'd* make it this far." Was it disbelief, he wondered, that he hadn't ended up a red puddle somewhere, or a grudging tip of the hat to his agility and chancy style amid crushing orthodoxy, his proficiency in beating the tricks and traps meant to wreck his cases and career?

Looking back, Levine figures he should have had his ticket punched long before that day. Son of a minor-league loan shark who deserted early, he should have died in the South Bronx, where he ran with a fifties gang, a "bad Jew kid" pretending to be a Puerto Rican in order to stay whole. After a couple of arrests before age sixteen, he joined the air force, thinking they'd let him be a fighter pilot. He should have died there, too, when a barracks argument evolved and in the scuffle the guy's gun didn't fire. The weapon was later tested repeatedly by his sergeant—no problem.

After the air force came marriage and the struggle toward an accounting degree at Hofstra, while he tended bar and played sax in a string of cheap-drink joints. The degree got him on as a US Treasury agent, then he made a stop at the Bureau of Alcohol, Tobacco, and Firearms. It was here that the road turned in a tragic way. His younger brother, David, had become a heroin junkie. Trying desperately to save him, Levine put him in rehab seven times and finally made him live with his wife and kids. He was soft with him, then dogged him to respond. Nothing worked, and as he watched what it was doing to his own family, he had to let him go. A few years later, David put a bullet through his own brain.

Levine switched to the narcotics wing of Customs, carrying a load of revenge and guilt made heavier each time he saw his mother's face or recalled the squish of his brother's brains under his shoes as he looked for the suicide note. No more tunneling into gun rings and holdup gangs at ATF; he had a widescreen enemy now—the drug dealer. Customs sent him to Thailand, where he made the first foreign penetration ever, a record heroin score back then, then stayed to work on the periphery of a case involving heroin shipments in the bodies of Vietnamese dead. The DEA was born in 1973. A friend and agent, Sante "Sandy" Bario, told him, "Mike, the future is drugs, and it's going to be a horror." He promptly joined the new agency. "Some agents in DEA," says a colleague, "didn't want to work with Levine. They liked slow motion. They thought he'd get them hurt. Mike went for the throat every time out."

The DEA and other agencies are wary of undercover men. They're too flamboyant, too far out in front of the machinery, so chameleon that the agency is never certain what it is seeing—a clever agent or someone just as corrupt as the dealer. "To agencies," says Levine, "it's often a given that you're unclean, as if they say, 'What kind of man could do this work?' And it is scummy. You turn father against son, brother against brother, all of them trying to save their own skins. Ends justifying the means, you never get used to it."

He recalls a time with the ATF when he infiltrated a neo-Nazi gang and was giving out pamphlets on Eighty-Sixth Street in Manhattan. A Jewish kid, a student, came along, took a pamphlet from him, and tore it up. All the Nazi eyes were on Levine, a new member. "I had to make my bones," he says. "So I started shoving the kid. He ran, his books falling out of his hands. And I gave him a kick in the ass. The Nazis cheered. I was made. I've often thought about that poor kid. I felt like a creep."

To Levine, undercover was personal expression, not an enforcement device. It demanded razor intellect, an intuitive command of psychology, and still-water calm, knowing that you are a potential victim locked in a zone with your murderer. "If you stumble," he says, "they'll recoil. If you're afraid, they'll smell it. Undercover is like living with a gun behind your ear. Death can come as slow as a thirty-year sentence or as quick as a jailhouse suicide."

"There is no drug war. It's a fraud. No other nation in the world has a drug war. The rest have *addiction* problems. We have war. Why? Because it's a toy, a grab bag with a lot of big hands in it."

To Levine, the real news—not the fingertip kind the media like—resides in the actions and motivations of secrecy fetishists, backroom rulers who despise limits, government employees who have begun to control their employers.

"The DEA," he says, "they want more power, more people, more funding, more headlines and glory. The politicians, they want a platform easily sold to voters, something that the public can identify and think something's being done, an illusion that they can throw millions of dollars at and show that they're challenging the drug barons; the war is great theater for politicians." The Pentagon and CIA: with the fade of communism, they are building a pretext for maintaining their budgets. *Everybody* wants a toy. All held together by a phrase: *war on drugs.* The black humor, the madness, is heartbreaking.

"God knows how many secret elements," he says, "are out there working under the guise of the drug war. Oliver North was the latest example. His operation was hip deep in contra drug smuggling. He was banned from Costa Rica for his involvement with drug runners. The DEA documented fifty tons of contra coke that was being routed into the US by a Honduran connection. An agent bought two kilos in Lubbock, Texas, and made the arrest. The CIA comes quickly to the rescue. A closed hearing is held. Case dismissed. In the meantime, an agent like my friend Ev Hatcher is murdered in New York over a couple of ounces, and there is the DEA wail of dying for 'a just cause.' A ghastly value is at work here."

Congressional hearings and the media skirted North's drug involvement; they burrowed for linkage to Bush and constitutional violations. North and his CIA cover skated free. "It was unbelievable," says Levine. "But if the conduct of the drug war is ever investigated, Watergate and Irangate will look like midgets. One day it'll happen. Like Peter Kelly, a federal judge in Kansas, said, eventually, in the public good some high people in the administration should be indicted for conspiracy."

These later revelations only underscore the truths that Levine recognized as far back as 1980. In the US, Bario's warning of "horror" was taking shape rapidly. Despite a previous decade in which drugs had become a visible issue, the stateside atmosphere was still one of complacency, from the White House down to the population, which had begun to view cocaine as a trendy indicator of personal success. Like other agencies, the DEA was arrogant and smug on the exterior, but had little or no grasp of its adversaries, their organizational capability, or their aim to mobilize giant, tentacled structures.

Posted to the embassy in Buenos Aires, Levine worked the boulevard cafés with informers, drug syndicators, and rip-off artists. The Argentine secret police were among the latter. They were fond of drug-world jewelry—not the drugs. The secret police (elements of which worked closely with the CIA) killed and tortured with an almost dull promiscuity; the bones of young ideologues filled the soil. "One of the cops," says Levine, "pulled me aside and showed me his new invention, a little electric box. Grinning from ear to ear, he said he'd throw a dealer in the car and hook his balls to it."

Marcelo Ibañez was different. The ex–minister of agriculture in Bolivia, he dressed like a banker going out of business. In undercover, it helps if you can adhere to a target, genuinely like him. Ibañez was a man of intellect and manners. As chief aide to Roberto Suarez, the padrone of Bolivia, he did not relish drug activity, but embraced it as a necessary act of patriotism. Posing as a Mafia prince, Levine said he wanted to expand his US operations. The crucial topic in a drug sting is not the money. It is logistics, delivery, when each side is vulnerable. Ibañez said Suarez could guarantee a thousand kilos a month. Levine negotiated an initial deal for five hundred kilos, to establish trust.

Levine was amazed at the size of Suarez's operation. What was going on here? He called the DEA and reported the prospect of a thousand kilos. "Come on, Levine," an official said. "What kind of scam are you trying to run?" Mike says now, "The largest bust by the DEA had been two hundred kilos. And get this, the name of Roberto Suarez wasn't even in the computer, despite our having five agents in Bolivia. "You don't understand," said Ibañez. "Don Roberto is a god there. He feeds our people. Politicians don't. He does what he wants in my country." Levine sighed. "That is precisely why I cannot go. I won't be safe," Ibañez smiled. "You are a smart man, my friend."

A dramatically expanded American market tantalized, and Ibañez agreed to see Levine in Miami to explore further options. Levine was ready to play out the hit of his career, and one that stands as the most crucial turn in drug-war history. He figured on having a big Hollywood setup for Ibañez's arrival. He would be looking to see criminal royalty. "What I got," says

Levine, "was a twenty-five-hundred-dollar budget, a tract home, not a villa, a pool that looked like a duck pond, a dented green Lincoln instead of a fleet of cars. No Spanish-speaking agent or pilots to collect testimony once our beat-up plane landed in the Bolivian jungle." With forty hours left before Ibañez's arrival, Levine and his agents rushed around town buying linen and family goods and renting a new Cadillac. Ibañez was all business when he turned up; no booze, no women. He poked through the house, looking in cabinets and closets. "Miguel," he finally said, "this house is not lived in."

Levine and his men agreed they would make the case in spite of the DEA; it was as if the agency had a motive for it to fail. He convinced Ibañez this house was temporary. To show good faith, he would send his wife (agent Frances Johnson) on the plane. Ibañez was happy again. But that night the head of the DEA in Miami contacted Levine. "You can't send Frances," the voice said. "She's a woman." Levine shouted, "She's not a woman, she's an agent!" He was in retreat again. He had to tell Ibañez that his wife had to stay, only she had the signature to get the money from the vault.

Ibañez was crushed, and Levine still doesn't know what made him continue. Did he feel excessive pressure to please Suarez? "Suddenly," says Levine, "he looked over to our agent Richie Fiano. He liked Richie. And he said, "I'll take Richie. I will tell Roberto that he is your brother." Going to bed that night, Levine was wary. He looked at Johnson and said, "We're husband and wife, you have to sleep with me." Frances bundled up in pajamas, and sure enough, at 2:00 a.m., Ibañez burst through the door and switched on the lights. "Oh, please forgive! But I want to make sure we start early in the morning."

Once the Bolivian pickup was made, two Suarez emissaries—Jose Roberto Gasser and Alfredo Gutierrez—met Levine at a

Miami bank to collect their $9 million. They were arrested leaving the bank. Levine was astonished at the progress of events in the next few months. Gasser was released by the US attorney. Gutierrez's bail was lowered, and he jumped back to Bolivia. Angry, Levine kept asking himself, Why did the judge not only lower the bail but refuse to grant a hearing as to the source of the bail money? Why was Gutierrez not tailed while on bail? Why didn't Gasser even reach the grand jury, a standard procedure? The execution of the case, once suspects were in custody, made a mockery of his operation.

Back in Argentina, he pieced together the why. With the expertise of Argentine factions, the CIA was whipping up a Suarez-backed revolution in Bolivia to deter what they perceived as encroaching communism; that was the priority. Suarez won, and the first thing he and his people did was destroy Bolivian drug-trafficking records. "It's embarrassing," an Argentine secret agent told Levine; even to these antidrug fanatics, communism was more evil. Levine says now, "From that point, our drug war became a South American joke. The moment we turned Bolivia over to drug interests, it was the surrender of our drug effort. The mechanism for mass cocaine production was being protected by our own government. It was a ridiculous, self-inflicted wound. After 1980, drugs soared to a hundred-billion-dollar business. We could have dealt a hard blow to the future of drugs with our Suarez operation. But powerful alliances were born with the CIA and DEA help. They turned Suarez into the head of the drug world's General Motors and the major supplier of coca base to the Medellín Cartel."

While simmering in Argentina, Levine thought back to the death of his friend Sandy Bario. In 1978 Bario was arrested by DEA internal security in Texas and accused of dealing drugs. He was soon dead. He took a bite out of a peanut butter sandwich and keeled into convulsions. Early tests showed he'd been poisoned. Later tests revealed no trace of strychnine. And a final autopsy concluded he had "choked to death" on the sandwich. "That didn't wash among agents," says Levine. "Many believed he was killed by internal security or the CIA because he knew too much about the US government's involvement in drug trafficking. Sandy was on my mind when I wrote to a pair of *Newsweek* reporters, outlining what took place in the Suarez gambit. They either leaked my name to the DEA to curry favor or did it by accident. Afterward, my life was hell. A year and a half of investigations into the tiniest corners. They found only that I kept incomplete records and played my radio too loud in the embassy." Settle down, a high official advised, ride it out. "The guy paused," Levine recalls, "and then said, 'Remember the peanut butter sandwich.'"

Working out in the DEA gym, Levine watches another agent violently curling barbells over his chest. Between gasps of air, the agent assails the DEA: "It's like they *want* us to go bad. The FBI gets an extra twenty-five grand working this jungle [New York]. They come to work in car pools, and we get nothing." Another agent, skipping rope, adds his opinion of DEA management: "Christ, they're all whores." The talk continues about "suits" and how they cleverly composed their big names and cashed them in: John Lawn, chief of the DEA, went to the Yankees; Robert Stutman became a drug consultant to CBS News. "Hell," says the rope skipper, "a fucking saint would go bad in this business looking at all this shit." Levine reflects later, "I won't go to the gym anymore. It's a sad situation. The DEA is an unhealthy agency."

Levine himself had been through five DEA administrators, even saw the rise of William Bennett, with his marquee title of *drug czar*. "None of them knew a thing about drugs," he says. "And Bennett was merely a bigmouth who was looking for a statistic. Drugs are like the stock market. They rise some points, drop some points. Bennett waited for the curve to come his way, then resigned, claiming the drug corner was turned. Big résumé success. How many corners have we turned since Nixon? Why do the people eat it up while the body count goes up in the cities, families and careers are ruined, and crack babies fill hospital wards? In New York alone, there are seven born per hour. Project that number, and you're looking at a nation down the road full with psychotics, sociopaths, and lost people. It is truly an American tragedy. How we fought drugs is criminal."

The danse macabre brushed Levine again toward the end of his career. His family was in ruins as his daughter began to disappear into the drug underscape. The guilt still ached from his brother's death, and now this. She didn't have money for drugs; suppliers were turning her on for the fun of it. His mind flashed back to when he was undercover with a biker gang in Buffalo, how he had to watch what they did to fifteen-year-old druggies—and he could do nothing. "I gave her and her suppliers no peace," he reflects. "I was a homicidal father who was a drug agent. I wanted them to know that." He once broke into a party and announced that everyone was under arrest. His daughter ran out the back door. He raced toward this guy squinting drunkenly at a stub of marijuana. Ready to put the cuffs on him, he realized that it was a crushed moth.

Only a court petition absolving the parents from responsibility and forbidding the daughter to associate with the family saved the day. "It was a hard line of take," he says. "Hard hadn't worked with David. But after wrenching wars, she chose us." He heaves a sigh, accenting an already engraved bleakness in his face. "Being a DEA agent takes its toll," he says. "They have an outside study going now. Misconduct for bribery and other things is up 176 percent in the last several years. Then, there are the suicides. I knew an agent, came in all smiles, went to his office, and blew his brains out. Why? These are some of the best men out there. I'm told the life expectancy of an agent is only five years after hanging it up. But somebody should also study the torture and murder of our brother Kiki Camarena in Mexico. He wrote letter after letter. 'Does someone have to die?' he concluded. He did—for Mexican loan debt, oil and trade agreements, and the secret Mexican support for the contras and other CIA programs."

The Andean Offensive, a growing Pentagon-CIA-DEA presence in Peru and Bolivia, is the most recent tactic in the war and the most dangerous turn in Levine's view. The objective is to attack coca-base exports and production at its source, with military equipment, even US troops.

This tactic, says Levine, won't work. "American bankers don't want it. Their huge loans are being serviced by the crop. Peru and Bolivia don't want the military because their economies would be in dust. The State Department isn't too happy, either. They know these people will starve, and hungry people rush toward guerrilla movements, and then you got your kids fighting others named Juan and Carlos who don't think it's a good idea to starve because the US can't handle its own hunger for cocaine. The Andean front is just another example of the Pentagon and CIA being lost without the Russians and KGB. We learned nothing from the Panama invasion, with twenty-three Americans and perhaps thousands of their people dead. For what? Noriega? He picked our pockets for twenty years, and we knew it. He was at best a midlevel drug facilitator, not even a dealer. All that show of force, and Panama still hasn't altered its banking laws to combat money laundering."

In becoming an antihero, Levine knows he has violated what he used to preach at DEA undercover classes all over the world: "Don't get involved any more than you have to. What happens after you've done your job is none of your business. Fuck what happens in the courts. The plea bargains. Ambitious prosecutors. Political judges. Bad verdicts. Wrong sentences. Fuck it all. Just learn to survive." Levine thinks, then says, "Still true. You'll get offed with all that crap on your mind. But I've done my time, and I've watched. I've earned the right to say no. All through the eighties, from the media to the people, there's been an Orwellian yes—yes to government, politicians, and agencies. And there's an awful game being played out there with drugs."

But when he speaks to groups or goes on TV or radio, he is the bearer of an unpopular message: Americans are believers. Perpetually amazed Phil Donahue smothers the message in irrelevancies. On PBS, Charlayne Hunter-Gault, bewildered for twelve minutes, finally asks, "You mean we're being outgunned?" His whole point misses her bat. "The DEA," he says, "is proud of the job they've done with the media." The PBS anchor Robert MacNeil slides back to a top DEA official named Terry Burke (Levine can't confront him). "What about it, Mr. Burke?" says MacNeil. "By the DEA's own admission, he was your top agent. Why shouldn't we listen to him?" Burke mutters something about "commercial enterprise," a reference to Levine's book, *Deep Cover,* an exhaustive, surgical dissection of a mideighties operation called Trifecta, which, "had it not been sabotaged by the DEA," would have led to the inner chambers of three nations: Mexico, Bolivia, and Panama. "They even tried to send me to Bolivia," says Levine. "Even though they knew a contract was out on me. I said, 'Sure, just put it on paper.' They don't like that stuff on paper."

Levine shakes his head at the commercial implications. "If I wanted to make money," he says, "I'd hire out to defense attorneys." The day before, the lawyer for Luis Arce-Gómez (an archenemy Levine chased for years and who was finally nailed) solicited his help in preparing a trial defense. Levine also turned down a consultancy to Pan Am, which wanted to prove the DEA was linked to the Lockerbie crash, that the bomb had been planted on a DEA operative. What bothers him most on his rounds are the closed minds. In Pittsburgh, a disc jockey says after Levine—an agent noted for his meticulous care with court evidence—leaves the studio, "Not a thing this guy said would stand up in court."

His most troubling media affair has been a scheduled segment on *60 Minutes*. It was a major piece on their storyboard. "I was told it was a crash program for Don Hewitt," says Levine. All the preproduction was done, and then suddenly it was canceled. "I always thought," he says, "that it was because of Robert Stutman, my ex-boss and CBS drug consultant. The last person he would want was me. So I let it pass. The producer said to me, 'This has never happened before.' Later, two different sources from CBS revealed much more. Stutman did figure in it, but not out of his dislike for me. Hewitt didn't want to upset Stutman with a segment on me. He was counting on Stutman for something far bigger." Stutman supposedly had the goods on the long-rumored marijuana use of a youthful Dan Quayle. Hewitt never got his story. "Why knows?" Levine chuckles.

With colleagues, Levine usually gets a better hearing. They like his rap about "suits" who are masters of phony outrage, "functionaries sexually fascinated by manuals." Young people support any adult glimpse of authoritarian malpractice. At a small place in Mississippi, a student asks, "Are you telling us not to be DEA agents?" Levine replies, "Certainly not, if you

want adventure and action. If you think you'll make a difference, forget it." But at CCNY in New York, he has his hecklers.
A kid shouts, "You're a CIA agent of misinformation!" And then
a Hispanic hits him with some cool: "Yeah, well, man, you look
like you ain't doin' too bad yourself." Levine says, "You wanna
see where I live?"

Back at his tomb of an apartment, Levine says, "Nobody,
you see, really wants to know, it's too confusing, the lie is nice
and simple." He runs the scale on his sax, then drifts into "Stardust." The next morning he will leave for the airport for another trip to a tiny, backland college, where he will try to give a
face to men like Ev Hatcher, Sandy Bario, and Kiki Camarena,
where he will let his hurt and truth out in therapeutic dribbles,
knowing fully that he surely must appear like the dead, ar-
mored body of El Cid strapped to a horse riding nowhere.

5 No Pain, No Game

(JOEY BROWNER)

Esquire
January 1992

Observe, please, the human skeleton, 208 bones perfectly wrought and arranged; the feet built on blocks, the shinbones like a Doric column. Imagine an engineer being told to come up with the vertebral column from scratch. After years, he might produce a primitive facsimile, only to hear the utterly mad suggestion: Okay, now lay a nerve cord of a million wires through the column, immune to injury from any movement. Everywhere the eye goes over the skeleton, there is a new composition; the voluting Ionic thigh, Corinthian capitals, Gothic buttresses, baroque portals. While high above, the skull roof arches like the cupola of a Renaissance cathedral, the repository of a brain that had taken all this frozen music to the bottom of the ocean, to the moon, and to a pro football field—the most antithetical place on earth for the aesthetic appreciation of 208 bones.

After nine years in the NFL, Joey Browner of the Vikings is a scholar of the terrain and a rapt listener to the skeleton, the

latter being rather noisy right now and animated in his mind. It
is Monday morning, and all over the land the bill is being pre-
sented to some large, tough men for playing so fearlessly with
the equation of mass times velocity; only the backup quarterback bullets out of bed on recovery day. The rest will gimp,
hobble, or crawl to the bathroom, where contusions are counted
like scattered coins, and broken noses, ballooned with mucus
and blood, feel like massive ice floes. Browner unpacks each leg
from the bed as if they were rare glassware, then stands up. The
feet and calves throb from the turf. The precious knees have no
complaint. The thigh is still properly Ionic. The vertebral column
whimpers for a moment. Not a bad Monday, he figures, until he
tries to raise his right arm.

The bathroom mirror tells him it's still of a piece. It's partially numb, the hand is hard to close, and the upper arm feels
as if it's been set upon by the tiny teeth of small fish. Pain is a
personal insult—and not good for business; he knows the politics of injury in the NFL. Annoyed, his mind caroms through
the fog of plays from the day before, finally stops on a helmet,
sunlit and scratched, a blur with a wicked angle that ripped into
his upper arm like a piece of space junk in orbit. He rubs an
oriental balm on the point of impact, dresses slowly, then slides
into an expensive massage chair as he begins to decompress to
a background tape of Chopin nocturnes, quieting and rumina-
tive, perfect for firing off Zen bolts of self-healing concentration
to his arm.

By the next morning, after re-creating his Monday damage
probe, he appears more worried about his garden of collard
greens and flower bed of perennials; given the shape of his arm,
most of hypochondriacal America would be envisioning ampu-
tation. That is what Browner would like to do, so eager is he to
conceal the injury, so confident is he that he could play with

one and a half arms. At six-three, 230 pounds, he is a diligent smasher of cupolas, who has made more than one thousand tackles in his career. He is the first $1 million safety in NFL history; a six-time All-Pro; and a two-time conscriptee to the all-Madden team, an honor given out to those who have no aversion to dirt, blood, and freeway collision.

His only peer is Ronnie Lott, with whom he played at USC. Lott put the safety position on the map, invested it with identity, separated it from the slugging linebackers and the butterfly cornerbacks. It is the new glamour position in the NFL, due in part to CBS's John Madden, a joyful and precise bone counter who always knows where the wreckage will lie. With schedule parity, the outlawing of the spear, the clothesline, and the chop block, with excessive holding, and so many tinkerings to increase scoring, pro football veered toward the static on TV. Madden, it's clear, wanted to bring some good old whomp back to the game, and he found his men in players like Lott and Browner. Now the cameras are sensitive to the work of safeties, the blackjacks of the defensive secondary.

Of all hitters, they have the best of it: time and space for fierce acceleration, unusually brutal angles, and wide receivers who come to them like scraps of meat being tossed into a kennel. Lott delineates their predatory zest in his book, *Total Impact*, saying that during a hit, "my eyes close, roll back into my head ... snot sprays from my nostrils, covering my mouth and cheeks." His ears ring, his brain goes blank, and he gasps for air. He goes on to broaden the picture: "If you want to find out if you can handle being hit by Ronnie Lott, here's what you do. Grab a football, throw it in the air, and have your best friend belt you with a baseball bat. No shoulder pads. No helmet. Just you, your best friend, and the biggest Louisville Slugger you can find."

Like medical students, pro players do not often dwell on

the reality of the vivisection room, so Lott is an exception, a brilliant emoter with a legitimate portfolio, but still a man who has a lot of pages to fill with body parts and brute-man evocations. Browner has no marquee to live up to—except on the field. He is a star, though not easily accessible in media-tranquil Minnesota, distant from the hype apparatus on both coasts, part of a team that always seems to avoid the glory portioned to it annually in preseason forecasts.

Tuesdays are black days at a losing team's quarters, soft on the body and miserable for the mind. It is the day when coaches slap cassettes of failure into machines, vanish, then emerge with performances graded, carefully selecting their scapegoats. Good humor is bankrupt. On this Tuesday, Vikings coach Jerry Burns looks much like Livia in *I, Claudius,* who in so many words scorches her gladiators, saying, "There will be plenty of money for the living and a decent burial for the dead. But if you let me down again, I'll break you. I'll send the lot of you to the mines of New Media." Browner smiles at the notion. "That's it—pro football," he says. "You don't need me."

"No tears like Lott?" he is asked.

"No tears," he says. "I guess I don't have much of a water-works."

"No snot?"

He laughs: "He must have some nose."

"What's total impact?"

"Like a train speeding up your spinal cord and coming out your ear. When it's bad."

"When it's good?"

"When you're the train. Going through 'em and then coming out and feeling like all their organs are hanging off the engine."

"You need rage for that?"

"Oh, yeah," he says. "The real kind. No chemicals."

"Chemicals? Like amphetamines?"

"Well, I don't know that," he says, shifting in his chair. "Just let's say you can run into some abnormal folks out there. I keep an eye on the droolers."

"Your rage, then?"

"From pure hitting," he says. "Controlled by years of Zen study. I'm like the sun and storm, which moves through bamboo. Hollow on the inside, hard and bright on the outside. Dumb rage chains you up. But I got a lot of bad sky if I gotta go with a moment."

"Ever make the perfect hit?"

"I've been looking for it for years."

"What would it feel like?"

"It would feel like you've launched a wide receiver so far he's splashed and blinkin' like a number on the scoreboard. That's what you're after mostly."

"Sounds terrible."

"It's the game," he says coolly. "If you can't go to stud anymore, you're gone."

"I get the picture."

"How can you?" he asks, with a tight grin. "You'd have to put on the gear for the real picture."

There is no dramaturgy with Browner, just a monotone voice, a somnolent gaze that seems uninterested in cheerful co-existence. Or, perhaps, he is a model of stately calm. His natural bent is to listen. He does not come close to the psychological sketch work of Dr. Arnold Mandell, a psychiatrist with the San Diego Chargers some years back who visited the dark corners of a football player's mind. Now in Florida, Mandell says, "Take quarterbacks: two dominant types who succeed—the arrogant limit-testers and the hyperreligious with the calm of a believer. Wide receivers: quite interested in their own welfare; they strive for elegance, being pretty, the stuff of actors. Defensive backs: very smart, given to loneliness, alienation; they hate structure, destroy without conscience, especially safeties."

Is that right? "I don't know," says Joey. "But it's not good for business if you care for a second whether blood is bubbling out of a guy's mouth." Highlighted by the cornices of high bone, his eyes are cold and pale, like those of a leopard, an animal whose biomechanics he has studied and will often watch in wildlife films before a game. An all-purpose predator with a quick pounce, no wasted motion, the leopard can go up a tree for a monkey ("just like going up for a wide receiver") or move out from behind a bush with a brutal rush of energy ("just what you need for those warthog running backs"). The mind tries for the image of him moving like a projectile, so massive and quick, hurling into muscle and bone. It eludes, and there are only aftermaths, unrelated to Browner. Kansas City quarterback Steve DeBerg served up the horrors in a reprise of hits he has taken: his elbow spurting blood so badly that his mother thought the hitter used a screwdriver; a shot to the throat that left him whispering and forced him to wear a voice box on his mask for the next six games; and his memorable encounter with Tampa Bay's Lee Roy Selmon. "LeRoy squared up on me. The first thing that hit the ground was the back of my head. I was blind in my left eye for more than a half hour—and I didn't even know it. I went to the team doctor and he held up two fingers. I couldn't see the left side of the fingers—the side Selmon had come from. I sat on the bench for a quarter."

Browner offers to bring you closer to the moment of impact. He put some tape into the machine and turns off the lights. The figures up on the screen are black-and-white, flying about like bats in a silent, horrific dream. Suddenly, there is Christian

Okoye, of the Chiefs, six-one, 260 pounds, a frightful excrescence from the gene pool, rocketing into the secondary, with Joey meeting him point-blank—and then wobbling off him like a blown tire. "Boooom!" he says. "A head full of flies. For me. I learned. You don't hit Okoye. He hits you. You have to put a meltdown on him. First the upper body, then slide to the waist, then down to the legs—and pray for the cavalry." Another snapshot, a wide receiver climbing for the ball, with Browner firing toward him.

"Whaaack!" he says. "There goes his helmet. There goes the ball. And his heart. Sometimes. You hope." The receiver sprawls on the ground, his legs kicking. Browner looks down at him. Without taunting or joy, more like a man admiring a fresco. "I'm looking at his eyes dilating," he says. "Just looking at the artwork. The trouble is, on the next play I could be the painting." Can he see fear in receivers?

"You don't see much in their eyes," he says. "They're con men, pickpockets."

"Hits don't bother them?"

"Sure, but you tell it in their aura. When you're ready to strike, you're impeding it, and you can tell if it's weak, strong, or out there just to be out there."

"So they do have fear?"

"Maybe for a play or two. You can't count on it. They may be runnin' a game on you. Just keep putting meat on meat until something gives. But a guy like Jerry Rice, he'll keep comin' at you, even if you've left him without a head on the last play."

"The film seems eerie without sound."

"That's how it is out there. You don't hear. You're in another zone."

"So why not pad helmets? That's been suggested by some critics."

"Are you kidding?" he says. "Sound sells in the living rooms. Puts backsides in Barcaloungers for hours. The sound of violence, man. Without it, the NFL would be a Japanese tea ceremony."

The sound, though, is just the aural rumor of conflict, much like the echo of considerable ram horn after a territorial sorting-out high up in the mountain rocks. NFL Films, the official conveyer of sensory tease, tries mightily to bottle the ingredient, catching the thwack of ricocheting helmets, the seismic crash of plastic pads, every reaction to pain from gasp to groan. Network coverage has to settle for what enters the living room as a strangulated muffle. But in the end, the sound becomes commonplace, with the hard-core voyeur, rapidly inured in these times, wondering, *What is it really like down there?* It has the same dulling result as special effects in movies; more is never enough, and he knows there is *more.* Like Browner says: "Whatever a fan thinks he's seeing or hearing has to be multiplied a hundred times—and they should imagine themselves in the middle of all this with an injury that would keep them home from work in real life for a couple of weeks."

What they are not seeing, hearing—feeling—is the hitting and acceleration of 250-pound packages: kinetic energy, result of the mass-times-speed equation. "Kinetic energy," says Mandell, "is the force that dents cars on collision." He recalls the first hit he ever saw on the sidelines with the Chargers. "My nervous system," he says, "never really recovered until close to the end of the game. The running back was down on his back. His mouth was twitching. His eyes were closed. Our linebacker was down, too, holding his shoulder and whimpering quietly. I asked him at halftime what the hit felt like. He said, "It felt warm all over." TV production, fortunately, can't produce Mandell's response. But there still remains the infant potential of virtual reality, the last technological stop for the transmission of visceral sensation. What a rich market there: the semireality of a nose tackle, chop-shopped like an old bus; the psychotic rush of a defensive end; the Cuisinarted quarterback; and most thrilling of all, the wide receiver in an entrechat, so high, so phosphorescent, suddenly erased like a single firefly in a dark wood.

Quite a relief, too, for play-by-play and color men, no longer having to match pallid language with picture and sound. Just a knowing line: "Well, we don't have to tell you about that hit, you're all rubbing your spleens out there, aren't you, eh?" But for now, faced with such a deep vein of images, they try hard to support them with frenetic language that, on just one series of plays, can soar with flights of caroming analysis. War by other means? Iambic pentameter of human motion? The misterioso of playbooks, equal to pro football as quark physics? For years they played with the edges of what's going on below as if it might be joined with a 7-Eleven stickup or the national murder rate. It is Pete Gent's suspicion (the ex-Cowboy and author of *North Dallas Forty*) that the NFL intruded heavily on descriptions of violence, as it has with the more killer-ape philosophies of certain coaches. If so, it is a censorship of nicety, an NFL public relations device to obscure its primary gravity— choreographed violence.

But claw and tooth are fast gaining in the language in the booth, as if the networks are saying, "Well, for all these millions, why should we struggle for euphemism during a head sapping?" Incapable of delicate evasion, John Madden was the pioneer. Ever since, the veld has grown louder in decibel and candid depiction. Thus, we now have Dan Dierdorf on *Monday Night Football*, part troll, part Enrico Fermi of line play, and Mother Teresa during the interlude of injury (caring isn't out— not yet). There's Joe Theismann of ESPN—few better with physicality, especially with the root-canal work done on quarterbacks. Even the benignity of Frank Gifford seems on the verge of collapse. He blurted recently, "People have to understand today it's a violent, vicious game." All that remains to complete the push toward veracity is the addition of Mike Ditka to the corps. He said in a recent interview, "I love to see people hit people. Fair, square, within the rules of the game. If people don't like it, they shouldn't watch."

Big Mike seems to be playing fast and loose with TV ratings—the grenade on the head of the pin. Or is he? He's not all *Homo erectus*, he knows the showbiz fastened heavily to the dreadful physics of the game. "Violence is what the NFL sells," Jon Morris of the Bears, a fifteen-year veteran, once said. "They say they don't, but they do." The NFL hates the V-word; socially, it's a hot button more than ever. Like drugs, violence carries with it the threat of reform from explainers who dog the content of movies and TV for sources as to why we are nearly the most violent society on earth. Pete Rozelle was quick to respond when John Underwood wrote a superb series in *Sports Illustrated* on NFL brutality a decade back. He condemned the series, calling it irresponsible, though some wits thought he did so only because Underwood explored the possibility of padding helmets.

Admittedly, it is not easy to control a game that is inherently destructive to the body. Tip the rules to the defense, and you have nothing more than gang war; move them too far toward the offense, and you have mostly conflict without resistance. Part of the NFL dilemma is in its struggle between illusion and reality; it wants to stir the blood without you really absorbing that it *is* blood. It also luxuriates in its image of the American war game, strives to be the perfect metaphor for Clausewitz's ponderings about real-war tactics (circa 1819, i.e., stint on blood and you lose). The warrior ethic is central to the game, and no coach or player can succeed without astute attention to the precise fashioning of a warrior mentality (loss of self), defined by Ernie Barnes, formerly of the Colts and the Chargers, as "the aggressive nature that knows no safety zones."

Whatever normal is, sustaining that degree of pure aggression for sixteen, seventeen Sundays each season (military officers will tell you it's not attainable regularly in real combat) can't be part of it. "It's war in every sense of the word," wrote Jack Tatum of the Raiders in *They Call Me Assassin*. Tatum, maybe the preeminent hitter of all time, broke the neck of receiver Darryl Stingley, putting him in a wheelchair for life; by most opinions, it was a legal hit. He elaborated, "Those hours before a game are lonely and tough. I think about, even fear, what can happen." If a merciless intimidator like Tatum could have fear about himself and others, it becomes plain that before each game players must find a room down a dark and distant hall not reachable by ordinary minds.

So how do they get there, free from fear for body and performance? "When I went to the Colts," says Barnes, "and saw giant stars like Gino Marchetti and Big Daddy Lipscomb throwing up before a game, I knew this was serious shit, and I had to get where they were living in their heads." Job security, more money, and artificial vendettas flamed by coaches and the press can help to a limited point. So can acute memory selection, the combing of the mind for enraging moments. With the Lions, Alex Karras took the memory of his father dying and leaving the family poor; the anger of his having to choose football over drama school because of money kept him sufficiently lethal. If there is no moment, one has to be imagined. "I had to think of stuff," said Jean Fugett of the Cowboys. The guy opposite him had to become the man who "raped my mother."

But for years, the most effective path to the room was the use of amphetamines. Hardly a book by an ex-player can be opened without finding talk about speed. Fran Tarkenton cites the use of "all sorts" of uppers, especially by defensive linemen seeking "the final plateau of endurance and competitive zeal." Johnny Sample of the Jets said they ate them "like candy." Tom Bass even wrote a poem about "the man" (speed), a crutch he depended on more than his playbook. Dave Meggyesy observed that the "violent and brutal" player on television is merely "a synthetic product." Bernie Parrish of the Browns outlined how he was up to fifteen five-milligram tablets before each game, "in the never-ending search for the magic elixir." The NFL evaded reality, just as it would do with the proliferation of cocaine and steroids in the eighties.

The authority on speed and pro football is Dr. Mandell, an internationally respected psychiatrist when he broke the silence. He joined the Chargers at the behest of owner Gene Klein and found a netherland of drugs, mainly speed. One player told him, "The difference between a star and a superstar is a superdose." Mandell tried to wean the players off speed and to circumvent the use of dangerous street products. He began by counseling and prescribing slowly diminishing doses, the way you handle most habits. When the NFL found out, it banned him from the Chargers. Mandell went public with his findings, telling of widespread drug use, of how he had proposed urine tests and was rebuffed. The NFL went after his license, he says, and the upshot was that after a fifteen-day hearing—with Dr. Jonas Salk as one of his character witnesses—he was put on five-year probation; he resigned his post at the University of California–San Diego, where he had helped set up the medical school.

"Large doses of amphetamines," he says now, "induce prepsychotic paranoid rage."

"What's that mean?"

"The killer of presidents," he says.

"How would this show up on the field?"

"One long temper tantrum," he says. "Late hits, kicks to the body and head, overkill mauling of the quarterback."

"How about before a game?"

"Aberrant behavior. When I first got up close in a dressing room, it was like being in another world. Lockers being torn apart. Players staring catatonically into mirrors. I was afraid to go to the center of the room for fear of bumping one of them."

"Is speed still in use?"

"I don't know," he says. "I'd be surprised if it wasn't, especially among older players who have seen and heard it all and find it hard to get it up. Speed opened the door for cocaine. After speed, cocaine mellows you down." He pauses, says thoughtfully, "The game exacts a terrible toll on players."

Joey Browner is asked, "At what age would you like to take your pension?"

"At forty-five," he says.

"The earliest age, right?"

"Yeah."

"Should the NFL fund a longevity study for players?"

"Certainly."

"Are they interested in the well-being of players? Long term or short term?"

"Short term."

"Any physical disabilities?"

"Can't write a long time with my right hand. This finger here [forefinger] can't go back. It goes numb."

"How hard will the transition be from football?"

"I'll miss the hitting," he says.

"If someone told you that you might be losing ten to twenty years on your life, would you do it again?"

"Wouldn't think twice. It's a powerful thing in me."

"They say an NFL player of seven years takes 130,000 full-speed hits. Sound right?"

"Easy. And I remember every one."

Browner was answering modified questions put to 440 ex-players during a 1988 *Los Angeles Times* survey. Seventy-eight percent of the players said they had disabilities, 60 percent said the NFL was not interested in their well-being, and 78 percent wanted a longevity study. Browner was with the majority on each question. What jolted the most was that pro football players (66 percent of them) seem to be certain they are dying before their time, and that 55 percent would play again, regardless. The early death rate has long been a whisper, without scientific foundation. "We're now trying to get to the bottom of this idea," says Dr. Sherry Baron, who recently began a study for the National Institute for Occupational Safety and Health. "From the replies we get, a lot of players are nervous out there."

The *Jobs Rated Almanac* seemed to put the NFL player near the coal miner when it ranked 250 occupations for work environment. Judged on stress, outlook, physical demands, security, and income, the NFL player rose out of the bottom ten only in income. With good reason. The life is awful if you care to look past the glory and the money; disability underwriters, when they don't back off altogether, approach the pro as they would a career bridge jumper. Randy Burke (former Colt), age thirty-two when he replied to the *Times* survey, catches the life, commenting on concussions, "I can talk clearly, but ever since football my words get stuck together. I don't know what to expect next." And Pete Gent says, "I went to an orthopedic surgeon, and he told me I had the skeleton of a seventy-year-old man."

Pro football players will do anything to keep taking the next step. As noted in Ecclesiastes, *There is a season*—one time, baby. To that end, they will balloon up or sharpen bodies to murderous specification (steroids), and few are the ones who will resist the Novocain and the long needles of muscle-freeing, tissue-rotting cortisone. Whatever it takes to keep the life. A recent report from Ball State University reveals the brevity and physic pain. One out of three players leaves because of injury; 40 percent have financial difficulties; and one of three is divorced within six months; many remember the anxiety of career separation setting in within hours of knowing it was over.

What happens to so many of them? They land on the desk of Miki Yaras, the curator of "the horror shop" for the NFL Players Association. It is her job to battle for disability benefits from the pension fund, overseen by three reps from her side, three from the owners. For some bizarre reason, perhaps out of a deep imprinting of loyalty and team, players come to her thinking the game will be there for them when they leave it; it isn't, and their resentment with coaches, team doctors, and ego-sick owners rises. Her war for benefits is often long and bitter, outlined against a blizzard of psychiatric and medical paperwork for and against. She has seen it all: from the young player, depressed and hypertensive, who tried to hurtle his wheelchair in front of a truck (the team doctor removed the wrong cartilage from his knee) to the forty-year-old who can't bend over to play with his children, from the drinkers of battery acid to the ex-Cowboy found wandering on the desert.

"It's very difficult to qualify," Yaras says. "The owners will simply not recognize the degenerative nature of injuries. The plan is well overfunded. It could afford temporary relief to many more than it does. I even have a quadriplegic. The doctor for the owners wrote that "his brain is intact, and he can move his arm; someday he'll be able to work.' They think selling pencils out of an iron lung is an occupation."

On Saturday, Joey Browner begins to feel the gathering sound of Sunday, bloody Sunday. He goes to his dojo for his work on *iaido,* an art of Japanese swordsmanship—not like karate, just exact, ceremonial patterns of cutting designed to put the mind out there on the dangerous edge of things. He can't work the long katana now because, after thirty needles in his arm a couple of days before, it was found that he had nerve damage. So, wearing a robe, he merely extends the katana, his gaze fixed on the dancing beams of the blade, making you think of twinkling spinal lights. What does he see? The heads of clever, arrogant running backs? Who knows? He's looking and he sees what he sees. And after a half hour you can almost catch in his eyes the rush of the leopard toward cover behind the bush where he can already view the whole terrible beauty of the game, just a pure expression of gunshot hits, all of it for the crowd that wants to feel its own alphaness, for the crowd that hears no screams other than its own, and isn't it all so natural, he thinks, a connective to prehistoric hunting bands and as instinctually human as the impulse to go down and look at the bright, pounding sea.

PART FIVE

DEAD END

(BEETHAVEAN SCOTTLAND)

Gentleman's Quarterly
April 2002

Imagine three centuries into the future and you are on a tour of a dimly lit building, actually one long corridor flanked by jars of preserved brains, spots of light over each, for as far as the eye can see. As you pass the jars—what's left of some spectacular lives—the brains don't look so special. Just like clumps of intestine or, as was once noted, when the matter is cut, like strawberry yogurt. The scientist who leads the visitors sees much more: van Gogh's sunflowers, expressways of blinking neurons, tracts of burnt forest, and little alien heads trailing ghostly tendrils. With every sound vibration, the brains sway in their liquids as if they want to come alive again, a visual that never fails to chill him, especially at night.

By certain displays, he stops and delivers a small, arresting sketch of the organ's long-ago owner, with a delivery sure of itself, though he knows it's all for show, a combination of myth and vagrant fact. Not a bad post, this curator role, for an elderly fellow no longer in the thick of research. Yet oddly annoying, for after the many huge advancements in neuroscience, the question always remains...why? Like that brain over there—why did Michael Jackson have such a furious aesthetic obsession with his face? Or Elvis Presley—what misbegotten fear drove him into a dark passage with no exits? Or over here—why did Isaac Newton, the king of paranoids, shout to the walls at Cambridge? The long, yellow-lit corridor echoes, tantalizes with the same question.

The trouble is that few are interested in a repository of old brains; most fail to make a connection to the three-pound universe of beauty and horror. Those that do stay poised over the exhibits of trauma. Brain stems crushed by car accidents; there are no cars anymore. Cerebellums grooved ugly by gunfire; guns have long faded from society. Often the scientist concludes he is conducting a freak show. In a society without random violence, where all risk—except intellectual—appalls, people seek the feel of danger from faraway cultures, of high emotions now totally without value in this world.

For the past year, the curator has found his curiosity drawn to the blood sports called football, auto racing, and boxing, expressions of maleness that have a vicarious pull. Boxing fascinates him, perhaps because of the brain of a young man named Beethavean Scottland, an obscure fighter killed in the summer of 2001 and survived by a wife and three young children. To a scientist, Bee's brain still shows the work of instruments used to relieve swelling. Through this one fighter, the scientist is able to visit civilizations he has never given a thought while he traces the roots of boxing from the Greeks to the dust of the Roman Colosseum to the English fairgrounds. It is intellectual leisure sometimes enveloped by the same fervor that drove ancient scholars to devote lifetimes to, say, the wings of a dragonfly.

None of his peers even know there was once something

known as boxing; they are more interested in the great military slaughters of that period. By the time Scotland was left on the ring canvas of the aircraft carrier *Intrepid,* his brain ballooning, his eyes vacant to the twinkling Manhattan sky above, the sport was at the tail end of its longevity, with thirty years left. The scientist wants to know the why of Scotland's death, one of five hundred in the ring since early in the twentieth century, one of thirty-eight in the two decades before his final fight.

On the face of it, that seems like a lot of lives given up to a sport, yet the wreckage has been just as profound in car racing, and Theodore Roosevelt, the bull male of presidents, even gave some thought to banning college football because of its body count. The only thing that divided boxing, albeit subtly, from those other maiming pastimes was *intention,* the weak parry used liberally for numerous subjects by professional arguers on television. The ring, without doubt, seemed to act on the reformational mind like absinthe. Just one sip of impropriety and morality entrepreneurs shot to the oldest whore in the bar to vent their outrage.

Not so in the ring's infant days. The curator thrills to that time. Milo of Croton is a favorite, the first vector of hype known to the world. Milo, it was said, could destroy a man with one hand and pull up the roots of a tree with the other; he needed both to dispatch an ox, then eat it raw. The Romans improved on the Greeks with quantity and spectacle. It is enough to say that even the refined Cicero could not resist the violence. "We hate those weak and suppliant gladiators who, hands outstretched, beseech us to live." Fighting disappeared for a thousand years, then turned up on the heaths and at the fairs of England, but this time as an asset of national character. For the splendid essayist William Hazlitt in 1825, the joy of the ring "showed pluck and manhood."

What was the subculture that beckoned to Bee Scottland? The twentieth century had been boxing's golden time until television strangled the sport. Put the small-club incubators of talent out of business. Boxing was a Big Town game, part of the mystery and glamour that charged the air in crowded, frantic, raw-human cities that moved to the beat of big-band music and jazz. A slinky riff on an alto sax was at its heart. The notes spoke of the whisper of cash, of the riffle of cards and tumbling dice, of bombshell blondes with fiery-red lipstick and a flip curve to their mouths, of men with big rings and immaculate tailoring to go with the pomaded hair, and of everyone on the make.

An old, old movie, *The Harder They Fall*, with Rod Steiger and Humphrey Bogart, caught the essence of the way business was conducted. Bogart, the press agent for a foreign heavyweight named Toro, is trying to get the hulk a fair shake after building him up and selling him out when the gambling payoff was right. The dissection complete, the inept Toro is being bargained to an undertaker, the once popular name for those who handled fighters on the way down.

BOGART: How big was the gate tonight?
LEO: $1,284,000—that's before taxes.
BOGART (angrily): Just tell me how much Toro has coming.
LEO: Exactly $49.07.

Nowhere near as venal or colorful as in Toro's time, boxing was low in popularity and full of money in the last two decades of the twentieth century. The stewards of the game were lawyers with steel-trap clauses for every situation, not that lower cadre of ganefs who worked the sticky telephone booths on Eighth Avenue. In the neuron-crushing age of MTV, when it was bad form to expect substance, the ring had become a faux ritual, with a heart of cable wires and sinew welded to a studio technician and animated by cutout fighters who screeched promises of scripted violence usually seen in the balloons of comic books, all of it choreographed by warring, obscuring factions out for their own big kills.

Bee Scottland didn't have a chance in this velvet alley. The curator noted the kid's wandering innocence—on a dangerous trip without compass, jumping from one subterranean, unclever manager to the next. "I have to manage myself," Bee told his worried father, James Scottland. Didn't Bee know that the common cold in his game was brain damage—a life sentence so ingeniously defined by that rogue of rogues Charles "Sonny" Liston? "See, all the brains are in sort of a cup, and after you get hit a few times it shakes them out of that cup. When they give you smelling salts, it pulls them back into the cup. It's when the brains get shook up and run together that you get punch-drunk."

That brings a smile to the curator's eyes; when portrayed on vaudeville stages and in certain movie comedies, "punch-drunk" seemed like a facial tic, an occupational triviality. Brain science called it traumatic encephalopathy, irreversible and on the march with age, often appearing a number of years after a fighter's retirement. Symptoms were clearly visible: deeply muddy speech, dramatic memory loss, unsteady gait, and mental confusion. The American Medical Association had been firing study after study at the boxing tribe for most of the century. Mildly annoyed, the sport's dedicated follower A. J. Liebling, in his book *The Sweet Science,* pointed to the battiness of a celebrated ballet star and noted, "Well, who hit Nijinsky?"

The tribesmen had their own arguments. The curator broke them down, chuckled as he gave each a name. First, there was the Konrad Lorenz Defense, named after a famed ethologist who was a critic of those who decried the violence of sports.

After studying the habits of birds and animals, Lorenz concluded that man was a walking bomb of aggression, that "the main function of sport lies in cathartic discharge." In other words, watch a fight and be purged. To the tribe, this was scientific entitlement.

Economics, or the lack thereof, had been central to the argument for boxing, so the scientist named the second prong of defense after John Maynard Keynes, the generous and visionary economist who rightly saw everyone supping at the state's table. No matter what its welfare at any given time, boxing was the last hope for many, their only aptitude. Historically, it was the escape for the immigrant Jews and Irish. Why shouldn't poor blacks and Latinos be allowed to fight their way up through the skylight away from apartments filled with skittering rats?

He called the final argument the Kenneth Clark Persuasion in honor of the art scholar. This was the favorite retort of the literati and romantics (perhaps like the curator himself). Men who aligned the intricacies of a left hook to what Clark saw in a Florentine fresco. For them, there were Noël Coward lyrics in the work of a couple of good, fast lightweights, there were the enveloping brushstrokes of Goya in a pair of severely concentrated heavyweights. Was all visual pleasure to be legislated out of existence? Would we ever free ourselves from the austere clutches of Cotton Mather and the urge to deny and deny the senses?

Although the curator was partial to the arguments, he probed the soft areas. First, Lorenz, near the end of his life, jettisoned his theory, having seen so much national and personal violence. "Nowadays," he said, "I have strong doubts whether watching aggressive behavior in the guise of sport has any cathartic effect at all." The economic thrust, though socially gallant, seemed pallid, too; the math didn't carry the day. In the last years of the ring, only a handful of fighters made life-changing money. The rest were condemned to the dark corners of gyms and perilous, insignificant nights, and if you looked into too many torn faces, it became clear what an economic mirage it was. As far as the art of the ring, the aesthete was a rare sighting. The audience was now more inclined toward the tenets of someone like Fritzie Zivic of 1940, who said, "You're fightin', not playin' the piano, ya know?"

Film and TV were critically seared quite often for marketing violence, but the same has been said of the ring. It put humans too close to ancestral black-night fires where rocks and bones were shaped into killing points. An ambiguous reach, yet Alypius of Rome, dragged to the Games by a friend, shamefully noted their impact: "He took away with him a madness which could only goad him to come back again and again." James Scottland was on the same page. Abjectly, almost with a whisper, he said in the April 2002 issue of a national magazine, "It's the man-on-a-ledge thing. People screaming, 'Jump! Jump!' When he jumps, they go quiet; then they begin lookin' for the next man. The chance to see more blood, more death."

In his search for Bee Scottland, through the history of the game and the sport that so seduced him, the curator came across a ragged, very old novel with brittle pages, *The Bridge of San Luis Rey*, by Thornton Wilder. A priest in the story witnesses the collapse of a bridge in Peru that sends five people to their deaths. He sets out to discover what lives they had led. Why these five? Was it divine intervention (a quaint idea in the curator's world) or capricious fate that ended those lives? This would be the curator's model for the Scottland search—who was this kid, and what confluence of beliefs and hopes and delusions conspired to bring him to his final day on a ship in

New York harbor, towered by the iron-palace buildings that blind with a success that was barely imagined by the kid?

The longer Wilder's priest pried, the more he felt he was stumbling among great, dim intimations, forever being cheated by details. So it was with the curator; only a few people had really known the young fighter: his father, his wife, and his best friend, all of them so stunned by grief long after his death that recollection was painful, deep hurt visible on their faces. Bee was twenty-six, born in Washington, DC, to a musician father and a mother who was a corrections officer. James Scottland named his son after the great Beethoven (another son was named Bach), corrupting the spelling to Beethavean because he didn't want the boy to be mocked in school. All of the Scottland children were into music, Bee with a horn. He was hard to handle as an adolescent, got into trouble on the streets, and the judge assigned Derek Matthews, an aspiring fighter and trainer of dogs, to be his mentor.

Buoyed by the relationship, Bee went to live with Matthews and, without prodding, fastened his spare time to "mixing it up" in the basement gym. At fourteen, the boy had a brooding presence, sort of a street glower, that concealed a kind, giving nature. For a good while, he was harassed by the police. Matthews, annoyed, looked into the problem. "Why you keep pickin' him up?" he demanded. The police said, "Well, he looks suspicious." Under Matthews's watch, Bee never even flirted with trouble. He had a lot of amateur fights, then turned pro in 1995 at the age of twenty. His father, James, remembered the night, saying, "He won, but he got whipped up pretty good and was scared after."

By June 2001, Bee's record was 20-6-2, all right but not likely to induce a satchel of money. He never made upward of $3,000; it was more like several hundred here and there, handed to him in some nondescript dressing room in an envelope he didn't even bother to look at. Bee worked as a bug exterminator during the day, but his hope for a career rocket shot never receded. Increasingly, to Matthews, the possibility of big money was quite secondary to Bee's primary motive, the chance at true recognition. "You have to understand a guy like Bee," said Matthews. "He found his manhood in the gym, even more his identity. You don't part with that easily. There are no losers in a gym, no ridicule. If you give what you have, there is respect. Bee wanted that more than money."

But young Scottland had an unusual bead on reality. When asked by a documentary filmmaker, David Snider, if he had considered the risk of the ring, Bee replied emptily, "I'd say I have a fifty-fifty chance of being killed." That was striking. Most fighters would never put the odds that high—maybe 90 to 10, 80 to 20. Most never even think of the probability; it argues too much against the nature of their work. Bee also went to a brother and told him that if he was ever gravely hurt, the family should pull the plug, even if his heartbeat was strong. He insisted he had no wish to live if he could not see, smell, or taste.

When the invitation to fight George Khalid Jones arrived, Bee hadn't fought in nearly ten months; such was the life of a disposable talent. The critic Wilfrid Sheed could understand the boxer's predicament. He once described the trials of a minor novelist (one of those cruel industry designations): "To see a chipped copy [of a previous book] in a second-hand bookstore is like visiting your own graveyard." When Bee reached for the swirling bauble above, he crashed to the dance floor. When he kept his dream grounded, he was ignored. No one watched him train. As he poured out his blood and sweat in the ring, people sat in their seats and talked about mortgages. In his own mind, Bee was a main-event guy. In the scuzzy, half-filled arenas where he toiled, he was, rightly or wrongly, perceived as a worker ant.

No wonder he leaped at the chance to fight George Jones. Just a week prior to the bout, Dana Rucker, who was scheduled to face Bee in a Maryland title fight, bowed out with a hamstring injury. One day later, David Telesco copped out on Jones with a broken nose. When that happened to a hot product like Jones, the likely response was to find a presentable gypsy. That's how Bee ended up going to his last fight. It was a fusion of weights—Bee the middleweight, Jones the natural light heavy. Matthews begged Bee to pass. Jones was a hitter, and Bee had nothing but trouble against southpaws. The lure was too much: a TV go on ESPN, the shot at name recognition, and a $7,000 payday; it would cost more to bury him.

Bee had no complaints before the fight; the required CAT scan came up clear. Yet, according to his mother, Lucy Ann, he was fighting on a twisted ankle. He didn't seem right to his wife, Denise, and to Matthews; maybe it was their nerves. Matthews was with Bee in the corner in New York, but he had no voice; that belonged to Adrian Davis, a known trainer in DC who was once a fighter and had left the ring with a glass eye. Denise watched the fight alone in her dark bedroom in the New Carrollton, Maryland, home she shared with Bee, while James, who had appeared at the Apollo several times and once did a gig with Duke Ellington, played his piano at a Virginia supper club, moving between Tchaikovsky and the blues, keeping his eyes on his son on a TV at the bar. Denise cringed at what she saw and at one point jumped and shouted, "Stop it! Stop the fight!"

After three rounds, Bee had absorbed a percussive drumbeat of shots. He wasn't in the fight. The exchange rate was 50 to 4 for Jones. Lucy Ann couldn't keep her eyes fixed on the screen. She had to turn away as the beating got worse. The TV at the supper club was switched to another channel; James would not see the end. Davis said to Bee, "If you don't do right,

I'm going to stop it." Matthews noted to himself how Bee seemed intent on featuring his toughness. To whom? Matthews was confused. The ring doctor, Barry Jordan, took a look at Bee, an exercise he had performed hundreds of times before. "He had a chance," said Davis afterward. No, he didn't. If Bee had been a puncher—maybe. But he wasn't; he was a cyclist (refusing to pedal), who should have been sticking and moving against a swarming puncher fifteen pounds heavier on an overly soft ring canvas that gave lots of traction to a big bopper. Well ahead on points, Jones took a breather in the eighth and ninth, and Bee responded some. And then in the tenth, Jones tagged him. After the bout, he said of his punching, "I hit him so hard, so often, my hands hurt."

Bee lay on the canvas under the hot lights for fifteen minutes as they tried to revive him. His eyes were open, and one of them floated up to Matthews, the last person he would ever see. Denise was on her knees praying now. Her father came up and said, as he often would later, "I wouldn't let a dog take that kind of whippin'." Then Matthews was with Dr. Jordan and the med techs, trying to get Bee, his head braced, on the aircraft carrier's elevator; the stretcher wouldn't fit, and they had to prop him up, a ghoulish sight to Matthews, who kept pinching the fighter to get a reaction. In the ambulance, diverted from St. Luke's–Roosevelt to Bellevue, Bee was snoring deeply. Matthews kept pinching him, saying, "Wake up, Bee! Don't leave me!" Before long they were in surgery. Matthews was kneeling just below the head of Bee when a doctor nearly stumbled over him, saw his sobbing, and advised that he retreat to the waiting room. Dr. Jordan came out a short time later.

The next morning, Bee was back in surgery for desperate work on a hematoma, or blood clot, that was strangling his brain. Six days later, he died. "Who would answer?" James Scottland

asked long after the funeral. "My son was murdered." The sadness, the red eyes and tears, granted him entitlement to his con-
clusion. The facts were less dramatic—but no less compelling
for their ordinariness. Bee had been endangered by indifference, by a woeful failure of the officials to engage what was before their eyes: styles and pattern.

The contour of the bout was set in concrete early on, and
the young fighter never had the one tool—a big punch—to save
the day. Adrian Davis, the trainer? His old idea that a fighter
always has a chance was reckless; Bee was a greyhound trying
to win the Derby. The referee Arthur Mercante Jr.? Far too generous to Bee, perhaps too distracted by emphasis on the *show*, he
was impressed only by Bee's ability to speak and sporadically
return punches. Dr. Barry Jordan? After hundreds of fights, did
his observation fail him? He did tell the ref after the seventh
round he didn't think Bee could take many more punches, but he
visited Bee's corner only once, to inspect a trickle of blood from
his eye.

George Jones brooded over his part in the horrid evening,
just like all the fighters who had been in his place before. Emile
Griffith, the joyous welter, killed Benny Paret in a big Garden
fight in 1962. He was never the same again; in his dreams he saw
Paret walking toward him, and when he looked in a mirror, Paret stared back at him. The masterful Sugar Ray Robinson
couldn't sleep for a long time after killing Jimmy Doyle without
revisiting the haunting vision of Doyle looking up at him from
the canvas, despite what was interpreted as an uncaring comment after the fight. Robinson was asked if he had intended to
get Doyle in trouble. Angry and with guilt spreading, Sugar
said, "Sir, it's my business to get him in trouble."

Unreasoned guilt never left James Scottland, a very religious man fond of Scripture. "I did not always do the best things

for Bee," said James. "I once asked him to forgive me. He was so giving. He was very kind to me. I didn't deserve his kindness."

So it was long, long ago, the curator thinks, in a sport with no more significance or meaning than the dancing ember of a fire, in a mere distraction that had come out of a prehistory of bedded primeval slime and bone and was finally cast away as preindustrial, as preorganization, and ultimately as culturally unrevolutionary with no analogue to daily life; a tinny conceit, he thinks, considering what humans did to one another day to day back then. He admires Bee Scotland. Whatever had been at the root of an injured psyche, the kid sought, much more than fame and money, an end to self-division within and found a unified person in the purifying habit of gym work and in rings where spectators barely knew his name.

With a sigh, the curator concludes the young man was done in not only by indifference but by a passion and heart far too large for a certain talent and reality. There was as well the eerie conjunction of forces, the trapdoors of life. You could say that the boxer was maneuvered to his death by a broken nose and a hamstring, bizarre injuries for an opponent just days before a fight when prep work was light. Had the fighters Telesco and Rucker kept their dates, Jones and Bee would have passed each other like strangers in a mist. He thinks of the father, James, and though the curator lives in a godless time with which he is in full accord, he anxiously wants the final belief of the priest in Thornton Wilder's book to be unimpeachably true: "That the very sparrows do not lose a feather that has not been brushed away by the finger of God."

Acknowledgments

I would especially like to thank George Witte, the editor in chief at St. Martin's Press, for taking on this project, and for the enthusiasm with which he embraced it. I am also deeply grateful to Andrew Blauner, my literary agent, for getting behind the book and for the continued guidance he has provided me through the years.

I owe a deep debt of appreciation to Frank Deford. Frank and my father were colleagues during the early years of *Sports Illustrated* (and both Baltimoreans). This collection would not have happened without his generosity of spirit.

Thank you also to Rob Fleder for his help and encouragement along the way.

At *SI*, I would like to thank Group Editor Paul Fichtenbaum, his predecessor Terry McDonell, and Karen Carpenter. At St. Martin's Press, I am appreciative of the assistance I received from Steve Boldt, Ellis Levine, and Sara Thwaite.

John Schulian was enormously helpful with what has always been sage advice. Thank you also to Alex Belth, Steve Carroll, Norman Chad, Mike Downey, David Hirshey, Eliot Kaplan,

Jackie Koenig, Tom Lachman, Chris Raymond, Patrick Robbins, John (Jack) Sherwood, and Jason Wilson.

Lastly, I would like to express my heartfelt gratitude to my mother, Joan; Greg and Tracey; Peter and Kerry; Rene; Raymond and Hoi-Ling; Robert; Alix; my daughters, Cory and Olivia; and—above all—my wife, Anne.